COOKING IN RUSSIA AND FINLAND

YouTube Channel

Companion Reader

Volume 4

by

Greg Easter

*Dedicated to Kelvin Wu
and the dear members of my
YouTube channel,
without whom this book would not
have been possible.
I sincerely thank all of you!*

TABLE OF CONTENTS

II. RECIPES

III. SPICE PASTES

IV. DIPPING SAUCES AND SALAD DRESSINGS

V. COCKTAILS

VI. APPENDIX

INTRODUCTION

The recipes in this book are all new to the printed page. Some are based on past videos that were not included in previous volumes. Those have been revised to ensure they are up to date.

New features of this volume include sous vide cooking, spice pastes, cold sauces and most of all, a strong focus on thermal physics and heat management in all aspects of cooking.

THE UNTIMELY DEATH OF ANNOTATIONS

After many years of posting videos on YouTube every week, each with annotations and many with navigation bars within the video that relied on annotations, YouTube suddenly decided to erase all annotations from everyone's videos without any choice or way to save them. Needless to say, this was rather heart breaking since it meant six years of my work had been rendered useless.

Some fans tried to salvage those annotations by printing them out in the comments sections, but naturally most people who view those old videos and encounter lengthy black screens with nothing happening simply close the video and go back to searching for whatever they had been looking for. One fan, Jeff Gabalis, made the colossal and unimaginable effort to actually go through every one of my older videos (more than 300 of them!) and restore the annotations in on-screen text. I have made these files available to paid members, and I applaud Jeff for his amazing work. Bravo!

One might wonder why I used annotations in the first place. Why not just print the text onto the video, as I have to now? Because I wanted to be able to go back and make minor changes to those videos without having to delete them, re-shoot and re-edit them... so that I could fix it in the mix, as the saying goes.

FIX IT IN THE MIX

Back in the days of music coming from actual musicians and singers instead of the mostly computer-generated stuff these days, recording studio time was very expensive and unless you were a very successful (and wealthy) act, everything was done to try and minimize the studio time spent because time was money. Albums were recorded on giant 5cm (2 inch) wide magnetic tape, usually being 24 tracks (but sometimes as many as 48). Even after the tracks were recorded, there was the laborious process of mixing them down, adding effects, adjusting equalization, etc. All of these services were very expensive and billed by the hour, so a recording session was like hemorrhaging money. This meant you couldn't do take after take just because some little thing went wrong. When something minor went wrong, the catch phrase that was used constantly was, "We'll fix it in the mix", meaning we aren't going spend hundreds of dollars now re-recording this entire track, because when it is mixed down we'll find a way to bury this little mistake under some other sound such as an extra cymbal crash, or just drop the volume of that track for a moment. Did the guitarist hit one note that was out of the key signature? Fix it in the mix! The vocalist went off pitch? Fix it in the mix! This phrase became a standard joke among recording engineers if an entire part was badly played due to the musician being drunk or on drugs at the time, because only small mistakes could hope to be fixed in such a way. Sometimes you just have to start over.

So why am I telling you all of this? What does it have to do with food? First, the older recipes in this book have been changed since the time the video was made years ago. The basic idea is the same, but there have been modifications to improve it. So if you watch one of those videos and it doesn't exactly match what it says here, go by this book instead.

Second, it is easy for cooks to rely on this "fix it in the mix" strategy to excuse mistakes that should have meant starting over. Cooking is always an opportunity for learning and improving, so don't be afraid to start over again rather than try to fix serious mistakes by burying your mess in hot chilies, honey or loads of cream. But what if you have ruined an expensive piece of meat? Then just find something else to use that for if you can't afford to throw it away. You can grind up almost any meaty catastrophe to use in a ragu for a lasagna or to supplement a meatball mixture or to use in the filling for a meat pie. The point is to accept that sometimes things go wrong and start over.

One question I see repeatedly is what to do if too much salt was added or too much spice (especially chilies). This can easily happen because you didn't account for the salt in the cheese or broth, or in the case of chilies, some can be much hotter than others even within the same bunch of the same variety.

You can't fix such mistakes by just adding more of something else, but sometimes there is a way to *FIX IT IN THE MIX!* Here's how: Set aside the over-seasoned item and start the recipe over again, this time without <u>any</u> of the seasoning you inadvertently overdid last time. Then combine the new batch with the old batch. Now you have cut the amount by 50%, which is probably now less than it should have had. Now you can add a bit more to slowly bring it up to the proper level. Although you now have twice as much in quantity, it may be better than having just thrown it out completely.

RIJSTTAFEL

On a related note, a creative way to use up things that went wrong is to invent small dishes for a rijsttafel. The direct translation of this is *rice table*. It is an elaborate cuisine back from the Dutch colonial period in Malaysia. The idea is that you are served many little interesting dishes and a plate of rice. People mix these things together and have fun discovering interesting exotic food combinations. It doesn't matter if something is too spicy or too salty because it gets mixed with rice and other items that break all of the rules. You can have marinated fish, deep fried vegetables, spicy pork, barbecued lamb and just about anything else all in the same meal. There are a couple of dishes in this volume that are especially suited for this.

Remember, if you are unsure about any technique

www.youtube.com/user/cookinginfinland

THERMAL EXPANSION

Materials expand and contract by different amounts during heating and cooling depending on their molecular structure. The mathematical number that expresses how much something will change in size when the temperature increases is the *coefficient of thermal expansion* (a number multiplied by 10^{-6} m / °C).

If you heat up glass and then plunge it into water, it will shatter because the part that first contacted the water will cool quickly and shrink away from the surrounding area, creating fractures.

Metal will warp upon repeatedly heating and cooling it unevenly, unless the metal is very thick, in which case it will develop microfractures that will eventually cause it to crack (depending on how brittle the metal is). This is why cast iron pans are made thick but they will still shatter eventually if they are repeatedly cooled under water when they are still hot. So don't do that.

The invention of borosilicate glass, better known as Pyrex, was an important breakthrough because it has a smaller coefficient of thermal expansion than ordinary glass. As materials go, glass actually has a fairly low thermal expansion coefficient of 5.9. Still, as most people know, it doesn't take too much for it to shatter. Pyrex has a thermal coefficient of 4.0, which is sufficiently lower to keep it from shattering under ordinary kitchen use.

If money was no object, quartz is even better. With a thermal coefficient of an amazingly low 0.55, it is one of the lowest of all known materials. It is used in equipment like telescope mirrors and where there are extreme temperature changes. Quartz is virtually indestructible by thermal shock. It can be heated until it glows white hot, then plunged into ice water over and over without cracking. Unfortunately it is a very difficult material to work with, and so any cookware that would be made with quartz would be very expensive. Note that this is not the same as the "Stone Quartz" cookware brand being marketed. True quartz is perfectly clear like glass.

THERMAL PENETRATION

Although this should be obvious, few people really think about this issue explicitly. Let's take the simple 2-dimensional view of heat striking a piece of meat. Whether you have a high heat for a short time, a medium heat for a medium time, or a low heat for a long time, the "doneness" will be roughly the same when measured just below the surface, as shown in the diagram.

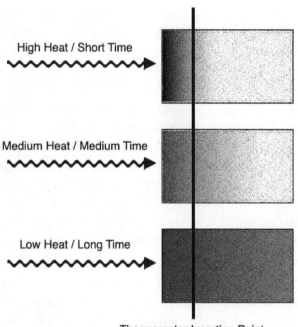

High Heat / Short Time

Medium Heat / Medium Time

Low Heat / Long Time

Thermometer Insertion Point

This is one of the inherent problems of relying on instant read thermometers, and a frequent cause of returned steaks by disgruntled customers. Getting an accurate reading on either a very large piece of meat or a very thin piece of meat can be impossible, but for different reasons.

For a large roast, you don't want to be plunging a thermometer down into it to check the temperature frequently because juices will come running out of every puncture. You can insert a thermometer one time and leave it in during the entire roasting time, but then you are only measuring a single part. Also, be sure to let the roast cool down before removing the probe, or it will leak juices out.

For thin pieces of meat, the problem is that your probe is reading an average of the surface and the interior—plus if you are trying to measure it while it is still on the pan, radiant infrared energy causes an artificially high reading.

Thus, you need to keep in mind that what you are actually measuring might not be what you are trying to measure. There is a well known piece of wisdom among restaurant cooks that *the best way to overcook or undercook something is to use a thermometer*. When food is returned to the kitchen for being underdone or overdone, the standard joke is, "But, Chef, I used a thermometer!" Everyone around chuckles. The best reliable method is practice.

SIZE MATTERS FOR PENETRATION (!)

You can brown **large** pieces of *anything* (including mushrooms) with much less risk of burning them because the rest of the thing you are cooking is drawing heat away from the surface. Smaller pieces will burn as they brown. That's the general principle, but there is more going on in the case of mushrooms and some vegetables because they are like little sponges. If you cut them up, all the moisture comes out. Leave them whole and the moisture is trapped inside acting like how antifreeze works in a car radiator.

The diagram on the previous page is ambiguous in regard to the size of the thing being heated. It also ignores heat coming from other directions. This is perfectly valid if we are talking about a steak on a hot pan (rotate the diagram 90° counterclockwise to visualize this). If you are cooking something round, such as a meatball, then the heat mostly spreads from a small point of contact. This is why you have to use a lower heat for a longer time, and why cooking them in a sauce is especially effective because then they are receiving heat from all sides much more evenly.

In the case of very small particles, such as ground spices in a dry pan, no matter what heat you are using, they will burn easily because every tiny particle is on the extreme left edge of that diagram on the previous page, receiving heat directly.

HOT SPOTS

No, this isn't about trendy nightclubs. It is about the uneven temperature that exists at the bottom surface of pans on the stove. While the common wisdom is that cast iron is ideal for even distribution of heat, this is mostly an urban legend. Iron is about the worst metal there is for heat diffusion. However, because cast iron pans are made very thick, the inherent inadequacy of this property is reduced. Aluminum is actually much better at diffusing heat, but cheap aluminum pans are so thin that overall they usually come up worse than cast iron for heating evenly (and please don't cook on aluminum!) Thin metals have a short lifespan in a busy kitchen, as they soon warp from being repeatedly heated and cooled.

The next urban legend is that gas burners heat more evenly than electric burners. Just one look at the heat source should tell you that this is not true.

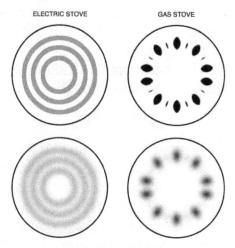

ELECTRIC STOVE   GAS STOVE

DIFFUSION THROUGH METAL PANS

Although gas enables instantly variable heat control, modern electric stoves respond quite rapidly, too. In the rare instance where you need super fast heat control with an electric stove, you can move the pan on and off the heat, or between two burners on different settings. It comes as a surprise to many people that the classic professional restaurant stove has a solid flat surface that is hotter in some places than others, and pans are simply moved from one part to another to control the heat. No dials or adjustments to the burners themselves are ever made. Because this type of stove is more expensive and requires a skilled chef to work with, they have largely fallen out of favor in recent times.

Some pans are much better at evenly diffusing heat. Steel clad is a popular example of these, but there are two problems with these that explain why they are rarely seen in a restaurant kitchen. First, they take a long time to heat up. Second, with heavy use, the layers begin to separate. This is less of an issue with a typical home cook, where such pans can last for many years, but in a restaurant they fall apart within a few months and are expensive. Pure stainless steel is the work horse of a <u>good</u> restaurant kitchen.

When it comes to many chain restaurants, aluminum is the most common choice because it is cheap, it heats rapidly and has good diffusion properties. However, there is the issue of aluminum's reactivity. Aluminum ions leach into food upon prolonged cooking at a high temperature, and despite what the aluminum industry tells you, aluminum in your food is a cause of a wide range of very serious health problems. This is akin to the tobacco industry dennying that smoking was harmful. Studies that claim aluminum is safe have been funded by the aluminum industry. Aluminum pans coated with Teflon are perfectly fine, though.

TEFLON PANS

While on this topic, it should be known that the fear mongering over Teflon is completely unfounded. The supposedly dangerous chemical that is targeted is *perfluorooctanoic acid* (PFOA). The PFOA is destroyed during the manufacturing process of Teflon cookware. The pan you buy does not contain any detectable residue of this substance. Why did this come up in the first place? Because a lawyer sued DuPont for dumping toxic waste from the manufacture of Teflon into landfills. That was a legitimate complaint. Then the media sensationalized the story into Teflon pans having toxic waste in them. This is an absurd claim, but the media usually prefers sensationalism to facts these days.

PARTICLE PHYSICS

That is, the physics of food particles. Think before you blend! Many times the flavor of the solids have already been extracted into the broth. Taste the meat or vegetables from a broth and you'll generally find they have almost no flavor. So why purée them and create a cloud of particles that will be very hard to strain off? Amateurs often feel bad throwing out this slime. Get over it.

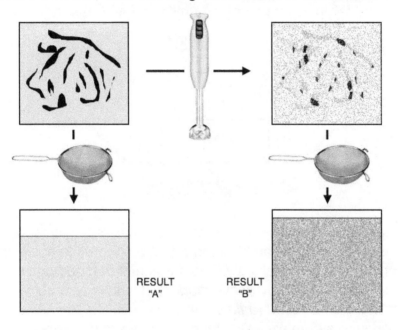

RESULT "A"   RESULT "B"

In the illustration above, a broth containing some boiled pieces of food is passed through a sieve to produce Result "A" without blending. A sieve can easily remove the solids. If you blend it first, you will have created a cloud of tiny particles that will pass through the sieve. This *might* increase the flavor slightly, but the grain of the solution will not be pleasant in most applications. Of course if you are making a ragu or a Mexican mole sauce, then it will be fine. If you are trying to make a beautiful glossy sauce for plating, then you have just made your work ten times harder as you now have to remove the particles you just blitzed up with your blender.

THERMAL RUNAWAY

With the exception of dry roasting spices and nuts, most food begins cooking in a state that is mostly water. Whether it is meat, fish, vegetables or fruits, most of the content is actually water. Some foods are almost all water. For example, mushrooms are 92% water and zucchini is 95% water! Water boils at 100°C (212°F), and so the temperature of mostly-water foods will not exceed that temperature by much until the water has escaped.

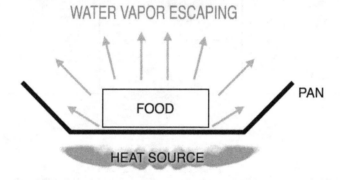

If the food has enough water in it, then there's a microscopic cushion of steam between the food and the pan that keeps it lifted above the surface very slightly. The surface of the food against that steam is being cooked by *convection*. That side is also being bombarded with *infrared radiation* that will result in some browning. When enough steam escapes, then the temperature increases due to *conduction*. These modes of heat transfer are explained in detail just ahead starting on page 20.

The turning point comes when enough water has escaped that the cushion of steam is gone. This has a cascade effect in which a higher temperature is reached due to the direct contact with the pan, driving off still more moisture, which allows the temperature to rise still higher, driving off even more water, and so on. This is *thermal runaway*. It is how food can go from golden brown to charcoal black quite rapidly. Especially for small bits of food stuck to the bottom of the pan that are subjected to both conduction and infrared radiation.

The following graph represents the typical pattern observed for pan frying foods. The temperature starts around room temperature. The pan gets hot until it comes to just over the boiling point of water, when steam begins to escape from the outer surfaces of the porous food. This continues with very little increase in temperature until enough moisture has escaped that the food can rise to above the boiling point of water, releasing water even faster, creating a vicious cycle in which the ever climbing temperature facilitates a higher temperature yet, and the food goes from brown to black in a relatively short span of time, depending on how hot the pan is.

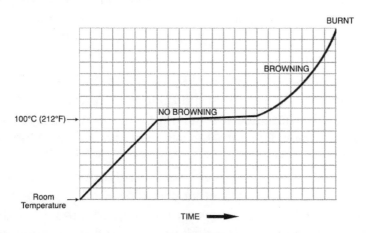

Your goal is to achieve a golden brown color, which means "parking" the reaction between the point the temperature climbs above 100°C, but before it burns. You can think of this like driving a car and trying to stop at a certain point. If you are driving at a modest speed, you can stop before an accident. Conversely, if you are driving like it's the final lap of the Indianapolis 500, you will almost certainly miss the optimum stopping point. Crash and burn.

The solution is to apply quite a bit of heat at the start, but turn the heat down as it begins to brown. In a high-throughput restaurant kitchen, it is common to use maximum heat to get the food cooking, then finish it completely off the stove using residual heat. Not only does this free up the valuable stovetop real estate as quickly as possible, but once you get the timing down, you won't have problems with burning food. Of course there is skill involved.

RISOTTO PHYSICS

Thermal runaway is usually something you try to steer well clear of when boiling a sauce, because it is the fast track to a scorched pan and destroyed food. However, risotto is a rare exception. There is a sort of "game of chicken" you play when making risotto properly. The idea is that you maintain such a low level of liquid that the rice is able to cook at an elevated temperature due to being on the edge of thermal runaway. From the graph on the previous page, you are operating in the region labeled "browning". In order to keep it from actually burning, you have to carefully add a little stock at a time and stir frequently.

Because the process of making risotto involves a great deal of stirring, the rice must be able to stand up to that treatment without turning to mush. The best rice for making risotto that you are likely to find outside of Italy is Carnarolli. If you can find Vialone Nano, grown in the Veneto specifically for risotto, that's even better. Many use Arborio rice because it is the easiest to find, but it has too little starch and turns to a pasty consistency very easily. If you are not extremely skilled, stick to Carnarolli for more reliable results—and <u>never</u> wash the rice first. You need all of the starch to produce the desired creamy texture that results from the constant rubbing of the rice grains against each other during the stirring with a temperature above the boiling point of water.

This is why *true* risotto is almost nonexistent in restaurants, even in Italy, because it is impractical to have a cook at the stove occupied for so long just to turn out a single dish. If you have only had risotto in a restaurant, then you probably have never tasted real risotto. Restaurants cook the rice ahead of time to speed up making it, but this alters the texture and the flavor. Risotto is a dish to master for yourself and make at home. In Italy it is prepared only after everyone is already seated at the table and awaiting it, because it is best very fresh. It is also a great way to use up leftovers because almost anything can go into it.

BROWNING OR BURNING?

The factors that determine whether food will brown or burn are:

MOISTURE CONTENT

Water will not boil above 100°C (212°F) at atmospheric pressure, so if something is mostly water, it will not begin to really brown until most of that water has been driven off as steam (see page 11). You can scorch the surface with very high heat (think in terms of a blowtorch on a mushroom) but that's not browning in the culinary sense of the word. Browning involves the loss of moisture.

SIZE OF THE INDIVIDUAL PIECES

The smaller the size, the faster it will cook because there is more surface area being exposed to the heat source.

AMOUNT OF HEAT AND TIME

Obviously nothing will brown at room temperature no matter how long you leave it out. So it is common sense that the amount of heat is a key factor in both browning and burning. But so is time. Anyone who has used a broiler knows all about this. The temperature of the broiler doesn't change, but food will go from brown to black sometimes within a matter of seconds due to moisture loss causing *Thermal Runaway* (as explained on page 11). Still, foods will cook at relatively low temperatures without ever browning. This is the principle of *Sous Vide* cooking (topic starts on page 35). Browning is usually still required at some point, though.

BROWNING

Since you are reading this book, you should already know the basics of the two types of browning that are both non-enzymatic (as opposed to the type of browning you see on cut potatoes or artichokes when exposed to the air for a while). They are:

CARAMELIZATION OF SUGARS

For all intents and purposes there are only three sugars that are important in cooking. Those are glucose, fructose and sucrose—but sucrose is just a molecule of glucose and a molecule of fructose joined as a disaccharide (glucose and fructose are monosaccharides).

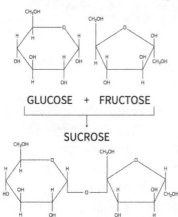

GLUCOSE + FRUCTOSE

SUCROSE

When sucrose is digested in the small intestine, the bond joining the two parts is cut by an enzyme called *sucrase*.

Sucrose is also broken down to its monosaccharides of glucose and fructose by heating it above 114°C (236°F) in the presence of water and an acid as a catalyst (it doesn't matter which acid is used). The solution of mixed glucose and fructose is given the special name of *invert sugar*.

If you slowly melt sugar in a dry pan without any acid as a catalyst, it goes through many changes gradually. Each stage is categorized by a specific temperature that begins at 160°C (320°F) for sucrose. The complexity arises largely because fructose begins caramelizing at only 110°C (230°F), so as soon as sucrose splits apart, the fructose is already well above the point it would caramelize at, so instead it decomposes into smaller molecules that react with the glucose and the remaining sucrose in the mixture. Glucose caramelizes at the same temperature as sucrose, coincidentally. The chemistry of these reactions is so complex that even today it is not well understood and only a tiny fraction of the intermediate reactions and products are known. The major product is *caramelin*, as in caramel. The specific thermal stages of caramelization are generally only important to pastry chefs and candy makers.

LACTOSE

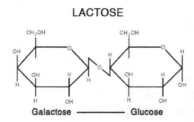

Galactose ———— Glucose

There are actually many different sugars. While on the subject of different sugars, one other sugar is also worth mentioning: the dreaded lactose. Well, dreaded by those who can't digest it. Lactose is another disaccharide. It is a molecule of galactose joined to glucose. Just as sucrose is split into its two monosaccharides by the enzyme sucrase, lactose is apart by the enzyme *lactase*. A lack of this enzyme is what causes lactose intolerance in some people. Pills of that enzyme are available.

THE MAILLARD REACTION

All serious cooks know the Maillard reaction is responsible for the delicious flavors of meats cooked over any high heat source, when stopped just short of turning your meal into charcoal. In fact, one of the things that so frequently separates novices from professionals is the reluctance of amateur to sufficiently brown foods in order to bring out those flavors. It is not only a matter of temperature and time, but also of bravery if you are not madly experienced. If you are madly experienced, then it is a matter of boredom—waiting and watching and, most important, smelling. The subtle changes in aroma that glide by as something is browning takes experience to identify. With enough practice, one can tell how brown something is from across the room while engaged in another unrelated kitchen task. No need to lift the food up to check it if you have been doing this 12 hours a day for years. I'm telling you this so that you (hopefully) begin to actively pay attention to the aromas produced during stages of browning that produce flavors.

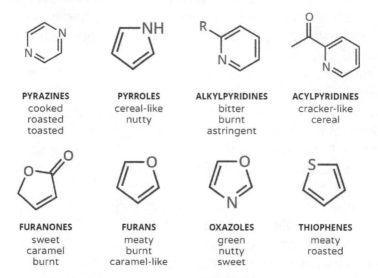

PYRAZINES	PYRROLES	ALKYLPYRIDINES	ACYLPYRIDINES
cooked	cereal-like	bitter	cracker-like
roasted	nutty	burnt	cereal
toasted		astringent	

FURANONES	FURANS	OXAZOLES	THIOPHENES
sweet	meaty	green	meaty
caramel	burnt	nutty	roasted
burnt	caramel-like	sweet	

If you read my book, *40 Years in One Night*, you will better appreciate why I included the above chart for Maillard products.

What makes things even more complicated is the factor of pH, or acidity. A more acidic environment favors caramelization of sugars and simultaneously slows the Maillard reaction of proteins.

Conversely, a neutral or slightly alkaline environment favors the Maillard reaction and retards the caramelization of sugars. You can shift the balance of these two reactions by adding ingredients that change the pH.

ONIONS AND OTHER VEGETABLES

When you char some vegetables like bell peppers, you really are <u>mostly</u> burning them because they contain very little protein and a lot of water that prevents the internal temperature from reaching the necessary temperature for caramelization or the Maillard reaction to proceed. On the surface when high heat is applied, the outermost layers burn black before the next thin layer down gets hot enough for caramelization or the Maillard reaction.

Different conditions exist for members of the allium family, especially onions. First, their cell structure is less dense which allows their water to escape as steam before the outside burns (providing they are cooked slowly) so they can caramelize easier. Onions are also rich in sulfur-containing compounds that leads to a meaty taste that is often misinterpreted as the Maillard reaction having occurred. In reality they have almost no protein, so you are mostly just tasting *thiophenes* (see chart on the previous page) and caramelized sugars.

Cauliflower also contains a significant amount of sulfur compounds, though not nearly as much as onions. Still, it can be coerced into tasting meaty on prolonged cooking, as in the Cauliflower "Steaks" recipe in this book (page 74).

One trick to cooking onions is to add a bit of baking soda to them. This is a catalyst, not a reactant, meaning only a small amount is needed. This is very different from ordinary browning. Onions contain *inulin*, which is a chain of sugars that break down when heated in an alkaline environment. The result is fructose, not glucose. So when you brown onions with baking soda, you are caramelizing fructose, which happens at a lower temperature than glucose. Because their structural starch inulin is broken down, the onions melts down into a jam-like consistency. The flavor is much sweeter because fructose is much sweeter than glucose. Some complex flavors develop, but fewer meaty ones because thiophenes don't form very well with so much moisture and a lower temperature. The flavor produced this way is very, very different.

The difference in pH often plays a much larger role in how foods brown than even most experienced chefs realize. **<u>Note: The same photos below are also on the back cover of this book in color.</u>** These are four slices of kohlrabi (a vegetable in the same family as cabbage, broccoli, turnips, etc.). After being pressure cooked for 17 minutes (see page 227), the slices were cooled and then drained for several hours on paper towels. A nonstick pan was heated on a gas stove. The burner setting was not changed during the four tests and the same pan was used (the pan was cooled for a few minutes and then wiped out with a cloth before the next test was started). Each slice was cooked by itself. All were fried in vegetable oil.

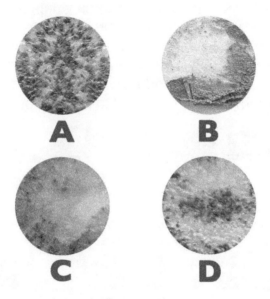

A = Just vegetable oil. Went from raw to starting to burn in a very short time. Not attractive and nothing special about the taste.

B = Sodium Citrate (Acidic): Developed a nice light skin on the surface. This one had the best flavor. Citric acid was problematic.

C = Sodium Bicarbonate (Baking Soda): Nice color, but too sweet due to the fructose released, as for onions mentioned on page 17.

D = Cider Vinegar (Acidic): The vinegar evaporated quickly, so the liquid just interfered with browning. This had an unpleasant bitter taste due to decomposition products of the vinegar itself, no doubt.

SIMULTANEOUS MAILLARD AND CARAMELIZATION

Rarely mentioned in literature about the Maillard Reaction is that meat also contains glucose. Zero sucrose or fructose, but some glucose. That glucose reacts with proteins during browning.

When you brown meat, water escapes as steam. With less water, the temperature rises and eventually reaches the 160°C (320°F) point at which glucose caramelizes, as explained in the previous section. Caramelization begins with the decomposition of sugar into smaller reactive molecules. These highly reactive splintered off groups quickly react with whatever is in their proximity. If amino acids are adjacent, that's what they may react with. This leads to the vast array of complex unpredictable products that contribute to the overall effect of browning.

The diagram below shows what takes place. Note that it begins with glucose reacting with proteins and the pH steers reaction pathways. I realize that few readers will be able to follow this, but for the sake of completeness and not to pull any punches, here it is:

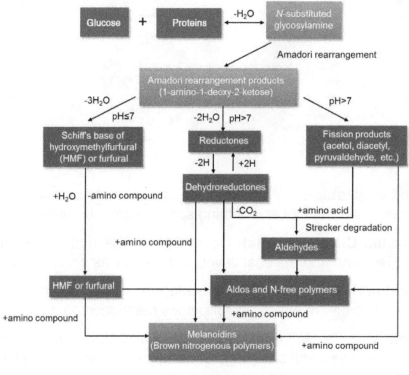

✵

HEAT TRANSFER PHYSICS

All cooking involves the transfer of energy to food. Whether that's from a caveman's fire or a high-powered laser. Conduction, convection and radiation are the three primary ways of cooking foods. Most cooking methods actually involve a combination of all three. Microwaves are in a separate category (see page 22).

CONDUCTION

One of the fundamental lessons in browning meat is to use only enough oil to enable conduction. You aren't cooking the oil. <u>Too much oil and you are deep frying the surface.</u> You usually only want enough to fill in the nooks and crannies to facilitate conduction. This is the crux of the issue. A little oil will enable the transfer of energy to the meat. A lot of oil will absorb the energy itself directly. On a microscopic level, meat and vegetables have a lot of little holes and ridges. They do not lie flat against the pan. The purpose of a fat is to fill in these tiny crevices and provide more even conduction. However, too much oil and the entire piece of meat or vegetable floats on top and the result is more akin to deep frying than searing. Unless you are cooking something liquid like eggs or pancakes, frying is actually a combination of conduction and convection to some extent.

CONVECTION

Boiling (convection of water) or deep frying (convection of oil) are both in this category as well as the convection of air in an oven. As explained above, the ratio between conduction and convection when pan frying is how much oil and/or water is in the pan. Baking something in the oven is primarily convection due to the circulation of hot air, however there is also the radiant energy from the walls of the oven. Depending on your oven design, there may be strong infrared energy from the heating element itself, too.

Inside your oven, there are hotter and colder places that cause air to circulate in the same way that a sea breeze is formed by the temperature difference in the air over land vs. water. This convection current, as you might imagine, is not very strong because inside a working oven it is pretty hot everywhere. There is air movement, but only slight. This is why fan assist and mechanical convection ovens were designed. They force the air currents around, producing more even browning and faster cooking. This is also the reason that you stir food on the stove. Stirring is mechanically forced convection of the liquid in a pot that both reduces cooking time and produces more even results.

The other form of heat transfer going on in your oven is the direct contact with the vessel in which the food is contained, which cooks by conduction on the bottom surface.

A form of convection that is often confusing for people is steam. This is termed convection, even if you are using an open steamer basket where the vapor only travels in a single direction—up and out. While it is tempting to think of it as radiation, it isn't because radiation *only* applies to electromagnetic energy waves. Technically there is also some conduction taking place during steaming, because some of the vapor condenses into liquid water and on a microscopic level is actually boiling the food on its surface.

RADIATION

Don't confuse the term *radiation* with radioactivity. All energy in the electromagnetic spectrum is radiation, including the visible light. **Refer to the spectrum diagram on the back cover of Volume 3**
Beyond the red end of the visible spectrum is IR (infrared) radiation, which causes the molecular vibrations that we call heat. Whether cooking over hot coals or under a broiler, these are cooking methods by infrared (IR) radiation.

Once again, there is a combination of effects taking place. Food on a charcoal grill is primarily being cooked by radiation, but where it touches the metal grates, there is conduction (the sear marks on the food are from this). There is also convection as steam leaves the surface of the food and circulates some before escaping.

Finally, even when pan searing, some radiant IR energy is emitted by the pan itself contributing to the total heat input.

COMBINED EFFECTS IN AN OVEN

For a vessel in an oven, the heat is a combination of conduction (direct contact), convection (circulating air) and IR from the hot vessel not in direct contact with food. The material of the vessel and whether or not the food is covered governs the ratio of these three.

MICROWAVES

Microwave cooking is an oddball and bears mentioning. It is distinctly different from any other form of cooking and does not exist in nature. The frequency employed has far too little energy to heat anything directly. It functions by rotating small polar molecules (especially water) which in turn interact with their neighboring molecules to produce the vibrational and translational energy that we term as heat. For a detailed explanation of the physics as to how and why microwave cooking works–and how it creates carcinogens in food, I urge you to read Volume 2, pages 46-47.

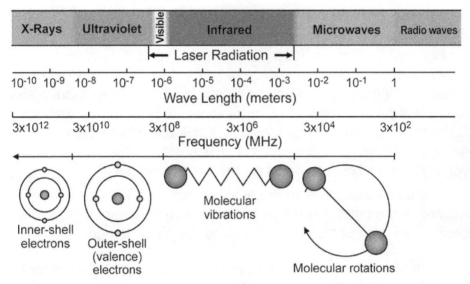

| X-Rays | Ultraviolet | Visible | Infrared | Microwaves | Radio waves |

← Laser Radiation →

Wave Length (meters)

10^{-10} 10^{-9} 10^{-8} 10^{-7} 10^{-6} 10^{-5} 10^{-4} 10^{-3} 10^{-2} 10^{-1} 1

Frequency (MHz)

3×10^{12} 3×10^{10} 3×10^{8} 3×10^{6} 3×10^{4} 3×10^{2}

Inner-shell electrons

Outer-shell (valence) electrons

Molecular vibrations

Molecular rotations

OVEN THERMOMETERS

Keep in mind that oven thermometers respond to the environment that they are in. If you place one next to the broiler element, you will record a much higher temperature than the average temperature inside of the rest of the oven. In the same way, if you place a thermometer between a baking tray and the heat source, you will register a lower temperature than is actually present. When checking the calibration of your oven thermostat dial—which you should do every few months—do so without any food or vessels in the oven. Also make sure the probe is not touching any part of the oven itself. This may seem like common sense, but I've seen cooks make this mistake many times.

OVEN POSITION / PLACEMENT

One of the most mysterious things to many cooks is if and why the position of food in the oven makes a difference. Indeed it does. This issue has been complicated in recent years by the change of oven designs. If you have an older oven, the heat (whether it is gas or electric) is likely to come from the bottom. There is usually a broiler element on the top inside of the oven, but that operates independently. In more recent electric ovens, the top and bottom element can operate at the same time, often along with some fan circulation. This produces more even heat distribution, but that's not always a good thing. Fortunately most of these ovens have controls in which you can select the heat source if you study the manual.

Because heat rises, food placed at the top of the oven will brown on the exposed surface, especially if you have an oven with a heating element running on both the top and bottom. Conversely, food placed on the bottom of the oven will brown on the crust-side faster than the top surface will cook. Think of pizza crusts as an example of why you would do this. The most extreme case is when you place your vessel directly on the floor of the oven.

The next issue is the material your oven dish is made of. Metal will brown the bottom and sides of your food the fastest. Glass and ceramic will be the slowest. Therefore the four rules are:

 • *For the maximum in <u>even cooking</u>, use a glass or ceramic vessel placed in the center of the oven.*

 • *If you want to <u>brown the top</u> of the food faster, use a glass or ceramic vessel at the top of the oven.*

 • *If you want to <u>brown the bottom</u> fast such as making a crisp crust, use a metal pan on the bottom of the oven.*

 • *And (of course) if you only care about browning the top or melting cheese, then use any ovenproof vessel you like and place it at the top shelf with the oven set to broil.*

HEAT TRANSFER MEDIUMS

Just as oil is thicker than water, a far more significant difference is that between air and water. Water can transfer heat much more efficiently than air. Boiling something at 100°C (212°F) will cook it much faster than putting it in an oven set to the same temperature. Cooking on a pan usually involves a lipid such as oil being the heat transfer medium, which is also much thicker than water.

Conversely, cooling something off by leaving it stand at room temperature is not nearly as efficient as it being in a large volume of water. Although there is essentially an infinite amount of air surrounding the thing you are cooling down, the problem is that air just isn't efficient at absorbing heat. If the same food is in a container of water, an equilibrium is soon reached in which the water is warm and the food being cooled down is still hot. This can be overcame by putting the item under running water in a sink, or by adding ice cubes periodically to maintain the lower temperature in the surrounding water.

Why does steam cook faster than boiling water, then? The density of the medium (steam) is much less than that of water, but steam has more energy than boiling water because it also has the *latent energy of vaporization*. For steam, all of the molecules had to have enough energy to escape the surface tension of the water. See the Boltzmann Curve in Volume 3, page 81. The amount of energy and the transfer medium are two different things.

THE PAN THICKNESS PARADOX

Something that most amateur cooks fail to consider is how adding food to a pan will lower the temperature of the surface, depending on the thickness and type of metal of the pan. In some steakhouses, there is a <u>very</u> thick plate of metal below the broiler element—sometimes as much as 2.5cm (1 inch). This gets extremely hot with the broiler heating it constantly, as you can well imagine. Putting a dozen steaks on that armor plated tank is not going to lower its temperature by any significant amount. This is quite different from cooking on any pan you would ever own.

Now here's where it gets counterintuitive. You are actually better off with a thin pan than a medium-thick pan for maintaining a high temperature. The surface temperature of a thin pan will drop faster and sharper, but it will recover faster, too. A medium-thick pan will drop in temperature slightly slower, but it will take longer to recover because the heat from the stove has more metal to penetrate. An extremely-thick pan (or grill) such as the one just described in steakhouses, will hardly drop in temperature and recover reasonably fast because of the massive amount of surrounding hot metal "feeding it". See the graph below.

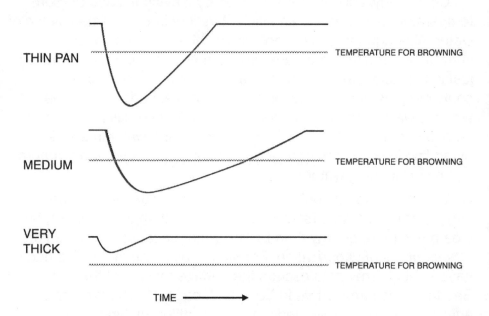

Note that the graph is only an approximation and there are other factors, such as the temperature of the meat being introduced, as well as it's thickness and density. That is, if you put a single strip of bacon on a pan, obviously it isn't going to alter the temperature as much as a tombstone-size steak straight out of the fridge, not that you should *ever* cook steak right out of the fridge (see page 236).

The real issue here is the time the meat spends below the browning temperature. This is the period when it is cooking mostly by convection on a cushion of steam produced by the water escaping the surface. In the case of the extremely thick griddle, the temperature never drops below the browning point. There is so much energy that the steam is blown off as fast as it can form, so it contributes almost nothing to convective cooking.

In the case of a very thin pan, the food is nearly on the burner surface itself. In fact, a lot of infrared radiation is actually coming directly through the pan, so you have both conduction and radiation doing the cooking. No slab-o-beast is so large that it will lower the temperature of a glowing red electric stove element, let alone the flaming jet nozzles of a gas range. That thin piece of metal separating the food from the fire is almost invisible when it comes to heat transfer. While with a medium-thick pan, we have a layer of metal that has to be reheated from below once it has been thermally quenched.

So, does this mean that the cheapest steel pan you can find at a 99 cent store is going to do a better job of browning than an expensive all-clad stainless steel pan? Yes, believe it, or not! That's why paellas are thin. However, it will also cause the meat to burn on the outside while it is still raw on the inside if you carry it too far—but maybe that's how you like it (some do). The downside is that cheap pan is going to warp pretty fast. If you are using an electric stove, a warped pan is completely worthless so you'll be replacing it often. If it won't sit flat on the stove, it won't heat evenly. While this isn't quite as much of a problem for a gas stove, a badly warped pan still produces uneven heating to some extent.

PIZZA STONES

In my considerable experience, a pizza stone is the culinary equivalent of a Pet Rock. If you aren't old enough to remember what those were, these were a gag gift in the mid-1970's. It was just an ordinary rock in a box with directions telling you joke things about all of the advantages of this pet has because it doesn't need to be walked, or fed or any other form of attention, but you were sure to fall in love with it. There is no necessity for a pizza stone, or the extremely long and wasteful preheating time that it requires, even if you have fallen in love with yours.

Why not? You say that commercial pizza ovens have stone decks inside and they make great pizzas! The difference in a commercial pizza oven reaches at least 400°C (750°F), so a stone cooking surface is good because it retains heat just like that metal plate in the steakhouse broiler mentioned in the previous section. A big slab of stone heats up slowly but it remains hot, and that's really important when you are shoveling in a dozen pizzas at a time over and over all night with the oven door being frequently opened. A metal deck would burn the crust before the rest cooked, thus stone.

The is a problem for you at home because stone is not nearly as good at transferring heat compared to a metal pan. That's not an issue if your oven is 400°C (750°F) or more, but your home oven is not even close to that temperature. So now what you have is a big rock that isn't very good at transfering heat but is doing great job of blocking the convection in your oven. Sure, it transfers some from what it retained before you put that big cold pizza on top, but you can get a better and far more energy-efficient result just by using a thin metal pan and cooking your pizza in two steps instead of one. Plus then you don't have to deal with getting that giant volcano-hot rock out of your oven later while trying not to drop and shatter it.

THE SOLUTION FOR HOME PIZZA

So here's what to do: Put the circle of dough down on a relatively thin steel pan. Use a fork to dock it (that's technical lingo for poking a bunch of holes in it). Bake it at about 220°C (450°F) for between 7 and 10 minutes depending on the thickness of the dough and how crisp you like your crust. Then take it out and put on the sauce, cheeses and whatever other toppings you fancy. Now put it back in the oven (same temperature) and continue cooking for another 6 to 9 minutes depending on how much topping was on it and (once again), depending on how crisp you like your crust given the thickness of the dough you chose to use.

One final note here. I continue to specify steel pans and not aluminum because please remember that aluminum cookware is reactive and ions leach from the surface every time you cook. Over years, these cause deleterious health effects, despite what the aluminum industry would have you believe. Anodized aluminum, or aluminum pans with a nonstick coating are fine. It bears repeating: Do not cook on plain aluminum.

ICEBATHS AND DEFROSTING

Convection is not limited to the circulation of air in an oven or steam under food in a pan. As a rule of thumb, the denser the medium is, the more efficient the transfer of heat will be (as explained on page 24). Thus, the water bath as used in sous vide cooking is far more effective and controllable than air in an oven. Still more efficient is the oil in a deep fryer, which is the next topic.

The same goes for cooling. Leaving something out at room temperature will eventually cool it down to room temperature (of course). Set it near a running fan and it will cool faster because more air is passing by, carrying heat away. Put it in the refrigerator or freezer and it will cool even faster because the cold air in the refrigerator is circulating by fans, so the cold air will carry away more heat per second. Still, these are all slow methods compared with cooling something down in cold water or an ice bath because water is far more dense than air. In fact, water is a peculiar substance for having a very high density and still remaining a liquid when very cold. The unique properties of water are what make life as we know it possible, but I digress...

It is often necessary to thaw seafood or meat quickly. This is best accomplished with running cold water. Never use hot water because you are partially cooking the surface before the interior is defrosted. In fact, if the piece of meat is large enough, you can actually cause it to turn rancid before it comes to room temperature.

In the case of shrimp, which are probably the most frequent item to require rapid defrosting (at least in a commercial kitchen), you can simply add them to a large bowl of cold water. Change the water after 5-10 minutes two times and you will have perfectly thawed shrimp or prawns from the freezer in only about 15 minutes.

The main application of ice baths is to stop the cooking of vegetables being blanched, or to rapidly cool down any stock after it comes off the stove. This will greatly extend its life before spoilage because the "danger zone" is where bacteria multiply quickly. Leaving it to cool at room temperature will allow bacteria to double every 20 minutes (more about this on page 38).

DEEP FRYING PHYSICS

A deep fryer is not an oven. This may seem obvious when it is stated directly, yet many novices treat the two as if they are the same. Adding food to a deep fryer immediately lowers the temperature of the oil. Especially frozen foods! Adding food to an

oven has very little effect on the temperature inside. Again, this is because oil is an excellent heat conductor and air is not.

Hot oil is what makes the difference between food coming out crispy and flaky or nasty and oily. Small home deep fryers are especially prone to this problem as people tend to overload them.

You can't put a kilogram of food in two kilograms of oil and expect good results. The less you put in at a time, the better because the temperature will not drop as much.

The other issue is that the oil becomes wet after using it. You may think that's impossible because oil and water don't mix, but they do to some extent when the oil is hot. The main factor is that the foods you are frying often contain natural emulsifiers (things that enable oil and water to mix). If you are deep frying something that was dipped in the classic flour, egg and breadcrumb mixture, or any batter containing eggs, some of that egg will get into the oil and greatly increase how much water the oil can retain. The water comes from the steam escaping from whatever it is you are frying. If you have a small amount of oil to start with (relative to the volume of food) it will become wet quickly, and that means that whatever you fry next will be increasingly oily. Deep frying vegetables like cauliflower and beer batters is the worst for this.

The problem is that many people do not regard the oil as an ingredient. It is! Frying is going to cost you money if you do it right because you must change the oil frequently for good results.

TWO PHASE COOKING

My very first video on YouTube was put there to teach cooks in my restaurant how to properly cook the basis of many recipes: Tomato sauce. It is so counterintuitive that I always have trouble getting cooks to follow the directions. They are sure the sauce will burn, but does not. This relies on physics similar to how foods are deep fried, only here you are actually deep frying a liquid—really!

This is to answer the questions that I have been asked in comments frequently for years. Namely, why does it work? How?

First a pan is heated with enough oil to completely cover the bottom surface. It must be smoking hot. Then passata is poured on top (use a splatter guard and fast reflexes!), but do not add so much as to drop the temperature of the oil drastically, or the whole process is ruined. As long as the oil remains far above the boiling point of water, the passata can not touch the bottom of the pan because the steam that it releases on contact with the hot oil will lift it back up away from the pan. This boundary layer is where the action is taking place. The passata is cooking at the temperature of the oil but can not burn except only at the edges of the pot where it actually does contact the hot metal, but that will be okay as long as you don't let it go for so long that it actually does burn. Caramelization of the passata at the edge of the pan only adds to the flavor (within reason).

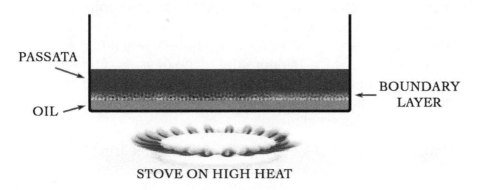

As you can see, if you stir this, you have destroyed the barrier between the passata and the hot metal of the pan. Now it will begin to burn because you have mixed the oil into the passata and cooled the oil down so it no longer provides a barrier.

Even though you can't see it, convection currents within the passata are actually doing the stirring for you, so you don't need to worry about that. If that wasn't happening then the layer next to the oil would just burn and the rest of the passata would still be raw. When you check on it, you see that it cooked evenly.

There are a couple of other considerations in using this method:

1. The pan must be stainless steel or (better) anodized aluminum. Do not use a nonstick pan for this because splattering will be far greater and the oil and passata will begin to mix after a short time due to bubbling disturbing the bottom layer on the slippery surface.

2. A very heavy pan is required. If you use a thin pan, the hot spots (see page 8) will produce uneven heating and once again the passata and oil will start to mix, ruining the process.

3. Be brave. Resist the urge to stir for several minutes. You can carefully pull back a tiny bit to inspect the progress being made, but as soon as you stir it or if you add anything to the pan that will lower the temperature, the two phases will mix and then game over! You can add things like sugar and spices (without stirring), and when it is well on its way to being done you can add chopped vegetables such as onion, but don't add any more passata or wine or anything else that will drop the temperature until the final stage is complete. Also, adding vegetables such as onions will slow the cooking down because they will release moisture slowly and that water will reduce the temperature of the passata. Adding a spice (typically paprika) is okay because it will float on top of the passata and not burn. It will infuse into the sauce providing you don't stir it.

I repeat: Do not stir it until it is finished caramelizing.

PRESSURE COOKER MAGIC

When you get right down to it, the only controls we normally have over cooking are temperature and time. Sure, there is the ratio of conduction, convection and radiation, but for foods that are mostly water (see table below), the maximum temperature internally is going to be in the vicinity of 100°C (212°F) until they have been cooked sufficiently to drive off most of the water. That is, unless you employ a pressure cooker (see chart on the next page).

90–99%	**Mushrooms, cabbage and many other vegetables**
80–89%	**Apples, potatoes, lemons, oranges, artichokes**
70–79%	**Red meats, bananas, many cheeses, corn, shrimp**
60–69%	**Legumes, salmon, chicken breast, breads**

Possible cooking methods are really quite limited, being only your stove, the oven, a deep fryer, a water bath for sous vide and a pressure cooker. Plus a charcoal grill if you have the luck of nice weather and live in a place where BBQ is allowed. Of these few methods, a pressure cooker is the one most often forgotten.

One reason why pressure cookers don't get the attention they deserve is that they require some different skills from ordinary frying and roasting. It take some practice and intuition to know what is going on is inside that "black box", because there is no way to see how the food is cooking until you stop everything, cool it down and release the pressure. In many cases the difference of just a few minutes of cooking time can decide the difference between deliciously moist meat or some inedible dry mummy that used to be your expensive roast. The stakes are high and the chances for success are definitely less than other cooking methods to the inexperienced user. However, with some practice one will find that pressure cooking shortens the cooking time, and increases both flavor and tenderness in a great many applications.

Even if you look up the official cooking time for a particular vegetable or meat, the information is often seriously flawed. Not only by telling you that everything can be cooked in a pressure cooker (only <u>some</u> things lend themselves to this method) but also

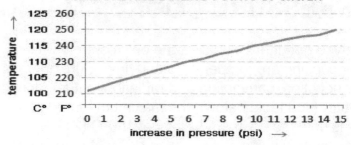

PRESSURE AND BOILING POINTS OF WATER

increase in pressure (psi) →

PSI	°F	°C
15	250	121
14.5	249	120.6
13.1	246	119
11.6	243	117
10.2	239	116
8.7	237	114
7.3	233	112
5.8	229	110
4.4	225	107
2.9	221	105
1.5	217	103
0	212	100

the times vary wildly from site to site and are hit and miss for accuracy. The tables at the back (page 224) are a guide to some tested times for foods that are recommended for pressure cooking.

CORRECTIONS ABOVE SEA LEVEL

The assumption is that you are cooking somewhere around sea level. If you are at a high elevation, this will limit your pressure cooker's power by just how far up you are. At 3 kilometers (10,000 feet) you have lost 40% of the power in both pressure and the increase in temperature, so now your 15 psi is only 9 psi because the atmosphere is thinner. As you can see in the table above, at 9 psi you can only reach about 115°C or 238°F. The rule is that if you are above 600 meters (2000 feet) elevation, add 5% time for every 300 meters (1000 feet) further up you are. Sea level is best by far.

INSTANT POTS AS PRESSURE COOKERS

The recently popular "Instant Pot" electric cookers only go to about 10 psi, while a traditional dedicated pressure cooker operates at 15 psi. This makes a bigger difference than you might think, being 33% more pressure as well as several degrees hotter. Some models claim to go to 11 psi, but in independent testing most did not even reach 10 psi, and cheaper models barely hit 8 psi. If you doubt this, it is easy to find reports on Google about Instant Pots coming in at 8 psi or even less. Bottom line: If you are serious about cooking, get a real pressure cooker. The days of them blowing up are long over. Today's models have interlock mechanisms and pressure relief valves as safeguards.

PRESSURE FRYERS

The pressure cooker and deep fryer in one is the real secret to the Colonel's famous chicken (aside from massive amounts of MSG). They are patented and not sold to the public. But even if you could buy one, they cost more than a luxury RV and require *more* electrical power than the central air conditioning of a huge mansion!

Enter the Genmine pressure fryer available on Amazon. It's still more expensive than any other kitchen appliance and it consumes oil like it was free, but it does work—if you have 220 volt power and you can afford the space it occupies and (of course) the price.

❊

SOUS VIDE APPLICATIONS

One of the most useful—and overused—tools in recent years is sous vide. This enables restaurants to prepare many items to the point where any novice (*i.e.* low paid) cook is less likely to screw up expensive proteins and can turn out consistent results. Depending on which food this is applied to, those results range from mediocre to excellent. This is the same range of results for home cooks, also because sous vide is not a one-size-fits-all solution. First, there is no Maillard Reaction or caramelization at low temperatures and there is no true solution to that, despite what advocates claim.

REVERSE SEARING

This is when you cook meat sous vide and then you sear it on a high heat to char the surface some. While this seems like a brilliant solution, it is not the same at all. To a large extent what searing does to sous vide cooked meats is to burn the surface a bit to add a little smokiness because, (a) there is not enough time for heat and flavor to penetrate into the meat before you overcook it since it has already been fully cooked, and (b) the flavor compounds near the surface have already reacted during the slow cook and will never react the same way again, even if you like your meat burnt. Keep this in mind when deciding if sous vide is really the best solution.

To be sure there are some great benefits in sous vide cooking in specific instances. Especially if the meat does not need deep browning such as delicate fish. Some specific advantages are the controlled tenderization of veal and the penetration of marinades.

THE VACUUM COMPONENT

Often vacuum sealing will infuse marinades without any hot water bath. There are some examples of that in this book, too.

Lastly, a Michelin Star type modernist technique these days is to squeeze out moisture from sliced fruits and vegetables by vacuum compression, leaving them denser and better looking. Unfortunately, for that you need a professional chamber-type vacuum sealer as shown on the next page. The home type "Seal-a-Meal" machine can not provide enough vacuum to do the job.

SOUS VIDE EQUIPMENT

To cook sous vide requires two pieces of equipment: A vacuum sealer and a precision temperature controlled water bath. There are many sources that claim you don't need a vacuum sealer and you can just use an ordinary plastic food storage bag and submerge it in water to push the air out. That's not creating a vacuum. The food inside is still at atmospheric pressure, which is poaching, <u>not</u> sous vide. *Sous vide* literally means *under vacuum.* You need proper equipment to actually cook sous vide. There are two types of vacuum sealers. The first one shown here is a pro "chamber" type:

These machines let you set the exact amount of vacuum. Far more important: no matter how much liquid is in the bag with the food, it will still seal cleanly—which certainly can't be said for less expensive "Seal-a-Meal" type vacuum sealers such as this one:

The reason is that the home consumer vacuum sealer slowly sucks the air out from the end of the bag, giving plenty of time to draw out any liquids along with it. Even if you are not adding olive oil or any other moist flavorings, most foods have natural juices that will come shooting up once the bag squeezes down on them during the slow vacuuming process.

Professional chamber machines create an entire atmospheric environment around the whole bag before sealing it up very quickly. The downsides are that the pro machines are big and heavy, plus they cost about ten times as much—but if you have the money and space, get the pro machine. It will pay for itself in the long run.

How? Because those rolls of specialty vacuum bags are rather expensive and the only way you can prevent liquid contents from gushing up with the cheaper machine is to cut your bag much longer than it needs to be for the food. Sometimes three times as long, and that means wasted money every time you use it. Plus the pro machines use a less expensive type of bag. Still, if you are only cooking sous vide on rare occasions, the cheap machine will be fine. Water baths are less critical. The stick type will work just well and can be stored away easily. The big tanks take up space.

Finally, you need to fold back the edges of the bags when loading them to keep the top edge clean for a good seal.

❋

SOUS VIDE SAFETY

The most dangerous aspect of sous vide cooking in the hands of an amateur is the failure to understand the great potential for food poisoning. The fairly low temperature and extended times of cooking can allow bacteria to multiply to very dangerous and even potentially deadly levels. There was a case in which some culinary pioneer tried to prepare a pork roast sous vide at 45°C (113°F) for 120 hours. There were no survivors from that oh-so-tender meat.

THE DANGER ZONE

Bacteria can reproduce less than once every 20 minutes under optimum conditions. So after just a few hours of pleasant warmth and humidity, thousands become billions. This is why sous vide can be dangerous if you don't understand how to avoid this pitfall.

The temperature range in which bacteria can multiply rapidly is called the "danger zone". See the chart in °F and °C below.

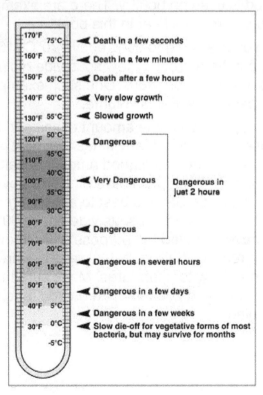

Most food hygiene courses and charts teach that the entire range from 10° to 60°C (50 to 140°F) should always be avoided. That conventional wisdom worked just fine until sous vide came along. Now people cook within that range, so those black and white days are over. What you have to understand is that near both extremes of that temperature range, bacterial growth slows down. It does not come to a halt until you get above 68°C (155°F), though.

If you are cooking above 58°C (136°F), you have less to worry about because bacteria only grow slowly in that range, despite what the old charts said about how they were reproducing quickly all the way up to 60°C (140°F). Still, with very long cooking times (which some recipes call for, all the way to 48 hours), care must be taken not to start out with meat that is laden with bacteria.

Obviously the fewer bacteria you have on your food to begin with, the longer it can be cooked without becoming toxic. So the best way to accomplish that is either quickly pan searing it first, using a blowtorch all over it, or poaching in boiling water a couple of times with an ice bath in between to keep it from actually cooking. The latter method is used on poultry. There are examples of these approaches in some recipes later in this book.

Of course if you are going to cook above 70°C (160°F) then you can ignore this, but there are very few sous vide recipes that operate at such a high temperature. One such example is the octopus recipe (page 109) in this volume.

The other consideration is the amount of salt and spices on the meat being cooked sous vide. Many times the meat is put in with a spice mixture or paste that has a good amount of salt in it. This also slows bacterial growth. Even plain olive oil alone slows down bacterial growth a tiny bit. Still it is best to always err on the side of safety. You can't cook everything sous vide above 60°C (140°F) to be safe, or you have defeated the purpose of the method. It is best to stick to proven recipes. Failing that, always beware of very long cooking times and of low temperatures. Make sure the recipe is from a reliable source and not someone on YouTube with no professional training.

BRAISING & VAPOR DENSITY

For any given size piece of food heated to any specific temperature, only so much vapor will be produced. This vapor is from the moisture in the food and the liquid that you added. If there is no containment of the vapor, then the moisture will be carried off into the surrounding atmosphere and the food will dry out. If the vapor is contained in a braising dish, then the concentration of the

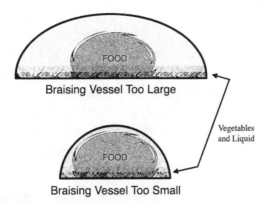

Braising Vessel Too Large

Vegetables and Liquid

Braising Vessel Too Small

vapor will be a function of how much space there is between the walls of the vessel and the food. For the maximum flavor retention, you want the highest possible vapor concentration *within reason*. Like most things, it is possible to carry the idea too far. If the braising vessel is too small, then vapor won't be able to circulate well. More important, the walls of the braising vessel radiate heat, so if the vessel is tight fitting, the food is being cooked by radiant IR energy instead of by the hot vapor. Ideally you want a vessel between 3 and 5 cm (1 to 2 inches) larger than the food on all sides. The bottom of the food must be protected from direct contact with the braising vessel by either vegetables or a metal steamer basket (mostly used when braising vegetables) to prevent cooking by *conduction* (page 20).

Remember to only use a small amount of liquid to braise foods. If your braised meat is dry and stringy, you had too much liquid so it boiled instead of braised and/or you had meat that was too lean.

DRY AGING BEEF

Up until the 1960's, most quality beef sold was dry aged to at least some extent. The shift from independent butcher shops to corporate chain supermarkets meant cutting corners to have the lowest prices. Today you only find quality dry aged meat in the most expensive small markets and steak houses.

True dry aging of beef can only be done on well-marbled prime grade beef because the fat helps prevent spoilage. Lean meat will rot before dry aging can occur. The potential of spoilage must be eliminated. There are two approaches. One is to leave the meat exposed to humidity-controlled circulating refrigerated air, and the other is to wrap the meat first in cheesecloth or some similar permeable membrane to slow the loss of moisture and the growth of microbes on the surface. The advantage of both methods is the breakdown of connective tissue by enzymes naturally present in the meat. The microphotographs below show this before and after.

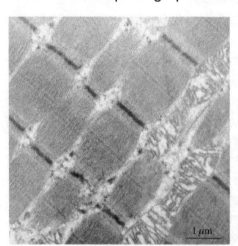

The cloth-wrapped method is more economical and will still render the meat more tender and slightly more buttery, but it is not the same as *true* dry aging, where about 20% of the moisture of the meat is lost (concentrating the beef flavor), but then there is a thick layer of microbial growth that has to be shaved off before cooking. True dry aging is controlled rot, and like blue cheese, it isn't for everyone—and actual moldy meat should not be consumed <u>ever</u>.

While dry aging is generally considered suitable only for beef, and certainly never for pork or chicken, it can be applied to veal and lamb, too. Recently a few top restaurants have began offering dry aged veal, and it can be quite delicious - but there are two serious problems. First, finding well marbled fatty veal is difficult because the animal hasn't lived long enough yet to have the sort of marbled fat you can get on beef. This makes it technically more difficult to dry age without it rotting. High tech solutions such as motorized racks turning large primal cuts in from of bactericidal ultraviolet lights can be employed with careful monitoring, but as you can well imagine, the cost of the final product is astronomical - especially considering that large pieces of the meat have to be cut away and discarded, as well as the loss of weight from evaporated moisture. Second, dry aged veal no longer tastes very much like veal. It tastes more like beef, but not exactly beef, either. It is a little bit strange, and so it will probably never see widespread popularity.

Dry aged lamb has the same problems, so mutton (older sheep) is usually chosen. Few Americans like mutton, especially after the flavor has been further intensified by dry aging, so this is a technique mostly seen in nations where mutton is appreciated.

The general scheme for all dry aging is to keep the meat at low humidity between -1 and +3°C (30 and 38°F) for 15 days or more, with the average being about 20 days.

KOJI RICE METHOD

This is another modernist technique. Steaks are coated with this special Japanese rice and wrapped up for 24 hours. Then the rice is washed off, leaving the steak more tender. This works because Koji rice has a type of fungus (*Aspergillus oryzae*) that is harmless to humans, but it breaks down connective tissue in beef. Because this special rice is often hard to find, people have tried the method using sushi rice (still from Japan, right?) but it doesn't do much at all because there is no fungal action. The reason sushi rice works a little bit is that the dry rice draws out some moisture from the steak, *slightly* concentrating the flavor. Koji is the only one worth trying.

MEAT GRINDER VS. FOOD PROCESSOR

A food processor is not a meat grinder. In most cases you can not substitute one for the other because the mechanical processes are entirely different. A food processor slices food into small pieces, but the blade is not sharp enough to finely mince tendons or connective tissues and there is no mechanism for removing these unchewable gnarly and stringy bits from the rest of the meat.

On the other hand, a meat grinder both cuts and tears fibers with enormous shearing force. The toughest fibers wrap around the auger screw and can't pass through the perforated plate, so they are left behind. The proof of that is when you disassemble a meat grinder after use and find the twisted wad of tendons and tough membranes that didn't get through. A food processor has no way of leaving anything behind. Whatever you put into it, you get back out.

Using a food processor on meat that has already passed through a meat grinder is fine, though. You've already eliminated the tendons and tough fibers. Finely ground meat is mostly useful in making sausages.

Boneless, skinless chicken breasts, fish without bones and most trimmed organ meats can be ground up using a food processor providing that care was first taken to cut away connective fibers. This is standard practice for preparing a mousse or pâté.

However, in the case of a mousse, it is generally necessary to rub the ground meat through a tamis (a fine mesh screen) in order to remove fine fibers, as well as any possibly missed small bone fragments (especially in the case of fish). This is a fairly tedious process, as you might well imagine. In commercial kitchens where this is a daily operation (especially in France), there are power strainers that accomplish that task effortlessly. Unfortunately, such machines are large and quite expensive.

TYPES OF SALT

There are countless brands and specialty salts sold all over the world. At one point I had a collection of more than thirty kinds. Here are a summary of the major types.

TABLE SALT

This is common salt that is inexpensive and little more than purified sodium chloride. It may be purchased with or without iodide added. Iodide is an essential element in the diet of most people for proper thyroid function. Table salt usually also contains a small amount of an anti-caking agent.

PICKLING SALT

Finely ground pure sodium chloride with no iodide and no anti-caking agents because they turn pickling solutions cloudy.

KOSHER SALT

Something surprising to many people is that kosher salt usually has nothing to do with it being blessed by a Jewish rabbi, unlike other foods labeled *kosher*. The name came from long ago when Jews used coarse salt for religiously dictated meat preparations requiring blood to be drawn out with salt. On rare occasions, one actually sees "kosher *certified* salt" that actually is overseen and blessed by a rabbi, usually kosher just means coarse salt that contains no iodine. It weighs less than regular table salt for the same volume because of the air between the chunks.

HIMALAYAN PINK SALT

This salt is mined in the mountains of Pakistan. Despite the pink color that leads many to imagine it is rich in minerals, analysis has determined it is 99% pure sodium chloride. Taste wise it is nearly indistinguishable from table salt, but it lacks iodine.

HAWAIIAN RED SALT

This is approximately 85% sea salt that is mixed with the red volcanic clay known as *alaea* in the Hawaiian language. This clay is rich in red iron oxide and other minerals that provide a slightly more complex taste. It may be beneficial for those on a low sodium diet.

BLACK SALTS

There are two main types of black salts that are quite unrelated. All get their color from charcoal. One is **Hawaiian Black Lava** salt, which is sea salt mixed with charcoal from coconuts. Related to this is **Cypress Black Flake** salt, which is sea salt from that area mixed with charcoal from birch and other trees in the region.

The other type is **Kala Namak** which is arguably more of a spice than a salt. It is Himalayan salt mixed with the bark of trees, spices, charcoal and sodium sulfate before being sealed up and roasted. The odor is often quite awful to most people who did not grow up with it, smelling of rotten eggs due to the hydrogen sulfide present.

SEA SALTS

Seawater is evaporated to produce a salt that is rich in flavorful minerals. The exact composition will depend on the origin, so simple "sea salt" is vague and can even be from polluted waters. The following three salts are examples of high quality sea salts.

FLEUR DE SEL

Harvested by hand from the surface of tidal pools in Brittany, France, this is known as the caviar of salts. Full of flavor.

SEL GRIS

Similar to Fleur de Sel, but harvested from the bottom of tidal pools in France. It is grey in color and retains over 10% water. Also very flavorful, but a bit too briny for applications other than fish.

MALDON FLAKE SALTS

Harvested from the banks of a river in Maldon in the UK. The water is evaporated over fires in ancient Roman clay vessels. Relatively high in minerals but oddly low in magnesium, making it less bitter than most sea salts. It is also sold in a smoked variety.

SMOKED SALTS

These are also more of a seasoning than a salt. Often preferable to liquid smoke for being more natural and subtle. For more about smoked salts, see Volume 2, page 49.

MUSHROOM CHEMISTRY

The most prevalent supermarket variety of mushroom is **Agaricus bisporus**, more commonly known as champignons, or button mushrooms when they are still white and immature. When they are more mature and brown, they are sold as criminis, or sometimes Italian brown or chestnut mushrooms. These are just different names for the same mushroom. When they are fully mature, they are marketed as portobello. This naming has been an invention of marketing. The general public remains largely unaware that these are all the same mushroom. In fact, portobello didn't even exist in stores a few decades ago. They were considered waste products and used for pig feed. Then someone got the idea of giving them a fancy name and selling them as a gourmet item. It worked remarkably well. The public had no idea that portobello mushrooms were just older overgrown regular mushrooms that they were paying a premium price for. They do have their uses, though.

GENETIC DIFFERENCES IN TASTE PERCEPTION

There are extreme genetic differences between individuals in how mushrooms are perceived. About 25% of the human population can not smell some of the bitter aromatic components in many types of mushrooms. These people have been termed *non-tasters*, but such labels are oversimplifications. Also, it has been discovered that age plays a role. Even those who were capable of making such distinctions in their youth lose this ability with the onset of age. This is a serious danger for older people who forage mushrooms, having learned to distinguish edible ones from similar looking bitter poisonous mushrooms when they were young.

Taste preferences are even more extreme when it comes to truffles, with about 25% saying they smell like old gym socks and 25% saying they are the best aroma ever. About 50% are neutral.

Bartoshuk, L. M. et al. (1998) "PROP (6-n-propylthiouracil) Supertasters and the Saltiness of NaCl", *Annals of the New York Academy of Science*. **855** pages 793–796.

Hallock RM. (2007) "The Taste of Mushrooms", *McIlvainea* 17: pages 33-41.

Manzi, P., et. al. (2004) "Commercial Mushrooms: Nutritional Value and Effect of Cooking", *Food Chemistry*, 84:2, pages 201-206.

THE EFFECTS OF DRYING AND COOKING MUSHROOMS

When mushrooms are processed in any way (frozen, canned or dried) the proportions of their flavor molecules are changed, yet they still retain mushroom flavor and aroma. This is because the key component common to all mushrooms is 1-Octen-3-ol, also known as *mushroom alcohol.* This has a powerful aroma and a

1-Octen-3-ol
"Mushroom Alcohol"

relatively high temperature for decomposition. Normal cooking won't reduce the amount significantly, but drying mushrooms does. In general, drying mushrooms tends to bring out the other aroma chemicals in their "symphony" of molecular components that all combine to produce the distinctive aroma and taste in each variety. By the way, 1-Octen-3-ol is a legal food additive that is commonly used by food manufacturers in many canned and frozen foods.

Porcini mushrooms are an extreme example of how flavors are changed when mushrooms are dried, as shown in this table:

COMPONENT	FRESH PORCINI	DRIED PORCINI	AROMA
1-Octen-3-ol	VERY HIGH	LOW	MUSHROOMS
1-Octanol	YES	NO	PUNGENT
3-Octanol	YES	NO	EARTHY, HERBS
3-Octanone	YES	NO	SWEET CHEESE
2-Octen-1-ol	YES	NO	VEGETABLE, FRUIT
Caprylic acid	NO	YES	GOATS, BEER
Furfural	NO	YES	ALMONDS, WOOD
2-Heptanone	NO	YES	GORGONZOLA
1-Hexanol	NO	YES	FUEL OIL, ALCOHOL
2-Hexanol	NO	YES	EARTHY, FLORAL

As you can see from the table on the previous page, many of the molecules responsible for the unique aroma and flavor disappear when porcini are dried. Yet when we smell the reconstituted dried porcini, they still have a porcini-like aroma and we tend to accept them as such. But if you actually compared them side-by-side with fresh porcini, you would realize just how muted and different the aromas are. It's just that such a situation rarely comes up for people. If you are using fresh porcini, you probably aren't reconstituting dried ones at the same time, and vice versa.

The natural aroma of foods is a symphony of molecules that are sometimes individually foul smelling. It is like an orchestra playing a melody with a pianist playing along with the theme. If the pianist starts playing off key, the rhythm and melody are still clearly audible. The key here is *audible*—but not the same.

As explained in Volume 3, most foods do not contain any single chemical that resembles the overall flavor of the food. A well known exception is vanilla, where a single component is responsible for about 90% of the flavor and aroma. However, such instances are rare in nature. Mushrooms are not as extreme, but every mushroom contains 1-octen-3-ol. Note that is practically the <u>only</u> aroma molecule in common champignons (also known as button mushrooms in supermarkets). Champignons have very little else in flavor molecules, so they just smell of faint generic mushrooms.

CHEMICAL DIFFERENCES BETWEEN SPECIES

The table on the opposite page here will give you some idea of the complexity of the topic. Only 23 of the established 64 aroma molecules present in mushrooms have been compared. Although these species are all edible European forest mushrooms, you have likely never heard of most of them. Two are well known, though:

B. edulis = Porcini, also known as Ceps

C. cibarius = Chanterelles

In each row the mushroom listed with 100 (%) is the benchmark with others being compared to it (in %) for that particular component. Where it says "nd", it means zero (nd = not detected).

Relative percentage (%) of some of the 64 volatile compounds of mushroom species

Compound	Samples (RA%)										
	A. rubescens	*B. edulis*	*C. cibarius*	*F. hepatica*	*H. agathosmus*	*R. cyanoxantha*	*S. bellini*	*S. granulatus*	*S. luteus*	*T. equestre*	*T. rutilans*
trans-2-Hexen-1-ol	nd	nd	33.1	nd	75.4	nd	100	nd	nd	nd	nd
1-Hexanol	nd	12.3	100	4.1	32.9	nd	29.8	21	nd	19.1	8.8
Methional	nd	100	nd	nd	nd	nd	nd	8	19	nd	nd
α-Pinene	63.6	11.2	4.9	6.7	13.1	31.9	15.8	9.1	100	10.2	13.3
1-Octen-3-one	15.7	8.9	100	nd	nd	nd	nd	nd	13	nd	nd
6-Methyl-5-hepten-2-one	nd	nd	nd	nd	nd	13.3	100	nd	40.6	nd	nd
3-Octanone	100	nd	nd	nd	nd	nd	nd	nd	nd	nd	nd
β-Pinene	18.1	nd	nd	21.3	32.8	nd	71.4	100	26.5	nd	nd
3-Octanol	100	nd	nd	nd	nd	nd	nd	nd	0.1	nd	nd
1-Octen-3-ol	17.4	31	100	1.6	64.4	16.4	40.3	4.9	nd	58.8	35.5
1.4-Cyneole	nd	nd	nd	nd	nd	3.1	nd	100	1.4	nd	1.3
Limonene	11.4	2.6	3.3	6.1	4.1	20.8	2.7	14.5	100	1.5	8.4
Eucalyptol	48.6	29.3	39.9	74.6	45.4	42	26.7	63.9	nd	16.6	100
Phenylacetaldehyde	7.3	2.2	1.5	12.3	5.5	16.2	3.5	30.6	100	19.4	4.2
trans-2-Octen-1-ol	20.7	nd	nd	3.2	nd	20.6	100	2.2	nd	81.2	82.7
Linalool	17	1	nd	1.6	4	22	18.7	100	25.2	nd	nd
2-Phenylethanol	6.6	18.4	1.6	30.8	9.6	13.8	3.8	100	25.9	40.5	7.2
Menthol	7.7	31	78.5	21.2	21.4	18.9	100	31.3	8.1	22.7	16.2
α-Terpineol	nd	nd	nd	21.7	nd	100	nd	63.1	50.7	nd	nd
trans-Geranylacetone	nd	4.5	nd	5.1	7.3	7.3	41.9	100	65.4	2.6	nd
β-Ionone	nd	59	nd	nd	79.1	nd	37.7	nd	100	87.1	17.4
trans-Nerolidol	nd	nd	nd	nd	nd	nd	11.3	84.8	100	nd	nd
Farnesylacetone	nd	nd	nd	nd	nd	nd	57.1	100	98.4	nd	nd

TYPES OF VINEGARS

DISTILLED WHITE VINEGAR

This is just dilute acetic acid, which is the chemical that makes all vinegars sour. Distilled white vinegar has no other flavoring. It is usually about 5% acetic acid to 95% water. The thing to know is that acetic acid has a relatively low boiling point of 118°C (244°F) and so a thick mixture such as a sauce or stew with vinegar that can boil at that temperature will gradually lose its acidity as it simmers. Acetic acid is also prone to reacting with other molecules when heated, and that will also slowly neutralize the sourness.

RED WINE VINEGAR

Much more punch and flavor than plain vinegar. This is red wine that has been fermented to the point of it being vinegar. This is what European chefs did long ago. You can also make your own from wine, and it will be far better that what you can buy in a supermarket as long as you use a quality wine. The method is described here on page 235. Inexpensive wine vinegars are made from cheap low-grade wine, naturally. The most expensive wine vinegars will state what type of wine was used to make it.

WHITE WINE or CHAMPAGNE VINEGAR

The same that goes for red wine vinegar, only white wine vinegar is a bit sweeter and more delicate. Champagne vinegar has some other notes in it and is classically paired with fish. Once again, what you buy is no match for what you can make yourself.

SHERRY VINEGAR

As in the case of red and white wine vinegar, this is fermented from sherry. The flavor is the richest and deepest of vinegars. This is used to deglaze pans in many classic French recipes, as most of the acetic acid will boil off after it has dissolved the fond in the pan.

CIDER VINEGAR

Also known as apple cider vinegar. Fermented from alcoholic apple cider. This is a fruity vinegar that is similar to white wine vinegar in strength. Especially important for barbecue sauces.

MALT VINEGAR

Fermented from ale (a type of beer) with a distinctive but relatively mild flavor. This is extremely popular in the UK on any type of fried potatoes, but seldom seen in some countries.

THE MANY RICE WINE VINEGARS

Rice wine vinegar runs the gamut of acidity from as much as 9% acetic acid down to less than 5%. The mildest ones are from Japan.

What most people don't know is that there are other types than the white rice vinegar you normally see. All types are made from fermented rice, but there is also red, brown and black rice wine vinegars. The red type is made from red yeast rice using a specific bacteria. The flavor is quite floral and delicate. Japanese brown rice vinegar is made from unpolished rice and is the *true* sushi vinegar, now rarely seen. Black rice vinegar is much stronger. It is from China and traditionally made from black glutinous rice. China has many unusual types that are too rare and exotic to detail here.

SUSHI VINEGAR or "SEASONED" VINEGAR

This is a mild white rice wine vinegar that already has the sugar and salt added to it as a convenience for making sushi rice.

BALSAMIC VINEGAR

As most foodies know, there are two distinct types: Cheap balsamic is just distilled vinegar with sugar and caramel color added. Authentic balsamic from Modena, Italy, is aged for between five years on up to a century, and is priced accordingly. Also, because the barrels used to produce the best balsamics are made from juniper wood, which is no longer legally allowed to be made into barrels, the price of the vintage balsamic is going up fast. The very long aged balsamics are thicker than maple syrup and are traditionally drizzled over aged Parmigiano-Reggiano.

FRUIT and HERB VINEGARS

For example, raspberry vinegar and tarragon vinegar. These are just infused white wine vinegars. Better results for a recipe can usually be had by using a good white wine vinegar and the other component in its fresh form (*e.g.* fresh raspberries or tarragon, *etc.*)

TYPES OF GARLIC

There are basically two types: hardneck and softneck garlic. Elephant "garlic" is quite different and more closely related to leeks in terms of its chemistry. Hardneck garlic has the most flavor.

Black garlic is fermented in hot, high humidity for weeks. The flavor is unique and as different as wine is to grape juice.

There is a common belief among cooks in the Mediterranean that one should never combine onions and garlic in the same pan. The origin of this is undoubtedly that long ago they noticed how onions and garlic changed the flavor of each other when they are mixed due to enzymatic action. For a full explanation of this, see Volume 3, pages 73-79. In garlic powder (and onion powder) the enzymes are denatured so they can't react in that way.

Many home cooks consider that using garlic powder is lazy, or they fear it will introduce an artificial flavor. Ironically many of these same home cooks use bottled minced garlic or garlic paste, which actually <u>is</u> lazy and has an artificial flavor from preservatives and sometimes vinegar. It has also lost all of its *allicin*, which is the chemical that gives garlic its characteristic pungent taste, because once you mince garlic, the allicin begins to self-destruct. It was all gone long before the bottle got to the store. Of course allicin is also missing in dehydrated garlic, but garlic powder is not a direct substitute for fresh garlic in any recipe. They both have their uses, but they are not interchangeable. When it comes to making meat rubs and seasoning mixes, garlic powder is the only reasonable choice. Bottled garlic paste and bottled minced garlic are worthless.

Dried garlic goes back over 2000 years. It was hung up in the sun to dry. Commercially available forms, which include garlic powder, granulated garlic, etc. are made by simply dehydrating freshly peeled garlic. There is nothing artificial added. You can even make your own if you have a dehydrater.

Remember that the two main advantages are that dehydrated garlic won't react with onions and it resists burning, unlike fresh garlic that burns easily.

SCALING UP RECIPES

One of the questions I am frequently asked on YouTube is if a recipe can be scaled up just by multiplying all of the ingredients. Within reason, yes they can. The problems arise when you are trying to scale up a recipe many times and you are using a home stove. While many of these recipes have actually been scaled down to work with home ovens and stoves, you can't just reverse them back up to gigantic restaurant portions and expect good results.

Why not? There are two problems. First, a restaurant stove is far more powerful than any home kitchen stove. A large volume of food requires much more heat to achieve the same results. Take this to the extreme and imagine trying to brown meat over a single candle. Ah, but you say that you can accomplish the same thing if you are just patient and take your time. No, you can't. You will be cooking the meat or vegetables all the way through while you are trying to brown the outside over this pathetic tiny heat source. Therefore the solution, if you absolutely must scale up a recipe by a factor of more than about two, is to work in batches and whenever necessary, use multiple pots for sauces and the like, each with no more than twice the original recipe's portions.

The second problem is in cooling down soups and sauces after you have cooked them. While a small volume can be cooled fairly easily, if you are working with restaurant size portions, you need a blast chiller to get your food out of the "danger zone" where bacteria flourish in order to prevent poisoning everyone. Since you don't have a blast chiller (they cost thousands and require high amperage and voltage to operate), again the safe option is to work in multiple small batches.

In the recipes here (and on my cooking channel), I don't bother mentioning these things because I expect people will work with the amounts stated in the recipe. If you are the exception and cooking for a large group, take my advice and work in batches that are no more than double the quantity stated. Preferably the amount stated.

MEATBALL MATHEMATICS

Believe it or not, a lawsuit by an Italian food critic was filed against NASA for their logo looking like an Italian fish ball and a fishing rod. Because *nassa* is a kind of fishing device in Italian, this "proved" to him that it was a case of cultural appropriation. This is the age we live in.

Like a great many classic simple dishes, meatballs are actually much more complicated than they seem if you want great results. Meatball composition is both science and art. Here are basic rules:

1. Good meatballs are almost never pure ground meat. The only notable exception being meatballs as a topping on pizza. Otherwise a good meatball is about 30% other ingredients and even more for a fish ball.

2. The fat content of the entire mix should be around 15%, and not only the *amount* of fat is important, but also at what temperature it will melt. For instance, see the cheese in the Italian Beef Meatballs recipe ahead.

3. For deep flavor, the Maillard reaction is critical (starts on page 16).

4. The dryness of bread used (if any) needs to be considered. Fresh bread adds moisture and if meatballs are too wet, they will fall apart.

5. The type of meat(s) used is important for both texture and flavor, as is the fat content of the meat. Everything must be taken into consideration.

6. Egg yolks add fat and also bind the meatball together. Egg whites tend to make meatballs dry, so they are only used if the mixture is rather wet. Fish balls are a good example of when egg whites are normally included.

CREATING A NEW MEATBALL RECIPE

FOLLOWING A RECIPE

The math may seem tricky so I am providing two examples:

SALMON FISH BALLS

INGREDIENT	WEIGHT	FAT
Salmon (no skin)	150g	20g
1 Egg, whole	60g	11g
* Chipotle in Adobo	8g	3g
Shallots	22g	0
Ciabatta bread, fresh	25g	1g
Dry Breadcrumbs	30g	0
Salt and Seasonings	5g	0

This adds up to 300 grams of the mix with 35 grams of fat, which works out to be 12% fat. This recipe will work, but it will taste a bit dry. If we <u>add 15 grams of butter</u> (at 80% fat = 12 grams fat) then the total weight is 315 grams with 47 grams total fat. This is now our at target of 15% fat. If you are ambitious, try making it without the butter, then with the added butter and then another version with 30 grams of butter instead of 15, which gives you 18% fat. In the latter case you will find the meatballs are a bit squishy and won't cook as well, even though it is only a little more.

SEASONING AND PROCEDURE

Now that the composition is calculated for the texture, you can move on to the art. Namely what seasonings you are going to use. For fish you should keep the seasoning relatively simple so that the fish itself doesn't get lost. For this recipe try 2.5 grams lemon zest, 1/2 teaspoon salt and 1/4 teaspoon each garlic powder and dry dill.

Melt the butter (if you are using it). Combine all of the ingredients <u>except the salmon</u> in a food processor. Add the melted butter and blitz to purée. Cut the salmon into cubes and add it. Now blitz again until reasonably homogenous. Cover and refrigerate for at least 30 minutes to give the dry bread time to absorb the liquid.

* Note that the Chipotle in Adobo called for in this recipe is the same product used in the Chipotle Chicken recipe on page 142.

AFTER REFRIGERATION

Dust a tray with flour. Shape the mixture into about 10 balls so each one is about 30 grams. Now sprinkle with a little more flour.

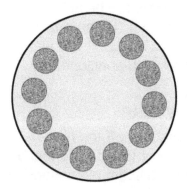

Slide the tray around briskly so the balls roll and get coated in the flour.

Alternatively you can make flattened cakes to fry up. The spherical shape only helps you with evenly cooking them if you turn them frequently, or they are submerged in a liquid that distributes the heat evenly on all sides simultaneously, but you still need to brown them first for good flavor. Put a little oil in a skillet and add the fish balls when it is warm. As I have shown in videos, line them up in a circle around the edge of the frying pan (diagram above left) for even cooking. Let them cook slowly so the inside is done by the time the outside is browned. That is unless you are going to finish cooking them in a sauce. In that case brown the outsides faster on a higher heat, turning them about every 60 seconds. Then transfer them to your sauce to finish.

ITALIAN BEEF MEATBALLS

INGREDIENT	WEIGHT	FAT
Ground Beef, 17% Fat	400g	68g
2 Egg Yolks	35g	10g
Garlic, crushed	15g	0
Cream	45g	8g
Dry Breadcrumbs	30g	0
Mushrooms	15g	0
Parmesan, grated	15g	* 0
Salt and Seasonings	10g	0

* Note that the Parmesan cheese actually does contain about 4 grams of fat, but it is not counted here because dry cheeses do not add moisture.

The total weight is 565 grams, comprised of 70% meat and 30% other ingredients. The total fat content is 86 grams, which is 15%.

The mushrooms in this formula will make the meatballs more tender because of enzymatic action on the meat, as I have shown in other recipes before. So when these meatballs are being browned care must be taken not to break them up. These are intended to be finished by simmering them in a sauce. If you want firmer meatballs then replace the mushrooms with additional dry breadcrumbs.

SEASONING AND PROCEDURE

Beef can stand up to stronger flavors, especially if the meatballs are going to be swimming in a robust sauce. For these I suggest a full tablespoon of freshly minced basil leaves, a scant tablespoon of freshly minced flat leaf parsley, 1/2 teaspoon of salt and 1/4 teaspoon each of dried oregano and ground black pepper.

Put the mushrooms, dry breadcrumbs and grated parmesan cheese in a food processor. Blitz to grind up well. Dump this into a large bowl. Add the seasonings and the rest of the ingredients except the ground beef. Mix to combine into a paste. Now add the ground beef and knead gently by hand until homogenous. Refrigerate for at least 30 minutes. A few hours is even better.

Now follow the exact same directions as those that begin at the top of the previous page for the Salmon Fish Balls titled *After Refrigeration*, only this time make the meatballs larger—about 12 of them at 45 to 50 grams each. Cook in the same way. They can remain in the warm sauce after they have simmered. This will only improve them. Grate fresh Parmesan over the top when serving.

FINAL THOUGHTS

Both of the examples in this section are rather basic. They are here to shed light on how to create meatballs that can be counted on as very good, but this is only a starting point. Even so, do try the Salmon Balls with some Tartare Sauce (page 203) for some serious good eats!

Borscht

Borscht is the quintessential example of how a recipe that is perceived as being from one nation actually has a much more complex history. This is a restaurant version, which is far more elaborate than what most Russians know Borscht as. A brief history of Borscht immediately follows this recipe (pages 60-61).

600g (1.3 lbs)	Beef, such as chuck roast
400g (14 oz)	Beets, cooked - see notes below
150g (5.3 oz)	Cabbage, finely sliced
120g (4 oz)	Tomato Purée (passata)
120g (4 oz)	Potato, peeled and diced
90g (3 oz)	Sausage, cured and lightly smoked
90g (3 oz)	Carrot
90g (3 oz)	Celery (or celery root)
60g (2 oz)	Red Bell Pepper
2 teaspoons	Red Wine Vinegar (page 50)
2 whole	Bay Leaves
2 Tablespoons	Butter
2 Tablespoons	Unrefined Sunflower Oil, or olive oil
1 Tablespoon	Garlic, crushed

1 additional whole onion and carrot for Step #1
Parsley and Dill, fresh
Knorr Beef Stock gel pack (optional - see recipe)
Black Pepper, Smetana (or Sour Cream)

THE BEETS

Either boil or roast the beets, but peel them first. The reason for this is explained in Volume 3 on page 172. The exact amount can vary between 300 and 450 grams (about 11 to 16 oz). More beets will make it more red.

PROCEDURE

1. Heat a cast iron pan (do <u>not</u> use nonstick for this) on a high. Slice an onion and carrot into halves and place flat-side down onto the heated

metal until they blacken some. Then remove and set aside.

2. Put 1.9 liters (2 quarts) water in a 4-liter stock pot (or pressure cooker). Cut the beef into large cubes and add it to the water along with the bay leaves and the charred onions and carrots. Bring to a simmer and then cover. If you are using a stock pot, it will have to simmer for 3 hours. In a pressure cooker it will be done in 45 minutes, plus 15 minutes off the heat.

3. Discard the vegetables and bay leaf from the broth. Strain off the meat and reserve, allowing it to cool to room temperature. Use a fat separating pitcher to get the layer of oil out of the broth. Depending on how much fat was in the meat, there may not be much. Discard the fat layer.

4. After the beef has cooled off, take a knife and trim off any bits of gristle or large pieces of fat so that only tender morsels remain. Set aside.

5. Grate the beets using the coarse side of a box grater.

6. Place a nonstick skillet and a sauce pan on medium heat and put one tablespoon each of butter and unrefined sunflower oil in each pan. In another pot at the back of the stove, heat the beef stock prepared earlier (skimmed of fat) to a slow simmer with the trimmed pieces of meat in it. Meanwhile, dice the carrots, bell pepper and celery.

7. When the butter in the nonstick skillet foams up, add the grated beets. Reduce the heat as needed to keep from burning.

8. When the butter in the stock pot foams up, add the diced carrots, bell pepper and celery to that pan. Continue cooking the beets and the vegetables for at least 12 minutes. If you use a lower heat setting and cook them longer, the result will be even better. Don't exceed 20 minutes.

9. Into the pan with the beets, add a teaspoon of salt, half of the tomato purée and the red wine vinegar. Stir and continue cooking slowly.

10. Add a teaspoon of salt to the bell pepper, celery and carrots that have been sweating. Also add the rest of the tomato purée. Cook 8 minutes.

11. Remove the casing from the sausage and dice it. After the 8 minutes are up, add the diced sausage to the red bell pepper, celery and carrot

mixture. Cook for another 4-5 minutes with occasional stirring.

12. Deglaze the stock pot containing the sausage with a ladle of the beef broth on the back burner.

13. Start a new large (8 liter) stock pot heating on the stove. Put the beef broth and trimmed beef cubes into this pot along with the beets and vegetables from the other pans. Now add the finely sliced cabbage and another 1 liter (1.1 quarts) of water or beef stock.

14. While this is coming up to a simmer, dice the potatoes and crush the garlic. After it reaches a simmer, add the potatoes and garlic. Simmer for 30 minutes.

15. Add more salt to taste, or (optionally) a Knorr brand Beef gel pack. if water was used in Step # 13. The Knorr gel pack is quite salty already, so if you are using that, make sure it is dissolved completely before tasting and adding any more salt. It will probably have all the salt you need.

16. Taste and add a little sugar if you detect any sourness.

17. Now add a couple of tablespoons each of freshly minced dill and parsley along with ground black pepper to taste. Simmer for another 15 minutes.

18. You can serve it now, or store it away for up to 4-5 days. Add sour cream and a little more freshly minced dill upon plating. Many Russians also add freshly minced parsley and scallions when serving it, but I suggest only dill.

HISTORY AND TYPES OF BORSCHT

I am going to ignore the soups known as Green Borscht and White Borscht that are similar only in name really. The type known to most of the world today is the purple beet soup. Although originally beets were not used. It was made from a wild plant called hogweed that can be poisonous if not prepared correctly, which might be why beets were substituted later, but no one really knows. Ukrainians claim they changed it to beets.

Depending on who you choose to believe, Borscht is either Ukranian or Polish originally. The problem in claiming it as Ukranian and not Russian (as most Ukranians fiercly insist upon) is that Ukraine was a part of Russia until 1922, and the soup was being made and consumed across a vast region long before that. Poland also claims it as their own invention, and to complicate matters more, Poland ruled Ukraine centuries ago. The geopolitics are so complex and intertwined that something as trivial as the origin of a soup recipe that uses ingredients that are common to the entire continent is impossible to say factually at this point. There is a very strong possibility that it had multiple origins because poor people making soup from ingredients they can get for little or no money would logically lead to many versions of Borscht springing up all over the Slavic nations. One thing is certain, though: outside of Ukraine and Poland, the world absolutely considers Borscht to be Russian.

There are so many recipes for Borscht that it is impossible to conclusively state what makes one Ukranian vs. Russian vs. Polish vs. Lithuanian (yes, there is a contingent claiming it is Lithuanian, too), but here are some notable differences (*generally speaking*):

Ukranian: includes salt pork, potatoes and parsnips. Hogweed tastes a lot like parsnips, by the way.

Polish: may have kielbasa sausage or no pieces of meat at all, although it does have a meat stock as the base—often chicken.

Russian: Sometimes includes potatoes and is heavy on cabbage in home versions. There is a further division between home style Russian Borscht and fine dining Borscht because of the history involved with nobility hiring private chefs from France and Germany. Those chefs elevated familiar peasant dishes for the wealthy. For more about that, see Volume 1 of my cookbook series. Home style Russian Borscht is usually very simple, with all the ingredients typically just boiled up in one pot at once. The upscale versions are more complex and may include red wine and also smoked sausage in place of the salt pork used in Ukranian Borscht.

Lithuanian: Uses buttermilk in place of the stock. Served cold.

"Navy Day" Chicken

This is named after a national holiday in Russia honoring veterans of the Russian Navy. Most of the year the only time you can get foods cooked over wood fires or barbecues is far outside of the city (usually at your summer house if your family still has one from the Soviet era). But on Navy Day there are licenses issued to permit grills to operate in some parks. Some enterprising people sell types of shashlik there. One old guy I saw several times was Georgian and he sold chicken that had been marinated in adjika paste (page 192). This is based on that, only using sous vide. You <u>really</u> need a barbecue to finish these, but you can sort of make it work with a broiler.

6 pieces	Chicken Drumsticks/Thighs bone-in, skin-on
60g (2 oz)	Adjika Paste (page 192)
100g (3.5 oz)	Onions peeled, cut in thick rings (see note below)
1 teaspoon	Citric Acid or 30ml (1 oz) Lemon Juice
1 teaspoon	Garlic Powder
1 teaspoon	Salt, or (better) Smoked Salt
40ml (1.4 oz)	Vegetable Oil, or (better) Unfiltered Sunflower Oil

THE ONIONS

Don't use finely cut the onion because you have to remove them later and it will be easier in thick rings that won't break down easily. Red onions are better, but that's optional. Also, the reason that garlic powder is used instead of fresh garlic is to prevent the enzymatic reaction from taking place, as explained in Volume 3.

PROCEDURE

1. Put the adjika paste in a large bowl with the citric acid (or lemon juice), garlic powder, salt and vegetable oil. Whisk until smooth.

2. Add the chicken pieces and make sure they are coated well on all sides. Then mix in the sliced onions. **You can also add a red chili or two** that has been sliced lengthwise in two pieces if you want it a bit spicier.

3. Put the chicken into a long vacuum bag. Then seal under vacuum.

4. Place the bag in a water bath at 62°C (143.5°F) for 2 hours.

5. Open the bag and empty the contents into a large bowl. Pick out the onion pieces and discard. Wipe off excess liquid from each piece of chicken, transfering the cleaned pieces to a platter to lay flat without being stacked on each other. Discard the rest of the liquid contents.

6. If you have a charcoal grill, you can just take the chicken outside and finish cooking it there. It is best loaded into a grill basket (shown below).

OTHERWISE: Preheat your broiler with a tray very close to the heating element. Also heat a cast iron grill pan on a high flame at the same time. When it is hot, blister the skin of each piece of chicken, leaving grill marks on it. Then move the pieces to a tray for broiling. When you have all of the pieces accumulated, put them under the broiler for a few minutes, watching carefully that they don't actually burn—but you do want some color on them. When you taste it, you'll see why BBQ is better.

6. Serve with wedges of lemon along side and French fries. Sliced tomato and sour pickles are typical.

Chashushuli

A Spicy Georgian Beef Stew

Although this is actually Georgian, not Russian, it is commonly seen in many Russian restaurants, due to the recent increased appreciation of spicy foods by younger Russians.

480g (17 oz)	Beef, cubed (see note below)
100g (3.5 oz)	Onion
45g (1.5 oz)	Adjika Paste (page 192)
45g (1.5 oz)	Vegetable Oil, ideally unfiltered sunflower oil
90g (3 oz)	Tomato Purée (passata)
60g (2 oz)	Red Bell Pepper, diced small
20g (0.7 oz)	Garlic cloves, sliced thin
1 teaspoon	Black Peppercorns
1 teaspoon	Coriander Seeds, whole
1 teaspoon	Red Pepper Flakes
1 teaspoon	Cayenne
1 teaspoon	Coarse Salt
1 1/2 teaspoons	Khmeli Suneli or ground fenugreek seeds
30g (1 oz)	Bacon Fat, or substitute vegetable oil
2-4 whole	Red Serrano Chilies, fresh
2	Bay Leaves, preferably Turkish
10-12 leaves	Basil, freshly cut into chiffonade
1/4 cup	Cilantro, freshly chopped leaves

THE BEEF

Use tenderloin for the best results. This may seem decadent, but tenderloin in Russia is not especially expensive. At the very least, try to get meat that feels soft to the touch when still raw.

PROCEDURE

1. Pulse the black peppercorns, coriander seeds, red chili flakes and coarse salt in an electric spice mill. Don't grind them all the way to a fine

powder. Leave a little texture, but crack all the peppercorns and seeds.

2. Put the onion, adjika and vegetable oil in a food processor. Run it until it is nearly a purée, but not quite.

3. Trim the beef and put it in a mixing bowl. Add the spices from Step #1 and the purée from Step #2. Mix well. Leave out to marinate 1 to 2 hours.

4. Heat a nonstick skillet on medium. When it is hot, add the meat mixture from the previous step. Fry just to get the pink off of the meat.

5. Add 120ml (4.25 oz) of water to the pan. Stir and then transfer it a pressure cooker. Sprinkle the Khmeli-Suneli (or ground fenugreek seeds) over the top and close the pressure cooker up. Heat until pressure builds.

6. When steam begins to vent, lower the heat to the minimum to maintain the point where steam is barely escaping for 15 minutes for tenderloin. If you have used a tougher cut of beef, leave it to cook for 30 minutes.

7. Turn the heat off and wait another 15 minutes before opening it up.

8. Use a spider or slotted spoon to transfer the meat to a colander. Save the broth from the pressure cooker for later use in this recipe.

9. After the meat is drained, put a large nonstick skillet on high heat. Add the bacon fat (or vegetable oil). Once it is hot, add the meat. Fry well, taking care not to burn it.

10. Remove the meat to a plate and reserve. Reduce heat to medium. Add the tomato purée to the pan. Cook until it is nearly completely dry.

11. Add the reserved broth from Step #8 along with the garlic, the red bell pepper and the bay leaves. Stir and cook for about 3 minutes.

12. Add the fresh basil. Cook another 1-2 minutes.

13. Add the meat back into the pan along with the fresh cilantro. Stir. Put the whole red chilies on top (don't cut them). Cover with either a silicone lid or a glass lid with a small hole. Reduce heat to maintain at a slow simmer for about 20 minutes.

14. Remove the lid. Discard the bay leaves. Adjust the seasoning, typically with 1/2 teaspoon of MSG. Serve with thinly cut rings of onion on top. Traditionally served over rice.

Georgian Grilled Shrimp

The ethnic authenticity of this dish has been cast in doubt because prawns were scarce for so long. Many versions are served in Georgian restaurants in Russia today, but restaurants change or invent recipes to satisfy local patrons for business. Just as Italians complain that Alfredo is not authentic even though it was created by an Italian chef in Rome using only Italian ingredients. In the end the taste is all that counts.

12 whole	Tiger Prawns, raw with shells on ("jumbo" size)
1 Tablespoon	Sesame Seeds
1/2 teaspoon	Coriander Seeds, whole
1/2 teaspoon	White Peppercorns, whole
3/4 teaspoon	Coarse Salt
30g (1 oz)	Onion, chopped
30ml (1 oz)	Vegetable Oil, or (better) Unfiltered Sunflower Oil
15ml (0.5 oz)	Lemon Juice, fresh
2 teaspoons	Paprika
1/4 teaspoon	Cinnamon, ground
30g (1 oz)	Adjika Paste, bottled or see page 192

To plate: Lemon and if desired, cucumber and tomato salad.

PROCEDURE

1. Put the sesame seeds, coriander seeds, white peppercorns and coarse salt into a hot metal pan and toast until the sesame seeds darken slightly. Be careful not to burn the spices. Remove to a bowl to cool. Do <u>not</u> grind.

2. When cool, transfer the contents to a blender. Add all of the remaining ingredients and purée. Put in a glass jar and refrigerate if you are making this in advance. It is best used within 2-3 days.

3. Make life easier by purchasing already deveined shell-on ("EZ-peel") prawns. These are ideal for many recipes because the shells are useful for making stocks and sauces, but <u>leave the shells on</u>. If your prawns are not

processed at all, you will need to devein them.

4. Combine the prawns with all of the marinade, making sure they are coated well. Leave at room temperature.

5. Marinate for 1 to 2 hours. Don't leave them overnight because the lemon juice will denature the proteins and make them tough, in spite of the shells being on. Also don't worry about them spoiling out at room temperature because the salt and acidity will slow microbial growth to a near halt. These are typically taken outdoors to cook where there is no refrigeration, so the safety of this approach is well proven.

6. Ideally you want to put the shrimp on double skewers so that they remain flat when grilling over charcoal. This allows you to flip them over as an entire kebab without having any fall between the grates. In this case you may want to put red bell pepper and onion slices between the shrimp on the skewers. If you are doing this indoors, then the best method is to cook them on a very hot cast iron grill pan for about 2 minutes on each side. Don't worry if they get a little charred on the outside because they will be peeled. When done, squeeze on a little fresh lemon juice.

RUSSIAN POSTCARD FROM 1928. TRANSLATED
CAPTION ON REVERSE: "GEORGIAN GRANDFATHER COOKS"

Solyanka

This classic Russian soup with a thousand different recipes can be made for vegetarians by leaving out the sausage, and it is still the best version I have ever had, if I do say so myself. Russian folk medicine prescribes this as a cure for a hangover.

140g (5 oz)	Mushrooms, large ones if possible
140g (5 oz)	Cabbage, finely sliced (see note below)
110g (4 oz)	Onion, medium dice
190g (6.7 oz)	Potato, peeled and in 1.25cm (1/2") cubes
140g (5 oz)	*Sausage, cured and lightly smoked
90g (3 oz)	Passata
30g (1 oz)	Celery, peeled and sliced
60g (2 oz)	Pickles, diced
30g (1 oz)	Green Olives, pitted and sliced
2 T	Unrefined Sunflower Oil, or vegetable oil
1 T	Tomato Paste, preferably Italian
1 T	Capers, rinsed well and chopped
2 whole	Bay Leaves
1/2 t	Allspice, ground

Fresh Parsley, sliced Scallions
Lemon slices and Smetana (or Sour Cream)

VEGETARIAN OR NOT?

* The sausage is optional. The soup is just as good without it.

ADDITIONAL TIPS

The cabbage is best cured ahead of time (see page 70). Plain uncured cabbage may be used instead, but then salt will need to be added.

PROCEDURE

1. Cut the mushrooms into 1.25cm (1/2 inch) slices. Put in a bowl and toss with 20ml vegetable oil and 1/2 teaspoon of salt. Place on a baking tray and broil for about 5 minutes depending on the broiler. Wait until they

have browned some. Then turn them over for another 3 minutes or so. They should be somewhat leathery and dried out. If you have a barbecue, you can put the slices on metal skewers and roast them. over hot coals for an even better and more authentic effect. They simulate meat and as they cook in the soup, they infuse flavor. Set them aside for now.

2. Optional: If you are using the sausage then brown it in a skillet first, or (better) cook this on a barbecue along with the mushrooms. Then cut it into pieces that will fit on a soup spoon and set aside for now.

3. Heat a large pot and add 2 tablespoons of oil. Ideally you should use unfiltered sunflower oil which is full of flavor, but this is very hard to get outside of Eastern Europe. Substitute ordinary vegetable oil. Fry the sliced cabbage in this with the 2 bay leaves on a medium heat for 3-4 minutes.

4. Add the chopped onion and celery to the pan. Continue cooking for about 5 more minutes.

5. Add the diced pickles, the tomato paste and a little fresh ground black pepper. Cook for another 3-4 minutes.

6. Add the passata and increase the heat. Fry for about 2 minutes.

7. Pour 900ml (30.5 oz.) water into the same pot. Add the cubed potato and the previously cooked mushrooms and sausage (if you are using it).. Simmer for 45 minutes.

8. Add the sliced olives, capers and ground allspice. Simmer another 10 minutes or so.

9. Serve in bowls garnished with chopped fresh parsley, sliced scallions, a dollop of smetana (or sour cream) and a wedge of lemon.

Salt Cured Cabbage

Salted cabbage is a common ingredient in Russia and some other parts of Eastern Europe. It is mostly for salads but sometimes it makes its way into cooked recipes. It is hard to find for sale elsewhere and is ideally made at home anyway.

The best tool for making this is an asparagus steamer pot because it has a large volume and the fitted wire basket allows for the cabbage to drain from all directions. The basket can be lifted and the liquid poured out easily.

PROCEDURE

1. Try to select a cabbage about the same diameter as your steamer basket. Cut it into slices.

2. Put a single slice down. There will be some stray bits from when you sliced it that you can use to fill gaps.

3. Sprinkle with a teaspoon or so of coarse salt. For additional flavor, sprinkle with Aquavit (Akvavit), which is a Scandinavian liquor flavored principally with caraway. Now repeat steps 2 and 3 until it is mostly filled.

4. Put a weight on top. A wine bottle or water bottle works well.

5. Every 12-24 hours lift the basket and empty out the liquid that has ran off. Repeat until 12 hours passes with almost no liquid (at least 3 days). You can leave it to ferment longer if you wish. Now rinse the cabbage very well with cold water in a colander. Slice finely.

Russian "Hat" Garnish

This is called a hat, a garnish, a salad or a pickle depending on which Russian restaurant kitchen you are in. There are many versions, but this one is my own and (naturally) my favorite.

120g (4 oz)	Salt Cured Cabbage (see previous page)
30g (1 oz)	Onion, chopped
30g (1 oz)	Carrot, finely grated
2 T	Unrefined Sunflower Oil, or vegetable oil
1 T	Parsley, freshly minced
1/2	Red Serrano Chili, fresh
1/2 teaspoon	Lemon Juice
1/2 teaspoon	Dijon Mustard
1/4 teaspoon	Coriander Seeds, ground
1/8 teaspoon	Black Pepper, ground
1/8 teaspoon	Sugar

PROCEDURE

1. Heat a nonstick skillet on a medium flame. Add the oil and fry the sliced cabbage. You can substitute plain cabbage for the salt cured one, but the flavor will not be as good.

2. Remove the stem and seeds from the chili. Cut into slices.

3. When the cabbage begins to soften, add the carrot and chili. Turn down the heat and cover the pan. Cook until the cabbage just starting to brown.

4. After it has cooled down, put this into a food processor along with all of the other ingredients. Pulse to combine, but don't turn it into a paste. There should still be considerable texture.

5. Store in the refrigerator for up to a week. It is especially used on grilled meats or grilled tuna as a little tuft on top (a "hat"), but it can also garnish potato salad and many other dishes.

Lemon-Smetana Chicken Drumsticks

This is based on a mostly-forgotten Russian recipe from the 1960's. To this day citric acid is in large Russian grocery stores.

8 whole	Chicken Drumsticks, bone-in, skin-on
60g (2 oz)	Sunflower Oil, unfiltered (or vegetable oil)
20g (0.7 oz)	Garlic cloves, peeled and chopped coarsely
1 Tablespoon	Citric Acid (see page 232)
2 teaspoons	Sugar, white granulated
1 teaspoon	Coarse Salt
1 teaspoon	Paprika (in all - see procedure below)
90g (3.2 oz)	Smetana or Crème Fraîche, but not Sour Cream
1 Tablespoon	Flour
2-3 teaspoons	Dill, freshly minced

PROCEDURE

1. Combine the sunflower oil, garlic cloves, citric acid, sugar, coarse salt and half of the paprika in a blender. Purée.

2. Put the drumsticks in a bag. Add the marinade and seal it. Preferably vacuum seal the bag, but do not try to cook this sous vide. Refrigerate for at least 4 hours and up to a day ahead, making it fast to finish up.

3. Place the drumsticks with the marinade still on them on a rack above a pan of hot water. Roast at 230°C (450°F) for 22 minutes with fan assist on.

4. Whisk together the Crème Fraîche, the flour and the other half of the paprika. When the drumsticks have cooled for 5-10 minutes, spoon this mixture over them, dividing evenly between the pieces.

5. Place under a broiler for about 5 minutes to slightly char the surface. You can use a blowtorch on them a bit to even out the browning.

6. Garnish with minced dill. Tabasco Green Pepper Sauce is also great!

Boudin Blanc
The Thai Chicken Dog

This is a type of sausage without any casing. There are many versions, especially in Cajun cooking. Asian flavors are not common, but this is delicious if you like spicy foods. Back in the 1980's there was a very successful take-away in Los Angeles selling artisanal skinless "hot dogs" with exotic meats and unusual flavors. They always had a line out the door, but they closed when the owner retired. This is a copycat recipe of one of their most popular menu items: The Thai Chicken Dog.

225g (8 oz)	Chicken Thighs, boneless/skinless
45g (1.5 oz)	Thai Red Curry Paste (page 200)
15g (0.5 oz)	Coriander stems and roots, washed well
15g (0.5 oz)	Green Serrano Chili, chopped coarsely
1 whole	Egg
2 teaspoons	Rice Flour
1 teaspoon	Salt

PROCEDURE

1. Cut the chicken into small pieces and combine in a food processor with everything else. Blitz to make a relatively smooth purée.

2. Lay cling film down and put a third of the mixture down. Roll it up into a sausage shape and twist the ends to secure it. Repeat two more times with the rest of the mixture. Multiply the ingredients if you want more.

3. Wrap these in foil, also securing the ends tightly. Refrigerate 1+ hours.

4. Steam for 15 minutes. Be sure to have a lid on the steamer.

5. Cool down to room temperature, then refrigerate until needed.

6. Fry in a skillet with oil, or on a BBQ, turning to brown evenly on all sides. These were served in a hot dog bun with onions and mayonnaise.

Cauliflower "Steaks"

This recipe requires sous vide equipment. There is no other way to do this well.

2-3 heads	Cauliflower
100g (3.5 oz)	Passata
60g (2 oz)	Mushrooms
30g (1 oz)	Soy Sauce
30g (1 oz)	Olive Oil, extra-virgin
1 1/2 teaspoons	Paprika
1 teaspoon	Dry Mustard, powder
1/2 teaspoon	Black Pepper, ground
1/2 teaspoon	White Pepper, ground
1/2 teaspoon	Smoked Salt
1/2 teaspoon	Chilies, ground, preferably Guajillo
1-2	Garlic Cloves, chopped
2	Eggs, whole
Flour, Panko Breadcrumbs	

THE CAULIFLOWER

There will be a lot of excess cauliflower florets because this recipe only uses the center section with the stem. Each head of cauliflower should yield two "steaks" that are 2cm (3/4 inch) thick each. Cutting these neatly may take some practice, so be prepared to use more than 2 heads of cauliflower to obtain 4 "steaks" the first time you make this. Of course you can use all of the other cauliflower florets that fall off from the heads for any recipe you like.

PROCEDURE

1. Combine the passata, mushrooms, soy sauce, olive oil, garlic and spices (not the eggs) into a blender and purée.

2. Coat the cauliflower "steaks" in the spice paste carefully. Try not to handle them too much.

3. Cut the vacuum bag from the roll much longer than you normally would (unless you have a restaurant type vacuum sealer where liquid doesn't get sucked in). Fold the top 5cm (2 inches) back from the bag's open end (see page 37).

4. Put the cauliflower "steaks" in the bag in a single layer so they do not lay on top of each other. Now pour whatever extra spice paste you have left into the bag. Fold the flap back and seal under vacuum. If liquid got sucked out, you didn't make the bag long enough.

5. Place in an 82°C (180°F) water bath for 1 hour and 5 minutes.

6. Run some cold water over to stop cooking, then refrigerate until cold.

7. Cut the bag open with a knife along three sides. Lift out the "steaks" one at a time using a spatula and place each one in a tray with an excess of flour. Turn over gently to coat both sides with the flour.

8. Whisk the eggs with a little water. Coat each "steak" in the egg wash and then gently shake in the panko breadcrumbs. Place on parchment or wax paper and refrigerate 1 to 4 hours until you are ready to fry them.

9. Heat enough oil in a skillet (ideally olive oil) to come up about 1cm (3/8 inch). Fry the pieces until golden brown on each side. For more flavor, continue frying until darker, as shown in the video.

10. Garnish with herbs, grated parmesan and a slice of lemon—or serve with BBQ sauce or mayonnaise, or just about anything you can think of.

Cornbread Mini Loaves

This was one of the first new recipes I had posted on YouTube after several years of my absence. It did not receive the attention it deserves. One reason may have been the poor photo shown of the product made in haste. Really anyone who tries this will find it quite delicious.

110g ()	Butter, softened at room temperature
60g ()	Corn Flour (not corn starch!)
2 whole	Eggs
1 Tablespoon	Muscovado Sugar, or Dark Brown Sugar
60g ()	Bread Flour (high gluten)
1 1/2 teaspoons	Paprika
1 teaspoon	Baking Powder (not baking soda!)
1 teaspoon	Cumin, ground
1 Tablespoon	Cilantro, freshly minced (or a bit more)
90g ()	Corn, canned (drained)
30g (1 oz)	Heavy Cream
1-2	Garlic Cloves, crushed
Aerosol lubricant, ideally Olive Oil	

THE BUTTER

Soften at room temperature for 1 hour if you are in a warm climate, or 2 hours if you are in a cold climate with the windows open.

PROCEDURE

1. Cut the butter into cubes and put in the bowl of a standing mixer equipped with the paddle attachment. With the motor running slowly, add the dark brown sugar.

2. Once it has combined, increase the motor speed to cream the mixture. Stop the mixer and scrape down the sides as needed.

3. Add the eggs and the corn flour (also known as corn meal).

4. Run the mixer on a medium speed to incorporate the ingredients, stopping to scrape down the sides and the mixer's paddle several times.

5. Stop the mixer. Add the cumin, the cilantro, the paprika, the baking powder and the bread flour. Run the mixer slowly again.

6. Use a garlic press to crush the garlic. Add this to the mixture along with the paprika. Continue blending until you have a homogenous mixture with batter consistency.

7. You can either add the drained corn directly or put it into a food processor to pulse it a few times if you don't want whole corn kernels in the bread. Now add the corn to the batter and run the mixer just enough to incorporate it.

8. Ideally you should bake this in rectangular silicone molds measuring 8x3x3 centimeters (a bit larger than 3 x 1 x 1 inches in all directions). Spray the mold with nonstick lubricant (preferably olive oil) first, then divide the mixture into 10 of the compartments.

9. If you want a more uniform appearance, dip a spatula into water and smooth the top of the mini-loaves. I did not bother with this in the video, which is why they did not come out as attractive as they can.

10. Preheat oven to 170°C (340°F) with fan assist ON. When it is at temperature, put the loaded silicone mold onto a baking sheet in the oven and cook for 17 minutes.

11. Turn them out onto a rack and let them cool for at least 30 minutes before consuming. Add a pot of whipped butter on the side and serve up as a first course. This is a classic accompaniment to many Southern dishes.

✦

Classic "Best Quality" Brown Beef Stock

This is the true classic method dating back centuries.

2kg (4 1/2 lbs)	Beef Bones
1kg (2 1/4 lbs)	Beef shoulder, bone-in
2 medium	Onions (each used at different times)
2 medium	Carrots (each used at different times)
300g (10.6 oz)	Celery Root or celery (used in two places)
2 whole	Bay Leaves
2 cloves	Garlic, cut in halves
60ml (2 oz)	Dry Vermouth, or dry white wine
1/2 teaspoon	Black Pepper, coarsely ground
1/2 teaspoon	Garlic Powder
2-3 branches	Thyme, fresh (or 1 teaspoon dried)
4 whole	Cloves (the spice - not garlic)
30g (1 oz)	Stock Fat or Butter (see note below)
Fresh Herbs (parsley, thyme, dill, etc.) for Bouquet Garni	

STOCK FAT

If this is the first time you are making this, then you will have to use butter. In the future, you can save stock fat that comes from making this by freezing it for the next time you make stock. This will produce better results, and the stock fat gets more flavorful with each time you make it.

PROCEDURE

1. Put the beef bones in a large roasting tray and sprinkle lightly with salt. Although stock is not salted directly, some salt on the bones will prevent (or at least greatly reduce) the chance of metallic notes developing. Note that in recent times it is common to brush the bones with tomato paste. It's not traditional, but it's up to you. Roast at 200°C (400°F) for 45 minutes.

2. While the bones are roasting, prepare the other ingredients. Peel and slice one onion in half. Stud each half with 2 cloves (the spice, that is). Peel and cut the carrot into a few large pieces. If you are using celeriac (celery root) then peel that. Cut half of the celery or celery root into large pieces. Tie some herbs together into a bouquet garni. If you have some green leaves from the upper part of a leek, you can use that, or use the wire cage shown on page 233 of this volume.

3. Put a large 8 to 10 liter stock pot on a medium-high heat (#7 out of 10). When it is warm, add 30 grams (1 oz) of stock fat if you have it, or substitute butter, as explained above. Cook the carrots and celery root (or celery) until golden, taking care not to burn the butter if that's what you are using. Then transfer to a bowl and reserve. Discard the excess fat and wipe out the pot. You don't have to be meticulous about it.

4. When the bones are finished roasting in the oven, use tongs to move them to the same stock pot. Add enough cold water to the pot to cover the bones plus about another 2.5cm (1 inch). Add the clove-studded onion halves, the bouquet garni prepared earlier, the garlic cloves, the browned carrot and onion (leave the fat behind as much as possible). Put this on a medium-high heat and bring it to a simmer.

5. Meanwhile, drain the fat from the roasting pan and discard if you used tomato paste on the bones. Otherwise it is a fantastic fat to brown potatoes in, but that's another recipe. This is not stock fat. Now heat the roasting pan on a burner and add the vermouth. Scrape to deglaze and continue heating until the aroma of alcohol is gone. Add the entire contents to the stock pot. Don't bother passing it through a sieve unless you have accidentally burnt the fond, which is *not* good.

6. When bubbles begin to break on the surface (which may take over an hour because of the volume of liquid), a frothy scum will form. Skim this from the top and discard. See the video (4:45 - 5:25) for this operation.

7. Reduce heat to maintain at a slow simmer. The temperature of the stock should be kept around 80°C (175°F) with a lid that partially covers the pot (leave it cocked to the side so that it is not completely covered). Maintain

at a slow simmer for 10-12 hours on a back burner. If the liquid level drops below the bones, add more water to cover them.

8. Turn the heat off and allow it to cool for 30-45 minutes before removing and discarding the bones with tongs.

9. Pass the remaining stock through a sieve into a container with a lid.

10. Stand the container in a bowl or other larger container in the sink and run cold water around it. Add ice cubes to the outside container, too. Get the temperature of the stock down to 24°C (75°F) or less before moving it to the refrigerator. If you put the hot stock directly into the refrigerator, it will remain in the "danger zone" for far too long and become sour, as well as potentially toxic from bacterial growth. Also, don't put it in the refrigerator with a tight fitting lid, because the volume will contract as it cools down the rest of the way, either rupturing the container or at the very least, making the lid extremely difficult to remove from the vacuum.

11. The next morning, the fat will have solidified on top. This is the stock fat that you will use the next time you are making this. Skim it off. You will be using some of it in a next step. Drain the fat on a sieve to remove as much of the aqueous phase as possible. Freeze leftover fat for next time.

12. Put the gelatinous broth in a stock pot on a back burner to melt it.

13. On a front burner, set a large nonstick skillet on a medium-high setting and add about 40 grams (1.4 oz) of the stock fat to it. Season the beef shoulder with coarsely ground black pepper. When the stock fat stops sizzling from the water boiling off, add the beef shoulder to the pan. Brown well on both sides. While this is browning, peel and coarsely chop the other carrot. Also chop the celery root (or celery) and the other onion.

14. When the stock is at (or near) a simmer, transfer the fried meat to the stock. Put the chopped vegetables into the pan that the meat was just browned in. Cook the vegetables in that fat until they are golden, scraping the bottom to pick up any fond.

15. Add the browned vegetables to the stock, including the fat. Add the branches of thyme (or dried thyme) and the two bay leaves. Bring the

stock up to a simmer.

16. Partially cover and maintain at a simmer for 1 hour. Use tongs to turn the meat around in the broth occasionally, returning the lid to partially cover it each time.

17. Remove the lid and increase the heat slightly to maintain the simmer. Continue to turn the pieces of meat around occasionally using tongs. Cook for another 1 1/2 to 2 hours.

18. Remove the meat and either discard or save for some other application (but it will have very little flavor left in it—what cooks call Russian orphanage steaks). Strain the stock through a sieve. Discard solids from the sieve. Do not rub the vegetables through the sieve or the stock will be very cloudy, as explained in this volume on page 10.

19. As before, put the stock in a container and cool it down with running cold water around the outside and some ice cubes. Bring the temperature down before transferring it to the refrigerator. Same as step #10.

20. After it has been refrigerated for several hours (or overnight), there will be another sheet of solidified fat on top. Skim this off, leaving the gelatinous stock below.

21. Transfer the de-fatted stock into a pot or sauce pan and heat on medium (#5 out of 10) to bring to a simmer and reduce to the point it weighs 1.2 kilograms (42 oz). You can check it periodically with a scale, or just estimate if you are comfortable doing that.

22. Finally, pass the stock through a chinois (China cap) fine mesh strainer.

23. Repeat Step #10 one more time, cooling it down in the sink before storing it in the refrigerator.

24. Once it has chilled, it will be a thick gelatin. You can cube it up and store it in the freezer, or transfer it to whatever size containers are good for you. In a restaurant it goes too fast to be frozen, but at home it might last you for months in the freezer.

✦

40 Clove Garlic Chicken
with Smoked Garlic

This dish was originally prepared using a capon that was spatchcocked (divided in two lengthwise). If you want authenticity, that's how to go about it, but capon is expensive and often difficult to find. Chicken is more delicate, so use care.

1.6kg (3.5 lbs)	Chicken, bone-in thighs and/or quarters
30ml (1 oz)	Bacon grease, duck fat, or vegetable oil
40 (or more)	Garlic Cloves, peeled
90ml (3 oz)	Dry White Wine or Brut Champagne (better)
8 branches	Thyme, fresh
1 teaspoon	Tarragon, dried (or sprigs of fresh if available)
1 Tablespoon	Cognac, or brandy
1-2 Tablespoons	Wood Chips (for smoking the garlic)
	SEASONING MIX
1 Tablespoon	Flour
1 teaspoon	Granulated Garlic
1 teaspoon	Salt
1/2 teaspoon	Black Peppercorns

SMOKED GARLIC

This technique is not worth the trouble for recipes that only call for a couple of cloves of garlic, but here it works very well. The type of wood used will have some influence on the flavor. Birch or alder are both very good. Hickory is too strong. Smoked garlic also goes great in a Paella.

PROCEDURE

1. Set up a stove top smoker by putting the wood chips in the bottom and lining the grate with foil. Poke holes in the foil to increase the circulation of smoke. A "smoking gun" won't work because you need hot smoking.

2. Center the peeled garlic cloves on top of the grate in a single layer. Close the lid on the smoker almost all the way and turn the heat on the stove to high (maximum). Wait until smoke begins to appear.

3. Now reduce the heat to medium. Wait 6 minutes.

4. Reduce the heat to low. Wait 4 minutes.

5. Move off the heat. Open to vent for a few seconds. Close again for 10 minutes longer (still off the heat). Store garlic in a closed jar until needed.

6. Crush the black peppercorns in a mortar to crack them. Don't grind them too fine. Combine with the rest of the Seasoning Mix ingredients.

7. Poke holes in the skin of the chicken pieces with a sharp knife. Put the chicken into a large box with a lid. Add the Seasoning Mix and shake well to coat evenly. Be vigorous to ensure even coating.

8. Heat a very large skillet or Dutch oven on medium. When it is hot, add the bacon grease (or duck fat or oil) to it. Brown the chicken pieces, skin-side down quite slowly over 15-20 minutes.

9. Turn the chicken pieces over and cook for about 5 minutes.

10. Add the wine (or champagne) and the tarragon. Scrape up any bits of fond, using the wine as a solvent.

11. Scatter the smoked garlic cloves and the thyme branches over the chicken. Now sprinkle the cognac on top and put the lid on the pan.

12. Transfer to a 160°C (320°F) oven for 1 hour.

13. Remove the thyme branches and discard. Transfer the chicken to a platter. Scrape up the garlic cloves and pan juices to use for plating.

14. Position a shelf in the oven about 15cm (6 inches) from the broiler element. Put chicken pieces that you wish to serve on a tray under the broiler. If they were previously refrigerated, this will warm them back up at the same time. Broil until the skin is crisp, but not burnt. The time is typically 6 minutes, but broilers vary. Divide out the garlic and pan juice mixture under each portion.

Split Pea Soup

Most recipes for this soup make it in a single pot, but that is not how it is classically prepared. The pork broth should be prepared separately, which facilitates removing the watery vegetables used to flavor the broth. Seasonings need to be kept to a minimum in order to let the natural pea flavor shine.

250g (8.8 oz)	Split Peas, dry
150g (5.3 oz)	Smoked Pork Ribs or Ham Hock
120g (4 oz)	Onion, peeled ⎫
90g (3 oz)	Carrot, peeled ⎬ Mirepoix for Pork Broth
90g (3 oz)	Celery ⎭
90g (3 oz)	Bacon, smoked
90ml (3 oz)	White Wine, dry
60g (2 oz)	Shallots, peeled and cut in large pieces
1 teaspoon	Beau Monde (see Volume 3, page 233)
3-4 branches	Thyme, fresh
1/2 teaspoon	Black Peppercorns, whole
1 whole	Bay Leaf
about 260ml (9 oz)	Duck Stock (optional - see note below)

ADDITIONAL NOTES

There are two types of dried peas sold: Yellow peas and green peas. Use green peas. Yellow peas taste more like potatoes in this soup. I prefer smoked ribs for this, but ham hocks are traditional. Don't use a ham hock that has no meat on it, or you won't have any to add to the soup.

DUCK STOCK

For optimum results, store the soup for 1-2 days and then thin it with duck stock when you reheat it. You really should try this!

PROCEDURE

1. Rinse the split peas under cold water in a sieve. Then soak them in

500ml (2 cups) of water. After 3-4 hours the peas should have swollen up to the top of the liquid. Don't soak them much beyond this point.

2. Meanwhile prepare the pork broth, ideally in a pressure cooker. Coarsely chop the carrots, onions and celery and put them into the bottom of the pot. Put the branches of thyme down and use the smoked ribs (or ham. Add 1.5 liters (53 ounces, or 1.6 quarts) water plus the black peppercorns.

3. Bring to a simmer and then close the pressure cooker. When steam begins to vent, turn the heat down to maintain it at the point where steam is just barely escaping. Cook for 1 hour, then move it off the heat without releasing the pressure. Let it stand for another 30 minutes before opening.

4. Remove the ribs to a bowl to cool to room temperature. Strain the liquid from the pressure cooker and discard the vegetables.

5. When the peas are finished soaking, strain about 150ml (5.3 oz) of the liquid into the pork broth. Strain off the rest of the water from the peas.

6. In a 4-liter stock pot, begin cooking the bacon strips on a medium heat without adding fat. Let them slowly cook until fat is rendered from them.

7. Add the cut shallots. Stir to break up the bacon and coat the shallots with the fat. Continue cooking on medium (#5 out of 10).

8. When some color begins to appear on the shallots, add half of the wine. Increase heat slightly (#6) and cook until nearly dry.

9. Add the other half of the wine and the bay leaf. Reduce until syrupy.

10. Add the strained peas to the pot, then the broth. Bring to a simmer.

11. Partially cover and adjust heat to maintain at a simmer for an hour. Stir occasionally. Pick the meat off of the rib bones and coarsely chop it.

12. Remove the bay leaf and add the Beau Monde. Now either purée all of the soup, half of it, or none of it. I advise puréeing at least half.

13. Return the puréed portion to the same pot. Add the meat and simmer for 15 more minutes with no lid on.

14. Adjust the salt level carefully (see index).

✦

Chicken Nuggets
Novel Method

The advantage with this method is that when you cut or bite into these, the ground chicken looks like whole fillets. Except it is impossibly tender and moist compared to any fillet. You can season these however you like. Originally these were served with a selection of six different dipping sauces, so the chicken seasoning had to be somewhat neutral to be compatible with all of the different flavored sauces (see page 203 onward).

*Ottoman Tertiary Additive (Volume 3, page 238) is **optional** but will add depth of flavor, which is always a good thing.*

250g (8.8 oz)	Chicken, ground (see notes below)
90ml (3 oz)	Chicken Broth, strong
or 90ml Water + half of a Knorr Chicken gel pack	
2 small sheets	Gelatin, or 1 1/3 teaspoons granulated
1 teaspoon	Ottoman Tertiary Additive (see note above)

You will also need: Eggs, Flour, Oil, Panko (or dry bread crumbs)

SPICE MIX

1 teaspoon	Thyme, dried
1/2 teaspoon	Rosemary, dried
1/2 teaspoon	Black Pepper, finely ground
1/2 teaspoon	Garlic Powder
1/2 teaspoon	Dark Brown Sugar
1/4 teaspoon	Turmeric

GROUND CHICKEN

Freshly ground chicken breast is what you need for this to work, rather than pre-packaged factory-ground chicken that is too wet. You can use a food processor in this unusual case (see page 43). You can use chicken thighs, but this will make breast meat super moist and tender.

PROCEDURE

1. Soak the sheets of gelatin in water. If you are using granulated gelatin, then stir it with 100ml (3.5 oz) of water.

2. In a small sauce pan, heat the chicken broth on a medium heat. If you are using the Knorr gel, wait until it fully dissolves.

3. As it warms up, add 1 tablespoon of flour, the teaspoon of Ottoman Tertiary Additive (if you are using it) and 1 teaspoon of the spice mix from the list of ingredients on the opposite page here (you will have enough of the spice mixture for several batches - just save what you don't use this time in a labeled bottle). Whisk to dissolve the flour. Cook for about 2 minutes.

4. Add 100ml of water, or if you are using the granulated gelatin, then add the 100ml of water with the soaked gelatin in it.

5. Increase heat slightly. Whisk to combine. If you are using the sheet gelatin, pull it out of the cold water it soaked in and add the sheets to the pot, whisking to melt and incorporate them.

6. Increase heat to medium-high and boil to drive off excess water. If you did this right, the mixture should now weigh close to 100g (3.5 oz).

7. Pour the mixture into a bowl containing 30 grams (1 oz) bread crumbs.

8. Stir to combine, and once it is cooled down a bit, mix in one egg yolk.

9. Fold in the ground chicken to make a homogenous mixture, but don't go crazy and over mix it or they will be tough.

10. Sprinkle a large plate with flour. Form the desired shapes from the mixture and place down on the plate. Dust with additional flour.

11. Dip each one in beaten egg and then Panko (or bread crumbs).

12. Heat a nonstick skillet with vegetable oil on medium-high (#7). When the oil comes up to temperature (about 160°C / 320°F) add the pieces. Now lower the heat slightly (#6) and position the pieces around the edge of the pan for even cooking, as shown in the video. Cook on both sides until golden brown.

✦

Breaded Chicken Strips
Novel Method

What is unique about this recipe is that you actually make the same sort of dough you would use to bake a loaf of bread. There are two options with this, providing very different results.

200g (7 oz)	Chicken, skinless (see note below)
2 teaspoons	MSG (optional)
1 teaspoon	Honey (or sugar)
90g (3 oz) + 1 T	Flour (in all)
60ml (2 oz)	Goat Milk or regular milk (optional; see Step #9)
1 teaspoon	Yeast, instant freeze-dried
2 teaspoons	Corn Starch
<u>SPICE BLEND</u>	
1 teaspoon	Thyme, dried
3/4 teaspoon	Rosemary, dried
1/2 teaspoon	Black Peppercorns
1/2 teaspoon	Salt
1/4 teaspoon	Oregano, dried
1/4 teaspoon	Turmeric
1/4 teaspoon	Paprika
1 teaspoon	Cayenne (optional - if you want it spicy)
1 1/2 teaspoons	Fuse Coating (Volume 3, page 241)

SKINLESS CHICKEN

Chicken breasts tend to look better because they can be trimmed into firm and regular sized large pieces, but the flavor of thigh meat is better. Just know that boneless skinless thighs produce irregular shapes.

PROCEDURE

1. Trim the chicken pieces of fat and irregular edges.
2. Use a Jaccard device on the chicken to tenderize it.
3. Slice pieces on the bias (diagonal cuts against the grain).

4. Stir 2 teaspoons of MSG (optional) and 2 teaspoons of salt into 250ml (1 cup) of water. When it is dissolved, add the chicken pieces. Set it aside. The total brining time should be around 45 minutes.

5. Put the honey in a bowl. Add 90ml (3 oz) of hot water. Stir to dissolve.

6. Now add a tablespoon of flour and whisk. By now it should have cooled down some. It needs to be just above body temperature. If it is still too hot, then wait. More whisking will cool it down faster.

7. Add the yeast and stir it in. Cover the bowl with a damp towel. Wait 15 minutes.

8. Put 60 grams (2 oz) flour in a bowl. Transfer the chicken pieces to this bowl, leaving behind as much of the brining solution as possible (wait a few seconds to drip off). Mix the chicken with the flour. Wait 2-3 minutes.

9. If you want a lighter flaky type of coating, add the milk to the yeast mixture now. Whisk to combine. If you want a heavier coating, then omit this step.

10. Pour the yeast mixture over the chicken pieces that are in the bowl with the flour. Gently combine.

11. Cover with cling film and refrigerate for between 3 and 12 hours, or if you are in a hurry, leave it out at room temperature with a damp towel over it for about an hour.

12. Grind all of the spices together. Combine in a bowl with the rest of the flour, which is 30 grams (1 ounce).

13. Heat oil for deep frying to 175°C (350°F). Pull pieces of chicken out of the breading mix one at a time. Dust with the seasoning mix and deep fry for 3-4 minutes. Drain on a wire rack over paper towel.

14. If you used the milk, then they are done. Otherwise they need a second frying. Let pieces rest for 5 minutes, then fry a second time at 190°C (375°F) for another minute.

Fried Chicken 2

This is an updated version of my fried chicken recipe that was posted as a new video to YouTube early in 2021. After several years of playing around with this, here is my best take:

6 pieces	Chicken Thighs and/or Drumsticks, bone-in
3	Egg Whites
2 teaspoons	Milk, lowfat

SPICE BLEND for each 6 pieces of chicken

1 teaspoon	Rosemary, dried
3/4 teaspoon	White Pepper, ground
3/4 teaspoon	Black Pepper, ground
1/2 teaspoon	Onion Powder
1/2 teaspoon	Thyme, dried
1/4 teaspoon	Nutmeg, ground
1/4 teaspoon	Oregano, dried
1/4 teaspoon	Sage, dried
1/4 teaspoon	Garlic Powder
1/4 teaspoon	Dry Mustard, powder
1/4 teaspoon	Paprika
1/4 teaspoon	Turmeric
1 teaspoon	Sugar
1 teaspoon	MSG
60ml (2 oz)	Kefir or Buttermilk (see recipe)

SCALING UP

If you are doing more than 6 pieces, just multiply the quantities, but mix the spices with the kefir/buttermilk only when you are ready to begin marinading your chicken.

MARINADE

Combine all of the dry Spice Blend ingredients (everything but the kefir or buttermilk) in an electric spice mill and grind to a powder. Whisk with the kefir or buttermilk. Use immediately.

PROCEDURE

1. Put the chicken pieces in the marinade (see above). Coat well and refrigerate for at least 3 hours and preferably overnight.

2. Mix up the dry coating in a large bowl by whisking together these:

180g (3 oz)	Pastry Flour (fine mill)
40g (1.4 oz)	Corn Starch
20g (0.7 oz)	Baking Powder (not baking soda)
2 teaspoons	Turmeric
2 teaspoons	MSG
1 1/2 teaspoons	Salt
1 teaspoon	Black Pepper, ground
0-2 Tablespoons	Kashmiri Chili Powder (only for spicy type)

3. Dredge the chicken pieces in the dry coating and then set aside on a platter. Do not throw out the dry flour mix.

4. Whip the egg whites together with the milk until frothy.

5. One piece at a time, coat each piece of chicken in the egg wash, then dredge it in the same flour mixture as before. Set it back aside on the same platter while you continue with the other pieces.

6. When all of the pieces have been coated as much as you can, put them back into the flour mix. Cover the container and shake it a bit to ensure the pieces are coated evenly. Try to make sure the pieces do not directly touch each other and that there is quite a lot of excess flour mix. Now refrigerate for at least 3 hours, but for best results, refrigerate for 2 full days.

7. Heat oil in a deep fryer to 170°C (340°F). Note this is lower than in the video. Also preheat your oven to 180°C (355°F).

8. Deep fry for 8 minutes, being sure not to overcrowd your fryer. Then remove pieces to a wire rack above a baking tray.

9. Put the wire rack/baking tray in the oven for another 7 minutes.

10. Turn pieces over on the wire rack. Let it cool for 15 minutes before consuming voraciously.

The Ultimate Ragu

This recipe takes days to complete, so plan well in advance. Because it takes so long, you may be tempted to try to scale it up. One word: don't. Use multiple pots each with the same amount of ingredients. That's the only way for quality.

700g (25 oz)	Beef Shank, whole
1 full bottle	Red Wine such as Chianti or Barolo (750ml)
100g (3.5 oz)	Red Bell Pepper, coarsely chopped
100g (3.5 oz)	Shallots, peeled and coarsely chopped
2 T	Paprika (in all)
1-2	Hungarian Eros Chilies, dried (see below)
10-12 cloves	Garlic (in all)
310g (11 oz)	Tomato Purée, in all (passata)
400g (14 oz)	Tomatoes, whole canned Italian
2 branches	Rosemary, fresh
4 branches	Thyme, fresh

HUNGARIAN EROS CHILIES

These are my favorite chilies for this, but they are hard to find outside of Hungary (which is where I got the ones you see in the video). You can substitute dried Hot Hungarian Paprika (labeled Eros in Hungarian) or a 50/50 mix of Cayenne and Paprika if you can't get that.

PROCEDURE

1. Tie the beef shank with twine around it to keep it from falling apart during the long cooking time, otherwise you'll be trying to pick shredded meat out of the broth later. Season with coarse salt and cracked black pepper. Coat it lightly with oil on both the top and bottom.

2. Put a 2 liter ovenproof stainless steel pot on a high heat. By ovenproof, that means it can't have plastic parts on the handles or the lid. When it is

92

very hot, add the meat. Don't move it around—let it sear well. After 5-6 minutes, turn the meat over and sear the other side well.

3. Remove the meat. Have a splatter guard ready. While the pan is still smoking hot, add 60 grams (2 oz) of the tomato purée and don't stir it for about a minute. Remember there is no oil in the pan, so it will burn if you let it go too long.

4. Now add the red bell pepper and the shallots. Scrape to pick up the fond and caramelized tomato purée from the bottom. Lower the heat to medium (#5) and stir vigorously to deglaze using the moisture that comes off of the vegetables. Add a splash of the wine to help. If you think it is getting away from you and on the verge of burning, use a steel spatula to scrape it up. You want deep, dark caramelization, but not charcoal burn. The skill involved here is what will make the difference between a good product and a great product.

5. Return the meat to the pan, placing it on top of the vegetables. Add the rest of the wine. The wine should come up more than half the height of the meat. If it doesn't, then your pan is too large. In that case, transfer everything to a smaller pan, but make sure that a lid will go down on it and not bump into the meat. Bring it up to a slow boil.

6. Sprinkle the top of the meat with 1 tablespoon of the paprika (the rest will be used later). Tie the rosemary and thyme in cheesecloth or the green part of a leek, or a metal wire container (see page 233) for the *bouquet garni*. Push it down into the liquid in the pan. Now put a well fitting lid on it. If you don't have a tight lid, put a layer of parchment paper on top and then foil over that, and then the lid you do have. Move into oven. Braise at 140°C (285°F) for an hour.

7. Turn the meat over. Replace the lid and braise for another hour.

8. Remove the lid and move the meat around slightly. Don't try to turn it over, or it will break apart. Return it to the oven for yet another hour.

9. Add 5-6 cloves of chopped garlic on top of the broth. Return it to the

oven for yet another hour—now without a lid.

10. If you have the whole Hungarian Eros chilies, then crumble them up into the pot. If you are using hot paprika then just sprinkle it on. Baste the meat with the liquid to keep it from drying out on top. Return it to the oven for one more hour, still with no lid on it.

11. Remove the pot from the oven and let it rest at room temperature for at least an hour, and two hours is even better.

12. Transfer the meat to a plate. Remove any bits of vegetables that adhere to it. Discard the bouquet garni. Also remove the string and discard it. The meat should have fallen off of the bone completely now. Use the handle of a spoon to push the marrow out from the bone. Refrigerate the marrow in a closed container for later use.

13. Pass the liquid from the pot through a sieve. Wipe out the pot and return it to the top of the stove. Put the sieved broth back into the pot. Also add the meat and 2-3 cloves of chopped garlic. Bring to a simmer on a medium heat. Maintain at a simmer for 30 minutes.

14. Add another teaspoon of paprika (not the hot paprika) and a little salt. Continue reducing until most of the liquid has evaporated and a spoon dragged along the bottom leaves a trail that doesn't close up.

15. Transfer to a closed storage container and refrigerate for 1 to 3 days before proceeding.

16. Pull off some of the long stringy bits from the top and set aside. Put the rest of the meat (and the heavy gel that formed on the bottom) into a food processor along with the marrow from Step #12 and about 4 cloves of garlic, coarsely chopped. Run the processor to chop it into small pieces.

17. Add the remaining 250g (8.8 oz) of tomato purée (passata) and run the processor again to make a smooth mixture.

18. Heat a 4 liter stainless steel pot on medium. When it is warm, add enough olive oil to coat the bottom (swirling to coat). Allow a short time for the oil to come up to temperature and then transfer the contents of the

food processor into the pan. Carefully spread it out to form a single layer, take care not to disturb the olive oil on the bottom. Leave it to cook without stirring it for about 10 minutes. Use a splatter guard if necessary.

19. Now stir it, using the wetter material on top to deglaze the bottom, scraping to pick up the fond. Once you have blended all of the fond into the mixture, cook another 5 minutes with occasional stirring.

20. It should now be a cohesive almost putty-like blob that you are moving around in the pan. Add the canned whole tomatoes and a teaspoon of salt. Stir to break up the tomatoes. Turn the heat down to low and put a lid on it. You might want to move it to a back burner.

21. Cook for 1 1/2 hours, occasionally removing the lid to stir it.

22. Add another 3/4 teaspoon of paprika. Cook for another 30 minutes with occasional stirring, maintaining a bare-simmer.

23. At this point you can refrigerate it and finish it up when you need it. If you are reheating it, then put it back into a pan with a little water (or better, half water and half dry red wine) and warm it up slowly while you fry the reserved meat from Step #16. Heat oil for deep frying to 160°C (320°F). Put an all-metal sieve into the pan (or deep fryer, if you have one). Do not rely on the wire basket of a deep fryer because the holes are too large and the meat will fall through. After the wire sieve has been in the oil for a minute and it is hot, add the reserved meat. You want it well fried, but not burnt. Drain on paper towels.

24. When it is cool, run a knife through it so it isn't as chewy. Now either add this to the ragu, which will produce better texture, or use it to put on top of the pasta you serve with this as an interesting garnish with a bit of a crunchy mouth feel. You have to try it to decide which you prefer. This ragu is well suited to a robust heavy pasta. Don't try to serve it on spaghetti.

✦

Lamb & Wild Mushroom Sausages

If you are going to go to the trouble of making your own sausages, you want to be sure your effort is rewarded with a delicious end result. This recipe justifies the work, for sure.

450g (16 oz)	Lamb, boneless with some fat
Zero to 85g (3 oz)	Pork Fat — see Step #9
100g (3.5 oz)	Shallots, peeled and chopped
100g (3.5 oz)	Mushrooms (see notes below)
12-14g (0.4 oz)	Parsley, freshly chopped
1 teaspoon	Coriander Seeds
1 teaspoon	Black Peppercorns
1 or more	Dried Arborio Chilies (more if you want it hot)
1 1/2 teaspoons	Coarse Salt
3 cloves	Garlic, chopped
30ml (1 oz)	Dry Vermouth or substitute dry white wine
1/4 teaspoon	Sodium Nitrite (see below)
1	Vitamin C tablet (see below)
1 Tablespoon	Olive Oil

THE MUSHROOMS

Oyster mushrooms can be used here. Most any wild type is better, except porcini because they are too strong and will overpower the lamb.

SODIUM NITRITE & VITAMIN C

Sodium Nitrite, also known as pink salt, is not only responsible for keeping meat an appetizing color (rather than turning gray), but it is also a flavor component that we associate with sausage and cured meats. The danger is that it chemically reacts to create a type of carcinogen, however by adding ascorbic acid (Vitamin C) to the mixture, that reaction is almost eliminated, but it is up to you. The taste is the same either way.

PROCEDURE

1. Chop the mushrooms up into large pieces. Heat a 3 or 4 liter pot on a high setting (#8 out of 10). When it is hot, add the olive oil. Wait for the oil to come up to temperature, then add the chopped mushrooms. Sauté for about 3 minutes. Don't stir too much. Let them brown some.

2. Add half of the shallots and stir. Cook for another 2 minutes.

3. Turn the heat down to medium (#6). Add the parsley and cook for 2 more minutes.

4. Turn the heat off, but leave the pan on the burner.

5. Grind the coriander seeds, black peppercorns, dried chilies and coarse salt in an electric spice mill.

6. Add the ground spices and the other half of the shallots to the pan. Stir, using the residual heat to soften the shallot. Stir for about 2 minutes.

7. Add the chopped garlic. Stir. The pan should still be hot. After a minute deglaze with the dry vermouth.

8. Grind up the Vitamin C tablet in a mortar. Mix the resulting powder with the sodium nitrite, then add the mixture to the pan. Stir well, then transfer the contents to a bowl and chill in the refrigerator for 1-2 hours.

9. Cube the lamb up for the grinder. If your lamb is very lean, add cubed pork fat to compensate. It should contain 85 grams (3 oz) fat <u>in all</u>.

10. Mix the cubed meat with the chilled mushroom mixture and cover with cling film. Refrigerate overnight (8 to 16 hours) before proceeding.

11. Pass the mixture through a meat grinder with the medium-fine disc.

12. Put the ground meat mixture into a food processor and grind until very fine, but not an actual paste—don't go *quite* that far.

13. Refrigerate the mixture for at least an hour before proceeding.

14. Pack this into casings as you would any other sausage. They are best cooked over charcoal.

Chicken Picatta
with Smoky Asparagus

This is based on an Old World classic, but one that is seldom seen these days. The original dish was Swordfish Picatta, but due to the rising cost and dwindling supply due to overfishing, the less expensive chicken breast was substituted. The problem is that when it is prepared in the usual way the chicken is invariably dry and lacking in flavor because chicken breast lacks the richness and delicacy of swordfish. so the dish soon lost its popularity. This approach solves those problems.

INGREDIENTS FOR TWO PORTIONS

1 whole	Chicken Breast, boneless/skinless
2	Asparagus Spears (see notes below)
2 (or more)	Garlic Cloves, peeled and sliced
45g (1.6 oz)	Butter
1 Tablespoon	Capers, preferably salt-packed
1/2 to 1 whole	Lemon, to be cut into supremes
1/2-3/4 teaspoon	Herbs de Provence (see notes below)
2 Tablespoons	Parsley, fresh
1/4 teaspoon	MSG (optional)

LARGE ASPARAGUS

Try to find thick asparagus so that even after peeling it is still at least a centimeter (0.4 inches) in diameter. If it is too thin it will burn and also there won't be anything for flavor in the chicken, either.

HERBS DE PROVENCE

The video for this dish stated only Herbs de Provence for the dried herb mixture, and that will work okay, but this blend is far superior here:

```
DRY HERB MIX (VERSION OF HERBS DE PROVENCE)
1 teaspoon        Thyme
1 teaspoon        Tarragon
1 teaspoon        Chervil
1 teaspoon        Marjoram
3/4 teaspoon      Parsley
3/4 teaspoon      Chives
1/2 teaspoon      Lavender (culinary grade)
```

PROCEDURE

1. Trim and peel the asparagus. Coat liberally with table salt and olive oil.

2. Heat a cast iron grill pan (or BBQ) on a very high flame to sear the asparagus until it has a smoky taste. Watch the video if you are not sure.

3. Trim the chicken breast so you have a nice even piece, then pound it flat between sheets of cling film. Again, the video is good to show details.

4. Sprinkle lightly with flour then place an asparagus spear on top and roll the chicken up to a log, using the cling film to secure it tightly. Refrigerate the pieces for at least 2 hours so that they retain their shape.

5. Cut the lemon supremes as shown in the video and reserve.

6. Wash the capers in several changes of water. Reserve.

7. Heat a nonstick pan with the butter.

8. Unwrap carefully and dust with flour. When the butter has foamed up, add the chicken. Cook slowly on a medium heat with occasional turning.

9. When the pink is gone from all sides add the garlic. Turn heat down.

10. When the garlic is slightly golden, add the capers. Fry for 1 minute.

11. Add the dry herbs, the parsley, the lemon supremes and the wine. After a minute, cover the pan and reduce the heat to low. Cook 2 minutes.

12. Remove chicken to a platter. Add the rest of the butter to the pan and increase the heat. Reduce to a thick sauce while stirring.

13. Pour over the chicken and add fresh green parsley for color.

Aloo Masala Gram Dosa

The cooking of the potato is a long and labor-intensive process, but the end result is not like any potato you have tried before. There are small armies of Indian women who make these for a few pennies a day in several cities.

300g (10.6 oz)	Potatoes, peeled and cubed
175g (6.2 oz)	Onions, sliced into rings
1 1/4 teaspoons	Coriander Seeds
1 1/4 teaspoons	Coarse Salt
1 teaspoon	Sambar Masala (see note below)
1/2 teaspoon	Fenugreek Seeds
1 whole	Green Serrano Chili, dried
1/4 - 1/2 teaspoon	Cumin Seeds
1/4 teaspoon	Asafoetida
3/4 teaspoon	Dark Brown Sugar
3 T	Cilantro, freshly minced
45g (1.5 oz)	Coconut Oil
Also Butter, Ghee or Vegetable Oil (your choice)	
<u>FOR DOSA BATTER</u>	
150g (5.3 oz)	Gram Flour
50g (1.75 oz)	Rice Flour
500ml (17.6 oz)	Water
1/2 teaspoon	Salt

SAMBAR MASALA

Sambar Masala is a South Indian spice blend. The product from India (such as MDH brand) contains ingredients that are difficult or even impossible to get outside of India. You can substitute the regular standard curry powder, but the flavor won't be as good.

PROCEDURE

1. The night before you want to make this, make the dosa batter by combining the gram flour, rice flour and water in a bowl. Do not add the

salt. Cover with cling film and leave out at room temperature.

2. Pass the mixture through a sieve. Put the thick gel-like material that didn't pass through the sieve into a blender along with 105ml (3.75 oz) of the liquid from the bowl and the salt. Discard the rest of the liquid. Blend very well to aerate. Then transfer back to a bowl. Cover with cling film and let rest 1 to 3 hours before using.

3. Remove the stem from the dried green chili. Put it in an electric spice mill along with the coriander seeds, coarse salt, Sambar masala, fenugreek seeds, cumin seeds and asafoetida. Grind to a powder.

4. Heat the coconut oil in a 4 liter stock pot on a medium setting (#6 out of 10).

5. When the oil is warm, add the onions. Cook for about 10 minutes, stirring occasionally.

6. Add the ground spices from Step #3. Stir and cook for 30-40 seconds.

7. Add the potatoes and lower the heat some. Cook for about 3 minutes.

8. Put a lid on the pan now that the temperature has been reduced. Cook for about 1 1/2 minutes, then remove the lid and stir, scraping the bottom to pick up any fond and keep it from burning. Replace the lid and repeat this step, stopping to stir and scrape the bottom about every 1 1/2 minutes for about 5 more times.

9. Remove the lid and add the dark brown sugar. Reduce heat to low and replace the lid. Wait for 5 minutes.

10. Stir and return the lid for another 5 minutes. Repeat one more time.

11. Stir and reduce the heat to very low (#1 out of 10). Replace the lid and cook for about 25 minutes.

12. Add the fresh cilantro. Stir and replace the lid. Wait 2 more minutes.

13. Transfer the mixture to a bowl and crush the potato mixture with a fork or other implement. You can refrigerate it for up to a couple of days at this point if you need to, but it will be best if you use it the same day. You can also add some finely diced green chilies if you want it spicier.

CONTINUED ON THE NEXT PAGE

ASSEMBLING THE FINAL PRODUCT

1. Whisk the dosa batter just before using it. Heat a good large nonstick pan with no fat or oil in it on a medium setting. When it is hot, add a 60ml (2 oz) ladle of the dosa batter in the middle. Don't let the batter reach the edges of the pan, and certainly do not swirl it around like you were making a crepe. The batter needs to be somewhat thick. Take a look at the video if you are unsure of how to ladle it out. That section is about 10 minutes into the video.

2. After about 3 minutes the dosa will have dried out enough on top for you to brush it gently with a little melted butter or ghee (or vegetable oil if you are vegan). Wait about 1 more minute.

3. Very carefully flip it over. Wait 1 more minute.

4. Using your fingers, position a heaping tablespoon of the potato filling in a crescent shape along one edge of the dosa.

5. Fold the opposite half over to enclose the filling. Cook for 2 minutes.

6. Flip it over and brush the other side with a little more butter (or oil).

7. Repeat Step 6 for the other side. Cook until golden brown.

8. Now fold it into quarters, if desired. There is no requirement to do this, but it is traditional in many areas. Use the edge of the spatula to make a slight indentation in the middle and then fold along the "dotted line" you just made.

9. Continue cooking slowly and gently pressing down with the spatula. Brush with additional butter or oil, as needed.

10. Serve with the curry of your choosing. It is typically served with vegetarian dishes and not meat, because it is a traditional part of Indian vegetarian cuisine.

Tropical Chicken Rolls

Based on a signature dish at the Sheraton Hotel in Hawaii.

1	Chicken Breast
2 thin slices	Ham
1 or 2 whole	Bananas, ideally a type called Baby Bananas
1/2 teaspoon	Angostura Bitters
1 whole	Egg, beaten
about 1/2 cup	Dried Coconut, shredded & unsweetened
about 1/4 cup	Flour
250ml (8.8 oz)	Orange Juice
1 1/2 T	Orange Marmelade
1 T	Sugar
1 whole	Passionfruit, or 1 T Passionfruit Syrup
1 T	Cointreau orange liqueur

PROCEDURE

1. Trim and slice the chicken breast into two thin sheets. Pound each one out gently under cling film.

2. Peel the bananas. Wrap a slice of ham around each. Add a few drops of Angostura bitters. Place on a pounded chicken breast piece and roll up as tightly as you can in cling film. Refrigerate for 3 hours or up to 2 days.

3. Put the orange juice, orange marmalade and sugar in a skillet and reduce on a medium heat until it starts to thicken.

4. Unwrap and dust each chicken roll with flour. Dip in beaten egg, then roll in the dried shredded coconut to coat as evenly as possible.

5. Deep fry at 165°C (330°F) for 5-7 minutes, depending on size.

6. Finish the sauce by scraping out the contents of passionfruit and adding the Cointreau. Heat to thicken more. Trim the ends of the rested chicken roulades and cut diagonally to stand up. *Lightly* sprinkle the banana ends with a little paprika.

Vitello Tonnato

This classic Italian dish has the seemingly odd combination of veal and tuna, but it didn't become a famous dish without good reason. This version is much improved over the one in my video from many years ago and now employs sous vide.

up to 900g (2 lbs)	Veal, Eye of Round
1-2 whole	Leeks, trimmed and rinsed
2-4 stalks	Celery
1 teaspoon	Marjoram, dried
2-3 branches	Thyme, fresh (or 1 teaspoon dried)

PROCEDURE FOR THE VEAL

1. Trim the veal eye of round of any sinew. Season with salt and freshly ground black pepper, then rub with a little vegetable oil.

2. Heat a cast iron pan very hot and sear the outsides, rolling it around evenly just to kill off bacteria. You aren't trying to actually cook it here.

3. Place it in a vacuum bag along with long pieces of leek and celery alongside of it to keep the bag from crushing the veal out of shape when vacuum is applied, as shown in this diagram below viewed from looking down into the open end of the bag before sealing (also see page 37).

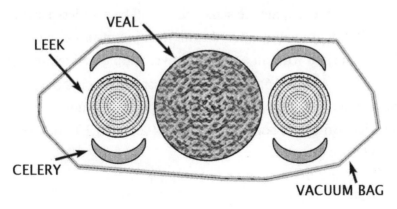

VEAL

LEEK

CELERY

VACUUM BAG

3. Add the marjoram and sprigs of thyme into the bag. The position is not important. Then vacuum seal the bag.

4. Place in a 55.5°C (132°F) water bath for 9 1/2 hours.

5. Cool the unopened bag down in an ice bath to get it out of the "danger zone" and then refrigerate it overnight (or longer).

6. When you are ready to use it, open the bag and discard the vegetables. Trim the ends of the veal off and then cut thin slices. If you have a deli slicer, this is the best tool.

PROCEDURE FOR THE SAUCE

150g (5.3 oz)	Tuna - see Step #1 below
*60g (2 oz)	Carrots, peeled and chopped
*60ml (2 oz)	White Wine, dry
*50ml (1.8 oz)	Apple Cider Vinegar
*1 whole	Onion, medium (cut into quarters)
*1 small bunch	Parsley, fresh
2 cloves	Garlic, peeled
1/2 teaspoon	White Pepper, ground
2	Egg Yolks
120ml (4.2 oz)	Olive Oil, extra-virgin
4 whole	Anchovies
2 teaspoons	Capers, rinsed well
25ml (0.9 oz)	Lemon Juice, fresh
1/4 teaspoon	Cayenne or Kashmiri Mirch

To Garnish: Caper Berries, Parsley and Lemon slices

1. You may substitute canned tuna. You will need 1 ½ of the usual size small cans. It won't be quite the same, but it will be a lot less expensive and easier. **If you are using canned tuna then you won't need the ingredients marked with an asterisk above.** Skip ahead to Step #5.

...Otherwise put 450ml (16 oz) of water in a small pot on the stove. Add the carrots, white wine, apple cider vinegar, quartered onion and the parsley sprigs. Bring to a boil on a high heat (#8 out of 10) for a few minutes to infuse the water.

2. Reduce the heat to bring down to a simmer.

3. Add the piece of tuna. Poach for about 5 minutes.

4. Remove the tuna and wipe off any vegetables stuck to it. Pass the liquid through a sieve. Discard the solids, but keep the broth for use later. Let the liquid cool for 1 hour. Crumble the tuna into a bowl.

5. Put the capers, anchovies, egg yolks, garlic, white pepper and cayenne into the cup of a stick blender. Add the crumbled tuna and about 60ml (2 oz) of the liquid that you passed through a sieve in Step #4. Purée. NOTE: If you are using canned tuna, then drain the tuna from 1 1/2 cans on a sieve over a bowl. Save the spring water that it was packed in from both cans to use in place of the poaching liquid. If you only have oil-packed tuna then discard the oil and use plain water for the liquid. Measure out 60ml (2 oz) of that liquid to add and discard any extra. Purée.

6. Drizzle the olive oil a little at a time while the blender is running to purée until all of the oil has been added and it is a thin mayonnaise.

7. Add the lemon juice now. Blend again, then adjust the seasoning with more salt and MSG if you are so inclined. Remember that it will thicken more after being in the refrigerator, so make it on the thin side for now.

8. Ideally refrigerate this for one day before assembling it. Put a layer of the mayonnaise sauce down on a plate. Slice the veal thin on a deli-type machine if possible. Make sure to remove any tough bits before slicing. Put circles of the meat down into the sauce. When the plate is covered, put another layer of the sauce on top. Put cling film over this and refrigerate the plate for at least overnight.

When ready to serve, remove the cling film and sprinkle with caper berries, lemon slices and fresh parsley leaves. Allow a little time for it to warm up at room temperature some. It should be cool, as in just below room temperature, but not refrigerator-cold.

Lamb Chops
To Truffle or Not to Truffle?

Usually the philosophy of the finest restaurants is to let the star protein of the dish shine. The exception is when it comes to truffles, where they are allowed to overpower other flavors a bit.

2 or more	Lamb Chops, bone-in
Salt, Black Pepper, Citric Acid, Olive Oil	

For the Truffled Lamb chops you also need:

20g or more	Black Truffle Meat Paste (page 194)
Black Truffles	

PROCEDURE

1. Preheat oven to 190°C (375°F). Season lamb chops with a little salt and freshly ground black pepper.

2. When the pan is hot, add about a teaspoon of olive oil per lamb chop.

3. Wait until the oil is hot, then put in the lamb chops. Without moving them, sear one side without actually browning it. You need a gray color.

4. Turn the lamb chops over, making sure to get them in the hot oil.

5. Sprinkle the other side with a little citric acid (see page 232).

6. After about a minute, turn the chops over to let the other side brown.

7. After another minute or so, flip them over and transfer them to a metal tray. If you are making the truffled version, spread about a teaspoon of the Black Truffle Meat Paste on each lamb chop. This will melt as it cooks.

8. Roast in the oven for between 4 and 7 minutes, depending on how well done you like them. Then for the truffled version, garnish with shaved black truffles, if possible.

Ribeye Steak
with Black Truffles

The ultimate luxury steak famous in Florence, prepared using sous vide so that the marinade can penetrate the meat.

1 or more	Ribeye Steaks (Entrecote)
10g or more	Black Truffle Meat Paste (page 194)
Salt, Black Pepper, Olive Oil	
Black Truffles	

PROCEDURE

1. Heat a flat-surfaced cast iron pan very hot. While it is heating, season your steak(s) with a little salt, black pepper and rub with olive oil on both sides. There is salt in the marinade, so go easy on it.

2. Cook the steak for 30 seconds on each side. Do them one at a time if you have more than one. The point here is to dramatically reduce the bacterial count on the outside, not to actually cook the steak.

3. Transfer to a tray and let them stand for 5-10 minutes before putting some of the Black Truffle Meat Paste on one side only of each steak.

4. Vacuum seal them, using a long bag to keep the liquid from running up into the machine (see page 37). Cook at 55.5°C (132°F) for 8 hours.

5. Put the bags into cold water (not ice water) for 3 minutes before opening it. Take the steak(s) out and carefully wipe off the surfaces from the paste. The flavor is in the meat now and burnt paste is not tasty.

6. Heat up a cast iron grill pan, or (<u>much</u> better) an outdoor BBQ.

7. Quickly grill the steak(s) on each side. They are already cooked through. You just want the Maillard reaction, grill marks and smokiness.

8. Garnish generously with shaved black truffles, if available.

Grilled Octopus

This is another example of how sous vide is truly useful because octopus is notorious for being tough and rubbery unless the cook is very skillful. This method assures excellent results every time. Plus it allows for preparation in advance.

1 or more	Octopus Arms, fresh
Olive Oil	

PROCEDURE

1. Only use fresh octopus, not that terrible pre-cooked frozen stuff. Separate the arms by slicing with a knife. The head is of no use here.

2. Bring a pot of salted water to a full boil. Keep a bowl of icewater nearby. Plunge the octopus legs into the boiling water for 20 seconds only, then into the ice bath.

3. Remove the legs and dry them off. Apply a little olive oil, then seal them in a vacuum bag. Put in a water bath at 77°C (170.5°F) for 5 hours.

4. Put the bag into a bowl with cold water to cool it down. Then either continue with the cooking, or store in the refrigerator for up to several days (as long as you don't open the bag).

5. Bring the sealed bag up to room temperature (or close to it) before opening. Then dump out the contents into a bowl. There will be some loose skin clinging to the octopus. Rub that off and discard it along with the liquid that has accumulated in the bag.

6. Dry the octopus well, then rub it with olive oil. Heat a cast iron grill pan very hot (or better, a barbecue outdoors). Grill the octopus to get some smokiness to it. The meat inside is already cooked and tender, so don't make it tough by overcooking it now!

Classic Fricassee
Chicken or Rabbit

"Fricassee L'Ancienne", as it is called in French, goes back to at least the year 1300 from one of the earliest known French cookbooks. In "more recent times", it was a favorite of King Charles V, who lived in the early 1500's. Those who say it is just another stew do not understand this dish. There are several key aspects that define it as a Fricassee. First, the meat must be skinless (not much choice in the case of rabbit, but most recipes you see today using chicken call for leaving the skin on, which completely ruins this dish as the fat dissolves into the sauce making it a greasy mess). Second, the meat must be marinated overnight with plenty of fresh thyme. The marinade recipe here (PAGE 195) contains the thyme. Third, it must include white wine. Fourth, the meat must not be allowed to brown—it must stay "white and pure". Truffles were added in the year 1590.

apx. 1kg (2.2 lbs)	Chicken (bone-in thighs/drumsticks) or Rabbit
1 recipe	White Truffle Fricassee Paste (page 195)
1 1/2 Tablespoons	Flour
90g (3.2 oz)	Mushrooms, cut in 1cm (0.4 inch) cubes
90g (3.2 oz)	Carrots, peeled and cut in 1cm (0.4 inch) cubes
90ml (3.2 oz)	Brut Champagne, or dry white wine
10ml (0.35 oz)	Champagne Vinegar (or white wine vinegar)
300ml (10.5 oz)	Chicken or Rabbit Stock (see notes below)
200ml (7 oz)	Cream
2 whole	Bay Leaves

THE STOCK

Use chicken stock for chicken. For rabbit, you can use chicken stock if you must, but I urge you to make your own rabbit stock from the scraps.

PROCEDURE

1. Prepare the seasoning paste (page 195). This is enough for six pieces of chicken (bone-in thighs and/or drumsticks) or one rabbit.

2. Section the meat. Remove the skin if you are using chicken.

3. Mix the marinade with the meat. Ideally put it into a vacuum bag and seal it under pressure for maximum flavor penetration (page 37), but you can just put it in a regular ziplock back. Refrigerate for at least 12 hours and up to 24 hours. Beyond that the texture of the meat begins to go mushy because of the mushrooms in the marinade.

4. Transfer to a bowl and sprinkle with the flour. Distribute evenly and then let it stand at room temperature for about 30 minutes.

5. Heat the butter in a skillet on medium-low heat. As soon as it has mostly melted, add the pieces of meat. Turn about every 30 seconds to prevent any browning. Cook for 4-5 minutes in this way.

6. Remove the meat and reserve. Add the mushrooms and carrots to the pan. Increase the heat. Cook with occasional stirring until the mushrooms are golden and starting to brown.

7. Drain the pan on a sieve. Discard the fat. Return the mushrooms and carrots to the pan. Add the wine and vinegar. Reduce the heat to medium-low. Cook until the liquid is mostly evaporated.

8. Add the stock, cream and bay. Stir, then return the meat to the pan.

9. Maintain at a very slow simmer for 25 minutes for chicken and 35 minutes for rabbit. Turn pieces over every 4-5 minutes.

10. Remove the meat to a platter and increase heat slightly to reduce the sauce for a few more minutes. Don't make it *too* thick, though!

11. Return meat to the pan to warm it back up in the sauce.

12. Ideally you should garnish this liberally with freshly shaved white truffles, but they are seasonal and the cost these days is astronomical. Even without that addition, your home will have a wonderful aroma that lingers through the next day.

Giabusada
Swiss Cabbage Stew

*This can be made as a vegetarian dish if desired, as explained below. The technique of cooking the cabbage in a **blanc** (explained below) is not typical for Giabusada recipes, but it produces a wonderful, creamy texture that is much more of a stew than the soup-like consistency this usually has, despite its name. This uses enzymatic action (see Volume 3).*

350g (12.3 oz)	Cabbage, trimmed
1/2 teaspoon	Citric Acid or 30ml (1 oz) Lemon Juice (see below)
30ml (1 oz)	White Wine, dry
15g (1/2 oz)	Garlic cloves
30ml (1 oz)	Cream
12 whole	Small Boiling Onions
2 T	Flour
2-3 T	Swiss Cheese, grated (optional)
	or substitute Maasdam cheese
4 strips	Bacon, smoked (see note below)
To finish: freshly picked Tarragon and Lemon juice	

WITH BACON OR VEGETARIAN

To make this a vegetarian dish, omit the bacon and when it comes to browning the onions in the bacon fat, just use a little butter instead.

THE *BLANC*

Do not confuse this with *Beurre Blanc*, which is a butter sauce. A *blanc* is comprised of water, flour, lemon juice and sometimes white wine. Here the lemon juice in the cooking phase is replaced with citric acid (see page 232). You can substitute 30ml (1 oz) of lemon juice if you like. The use of a blanc with cabbage seems to be forgotten in food lore, curiously.

PROCEDURE

1. Trim the cabbage of the stem and all heavy ribs. Be sure you have the correct weight of cabbage *after* you trimmed it. Roughly chop all of it.

2. Combine the garlic with 100g (3.5 oz) of the cabbage in a food processor. Pulse to combine, but don't purée. Add this mixture back to the rest of the chopped cabbage and stir. Wait 10 minutes, stirring sometimes.

3. Put 700ml (25 oz) of water into a pot. Add the citric acid, white wine and flour. Whisk to combine. Now add the cabbage and garlic mixture.

4. Stir some as you bring to a boil on a high heat.

5. Turn the heat down to maintain a slow simmer for 45 minutes or so.

6. Now increase the heat a little and stir to get the mixture to a somewhat thick, velvety texture. You want to drive off most of the water. After about 20 minutes it will weigh about 310 grams (11 oz) if you have done everything right. Transfer it to a bowl and set aside. It can be stored in the refrigerator for up to three days if you are not proceeding right away.

7. Cut the tip end and the root end off of the boiling onions. Don't bother trying to peel them. Heat a pot of salted water to a good simmer. Add the onions and cook for 5 minutes.

8. Transfer the onions to a bowl to cool down. Rub off whatever skins didn't come off.

9. Cut the bacon into small pieces. Heat a large nonstick skillet with the bacon. When some fat has rendered, add the onions and coat in the fat.

10. Transfer the onions to an ovenproof dish and broil at 180°C (355°F) for *about* 20 minutes. However, broilers vary greatly. Watch carefully!

11. Add the velvety cabbage to the skillet with the bacon. Lower the heat.

12. When the onions are done, add the cream to the cabbage and bacon. Stir to incorporate, increasing the heat some. Then plate, adding the onions, freshly picked tarragon and lemon wedges on the side. Serve with a cold Grüner Veltliner wine.

Saltimbocca

The name is Italian for "jumps in the mouth" because it was considered so delicious. This dish is seldom seen on restaurant menus these days. One reason that has been suggested is that people now want more complex and interesting flavors, which is what this version provides by adding a very non-traditional seasoning paste inside of each one. Although this is widely considered an Italian dish, some in Switzerland argue that they made it first. This is plausible since the Swiss have similar cured meats and stuffed veal dishes are common there.

2 whole	Veal or Chicken Breast pieces
4 slices	Prosciutto (see recipe)
about 12	Sage leaves, fresh
100ml (3.5 oz)	White Wine, dry
apx. 30g (1 oz)	Flour
	THE SEASONING PASTE
30ml (1 oz)	Olive Oil, extra-virgin
22g (0.75 oz)	Green Olives
2-3 T	Basil leaves, fresh
2 T	Parsley, fresh
15ml (0.5 oz)	Lemon Juice, fresh
2 cloves	Garlic. peeled and sliced

PROCEDURE

1. Put all of the ingredients for the Seasoning Paste into the cup of a stick blender and purée.

2. Trim the veal or chicken breast uniformly 6cm (about 1/4 inch) thick. Use a Jaccard device to tenderize the pieces (as shown in the video), then pound them flatter under cling film using a mallet. If you are going to pound out veal, then start with slightly thicker pieces.

3. Put the white wine in a dish and soak the meat in it for 15-30 minutes.

4. Drain and dry the meat on paper towels. Reserve the white wine.

5. Cut each piece in two so you have a total of 4 pieces. Divide the Seasoning Paste among the pieces of meat and spread on one end only.

6. Place a thin slice of prosciutto down. on a piece of cling film Put one of the slices of meat on time of it and then place 2 or 3 sage leaves on it. Now fold it over so that the seasoning paste is enclosed. Note that if you use a lot of prosciutto (wrapping the chicken or veal in more than one layer), it will taste mostly of prosciutto and not look very good aesthetically. If you love prosciutto and don't care about the appearance, then this is perfectly fine, of course. If you want it to look nice, then make sure there is only a single thin layer of prosciutto and that the sage leaves are uniformly distributed so that can shine through, as shown in the photo at the start of the video for this. Once they are at this stage you can keep them in the refrigerator (covered) for up to 3 hours before you cook them.

7. Dust one side with flour.

8. Heat a nonstick skillet on medium-high (#7 out of 10). When it is hot, add a little olive oil. Let the oil get hot, and then add the pieces, floured-side down. Move them through the oil in the pan briefly to make sure there is oil beneath each piece as it fries.

9. Add another dusting of flour to the side facing up as they cook.

10. Flip them over after they have been browned slightly on the first side. Now add the sliced garlic.

11. After the second side is lightly browned, flip them back over and reduce the heat to low. Add the reserved wine they marinated in back from Step #4. **Sometimes Mozzarella is added at this point. Another version also adds Pomodora.** Cover with a lid and steam for 5 minutes.

12. Check to make sure they are cooked through, and then remove to plate up. Continue boiling the pan juices until they are thickened. Add a little butter to make it glossier and richer, if desired. Caper berries pair nicely with this. Also buttered pasta, though that is not traditional.

Vegetarian Crumble

This was the first cooking video that I posted after several years of my absence from YouTube. A bit of trouble to make and so it seems to be unappreciated, which is unfortunate because this is an extremely useful concoction that can instantly elevate the most mundane of dishes into something quite delicious.

100g (3.5 oz)	Eggplant, cooked (see below)
100g (3.5 oz)	Black Beans, canned or cooked
100g (3.5 oz)	Red Lentils, canned or cooked
30ml (1 oz)	Black Truffle Oil
1 whole	Egg
2 cloves	Garlic
15g (1/2 oz)	Tomato Paste, Italian type in tube
15g (1/2 oz)	Black Beans in Chili Oil (see below)
2 teaspoons	Black Soy Sauce
1/4 teaspoon	Salt
1/2 teaspoon	MSG
Fresh Basil, a handful of leaves (no stems)	

NOTES ON INGREDIENTS

The weight of the eggplant is after it has been cooked in Step 1 below. Both black beans and red lentils are often available canned or in cardboard packages already cooked, or you can cook them yourself ahead of time. Black beans in Chili Oil is a product sold in jars in Asian food specialty stores (see page 233). Black Soy Sauce is also available in any Asian food store and is different from ordinary soy sauce (thicker and more intense).

PROCEDURE

1. Peel and slice an eggplant into about 2cm (3/4 inch) pieces. Fry gently in oil until soft. Once the first side has started to cook, flip the pieces over and season with smoked salt and fresh ground pepper. Continue cooking

until lightly golden, turning about every 5 minutes as shown in the video.

2, Leave eggplant pieces to cool in the pan on the stove with the heat off for about 40 minutes before proceeding.

3. If using canned black beans and/or lentils, drain them well on a sieve.

4. Combine all the ingredients except the MSG and the basil in a food processor until it is homogenous, but don't keep going until it is just liquid. See the video if you aren't sure.

5. Preheat oven to 200°C (400°F).

6. Use a spatula to spread the mixture out on a silicone mat. The depth should be 5 to 6mm (just under 1/4 inch). If you don't have a silicone mat you can try using two layers of parchment paper, but it may burn some on the bottom. The silicone is an insulator.

7. Roast for 5 minutes.

8. Leave it in the oven and reduce the temperature to 140°C (280°F). Open the oven door for about 30 seconds to help lower the temperature inside. Then close the door and continue roasting for about 15 minutes. Depending on your oven it could take up to 20 minutes. It should be dry but not burnt.

9. Let it cool at room temperature for at least 15 minutes, then scrape it off of the silicone mat back into a food processor bowl. If you did burn the edges by mistake, just scrape those parts away into the trash.

10. Spread it back on the silicone mat and dry at 120°C (230°F) with fan assist on for 20-30 minutes. Stir it around and leave to cool 1-2 hours.

10. Now it goes back into the food processor. Add the fresh basil and MSG. Grind it to a crumble. Stored in the refrigerator in a glass jar, this will keep for 2 weeks

This works absolute magic on simple pasta dishes because it is so complimentary to olive oil and Parmigiano-Reggiano. Once you try this, you will be sure to make it often.

Royal Persian Rose Duck

This recipe was originally prepared for a Saudi prince by his Persian (now Iranian) chef. The colorful history of this dish is explained on the page following this recipe. I have revised this recipe dramatically since it first appeared on my YouTube channel. The flavor is the same, but the preparation using sous vide here is easier and the meat is more reliably tender.

400g (14 oz)	Duck Breast, boneless
200g (7 oz)	Apricots, fresh
60g (2 oz)	Cherry or Small Plum Tomatoes
60g (2 oz)	Shallots, peeled and sliced
60g (2 oz)	Butter
4-5 cloves	Garlic, peeled and cut in halves
3 whole	Kaffir Lime Leaves, dried
1/2 teaspoon	Cumin, ground
pinch	Saffron threads or powder
1 small	Dried Red Chili
1/4 teaspoon	Cardamom Seeds (from the pods)
1 whole	Bay Leaf
1 teaspoon	Muscovado Sugar
45g (1.5 oz)	Feta, fairly mild and semi-soft
15g (0.5 oz)	Scallions, green part only
1 teaspoon	Rose Petals, dried (see note below)

NOTES ON INGREDIENTS

Both kaffir lime leaves and culinary grade dried rose petals are available in Middle Eastern specialty grocery stores, or online. Dried rose buds are often sold for making a kind of tea. Whole rose petals are even better, but don't use the kind you get from a florist because they are sprayed with pesticides and not intended for human consumption.

The original cheese for this was Kashk, but this is very hard to find and a quality semi-soft feta is just as good. Get it in small cubes.

PROCEDURE

1. Nick the bottom of each cherry tomato to facilitate peeling them. Bring a pot of water to a boil and blanch the tomatoes for about 30 seconds, then drop them into an ice bath. They will be easy to peel now.

2. Squeeze the cherry tomatoes to separate the skin from the pulp inside. Save both parts.

3. Melt the butter in a 1 liter (1 quart) nonstick pot over a medium-low heat. When the butter has melted, add the tomato skins, the bay leaf and the cardamom seeds. Start a timer.

4. While this is slowly cooking, put the cumin seeds, coarse salt, chili pepper and kaffir lime leaves in an electric spice mill and grind fine. Now pass the resulting powder through a fine mesh sieve, discarding any solids. Add the part that passed through the sieve to the butter and tomato skins.

5. When the tomatoes have been cooking for 15 minutes, turn off the heat. After a few minutes pass the mixture through a sieve and discard the solids. Reserve the flavored butter for later use.

6. Trim the duck breast of any sinew as well as the irregular edges so there is a nice clean piece. Salt the fat-side. Put it into a cold nonstick pan and set it on a medium flame, fat-side down. Cook for 6 minutes. Use a splatter guard.

7. Flip the duck breast over and sear briefly for only about 30 seconds. The point here is just to reduce the bacterial count so it doesn't spoil (as explained on pages 38-39). Now remove the duck to a plate and reserve.

8. Add the sliced shallots to the pan with the accumulated duck fat. Cook for about a minute, then pass through a sieve. The duck fat has no further use in this recipe, but save it for other things.

9. Put the shallots back in the pan. Add the flavored butter from Step #5 and the apricots (pitted and coarsely chopped) and the cinnamon stick and the bay leaf. Cook for about 5 minutes.

10. Add the tomato pulp from Step #2 and the garlic and the muscovado

sugar. Cook 5 minutes more with occasional stirring.

11, Turn the heat off and add the saffron. Stir to break up the apricots more (you should have been doing this all along, actually) and allow it to cool to near room temperature.

12. Put the duck breast into a vacuum bag. Add the apricot mixture (including the cinnamon stick and bay leaf). Seal under vacuum.

13. Ideally store in the refrigerator overnight first, but you can skip this and still have a good result. Heat a water bath to 57°C (134.5°F) and add the vacuum sealed package. Cook for 3 hours.

14. Cut the bag open and empty into a large bowl. Pick the duck out and put on a plate. Wipe the skin clean of the marinade. Reserve.

15. Add the scallions and the cheese to the pan and stir to slightly melt the cheese. Remove and discard the cinnamon stick during this time. You can refrigerate everything at this point and proceed when guests arrive, or when an order comes in, if you are in a restaurant.

16. Set a shelf in the oven about 10cm (4 inches) from the broiler element. Put the duck on a rack above a foil-lined baking tray. Poke holes in the skin with the tip of a sharp knife. Broil to crisp up the skin. The exact time will vary with your broiler, but watch it closely because it will go from being still flabby and soft to black in a very short span of time, especially if you are using a commercial restaurant salamander.

17. When the skin is crisp, put some of the warm sauce down on a plate, add the duck (skin-side up) and sprinkle with rose petals. You don't need very much rose because most of the rose flavor is largely from the synergy of the other ingredients, as you will see. For the authentic more elegant (though wasteful) version, trim the broiled duck of the edges before positioning it on the sauce. You can cut it into a rectangle using a very sharp knife so as not to tear the skin. This is how duck breast is frequently presented in the finest restaurants.

HISTORY OF ROYAL PERSIAN ROSE DUCK

Back around 1980, a Saudi prince with a mansion in Beverly Hills decided to leave the United States. One of his problems was that he wanted to take his palm trees from his estate back with him. He hired an expert from UCLA's horticultural department to supervise the removal and transport of the trees. He also chartered a ship to transport them across the Atlantic.

If you have read my cocktail book, you know my father spent decades as a navigator on cargo ships. This was one of his voyages, but because it was a single purpose trip, on arriving he was treated to a gala dinner at the prince's palace. The prince had a Persian (*i.e.* Iranian) private chef and one of the dishes that my father took special note of was this one for two reasons. First, because he normally didn't care for duck, but loved this.

He also found it a bizarre exception for being flavored with roses but not tasting like a bar of soap, which is the usual problem you face with roses or lavender in cooking. He asked for the recipe, but the chef's English was so bad that most of what he wrote down was impossible to read. I reconstructed it as best I could, and my father reported that this was perfect...except for the unfortunate lack of belly dancers performing.

Mac and Cheese Risotto Style
with or without Lobster

This produces a very creamy pasta with a crunchy and buttery topping that is a favorite for people of all ages. This can be vegetarian, or include lobster, or even smoked fish. In the latter case, use only a little or that's all you will taste. This recipe is for 2 servings as an entrée or 4 as an appetizer.

110g (3.9 oz)	Elbow Macaroni, small
325ml (11.5 oz)	Milk, preferably rich (4% fat)
250g (8.8 oz)	Stock (see note below)
22g (0.75 oz)	Shallots
45g (1.5 oz)	Butter (in all), softened some at room temperature
30ml (1 oz)	Dry Vermouth, or substitute White Wine
1/2 to 1	Dried Jalapeño Chili (see notes below)
60g (2 oz)	Monterey Jack Cheese or Cheddar (notes below)
30g (1 oz)	Bread Crumbs, dry
2 T	Parmesan, grated
50ml (1.75 oz)	Cream
1/2 teaspoon	Fennel Pollen or substitute ground fennel seeds
30g (1 oz) or more	Lobster (cooked) or Smoked Fish
	...or aternatively Lobster Pâté (page 234)

CHOICE OF STOCK

The optimum stock will depend on what you are going to combine this with. Vegetable stock is the only choice if it is going to be served as vegetarian. Lobster stock is your Michelin star choice if you are going to make this with lobster. Don't have stock? Okay - mix half a Knorr gel pack (either Vegetable or Beef) with 250ml (8.8 oz) of water. Heat in a microwave or on the stove briefly to combine. Veal stock is also an excellent choice, whether homemade for from a concentrate.

THE CHILIES AND CHEESE

If you are making this with lobster or smoked fish, use Monterey Jack and then you don't need the jalapeño. If you are making it without fish, then cheddar is best. There is a natural flavor resonance between cheddar cheese and jalapeño chilies. Even a tiny amount below the threshold of conscious flavor perception will enhance the "cheddariness" of cheddar. If you can't dry your own, then you can use a fresh one. Commercial dried jalapeño chilies are nearly always smoked (known as chipotle chilies) and are very different. Chipotle chilies can easily overpower everything else.

PROCEDURE

1. In a 1 or 2 liter pot, combine the milk, stock, dried jalapeño (crumbled - no stem) and fennel pollen. If you are using homemade stock and not a Knorr gel pack, then add 1/2 teaspoon salt since the Knorr product already contains salt. Heat on medium (#5 out of 10) to a slow simmer, whisking occasionally. Keep this on a back burner.

2. In a 3 or 4 liter pot, melt <u>half</u> of the butter on a low heat (#3 out of 10). Mince the shallot while the butter is melting, then add the shallot in. Sweat the shallots—don't brown them—for about 3 minutes.

3. Add the dry macaroni to the shallots and butter. In the same way you would make a risotto, stir the pasta around for 3-4 minutes, toasting it.

4. Add the vermouth and stir. Cook until it is almost dry.

5. Now add a 60ml (2 oz) ladle of the milk stock from the pot on the back burner. Start a timer now. Stir frequently until it is nearly dry again.

6. Add another ladle of the milk broth. Once again, cook until nearly dry.

7. Add the third ladle of stock and increase the heat to medium-high (#7). Cook with frequent stirring until nearly dry, as before. Be sure to continue scraping the bottom to keep anything from sticking and burning.

8. Continue adding the milk broth a ladle at a time until you used all of it. This should take roughly 10 minutes counting from Step #5.

9. Stir in the cheese. Make sure it is all well combined. This will take

between 1 and 2 minutes.

10. Cook for 2-3 minutes more, then move the pan off the heat.

11. Stir the 50ml (1.75 oz) of cream in. Also add a dash of orange food coloring, if desired. If it is too thick, add a little water. Remember that it will thicken further on cooling, and you don't want it to be a single blob of pasta glued together by cheese. Set it aside with the lid back on while you make the topping.

12. Put the bread crumbs into the bowl of a food processor. Add the butter and the grated Parmesan cheese. Process until it is fine crumbs.

13. Now if you are going to do so, either stir in the cooked lobster pieces or a little smoked fish (crumbled) in with the pasta. Depending on the strength of the smoked fish, add judiciously or it will have an excessively fishy taste. Also, it helps to have slightly undercooked the lobster and then put it in the freezer for about 15 minutes first so that it warms back up and is perfectly tender after cooking in with the pasta. For getting some little extra bits of lobster meat that most people miss, see page 232.

14. Spoon the macaroni mixture into a casserole dish or individual ramekins. Spread the topping over the pasta.

15. Roast directly under a preheated broiler for a just a few minutes to give the top a golden brown color. Keep a very close watch on it that it doesn't burn. A good way is to set a kitchen timer for 1 minute. When it goes off, check the condition of the dish and reset the timer for another minute if it isn't ready yet. This method has saved countless dishes from turning into smoldering ash. Broiling will likely take about 5 minutes.

16. Cool for a few minutes before serving. If you are making it with lobster, a few choice pieces of claw meat or medallions of tail meat are a beautiful addition. Alternatively for an interesting twist, try putting a little tuft of the Momiji-Oroshi (see recipe on next page) on top of each of the ramekin portions, if you decided to make it as individual portions.

Momiji-Oroshi Daikon

This is not a pickle in the western sense of the word. This is that little mound of relish served with some types of sushi and also with Japanese Steak Tataki. Originally this is nothing more than grated daikon and minced red chili peppers. Here is a more sophisticated version that is more floral and complex, but still spicy.

120g (4.25 oz)	Daikon Radish
1 T	Sea Salt
22g (0.75 oz)	Vodka Chili Elixir (page 210)
3/4 teaspoon	Apple Cider Vinegar
1/4 - 1/2 teaspoon	Sesame Oil
1/8 - 1/4 teaspoon	Cayenne
a few twists	Black Pepper, freshly fine ground

PROCEDURE

1. Grate the daikon on the fine side of a box grater. Put into a bowl and mix well with the salt. Cover with cling film and refrigerate overnight.

2. Cover with cool water and stir. Drain on a sieve, pressing down to expel water. Repeat this washing three times in all.

3. Wrap it in a towel and squeeze. Bang the towel over the sink to remove the last drops of water.

4. Put it in a bowl and mix with the Vodka Chili Elixir, sesame oil, cider vinegar, cayenne and ground black pepper. Stir well to combine. Let it rest for 1-2 hours.

5. Drain it on a sieve again and press out most of the liquid. Store it in a closed container in the refrigerator. Ideally it should be left for a couple of days before consuming. The flavor improves on storage, with about 3 weeks being the upper limit.

Chicken Saag
Indian Curry with Spinach

Note that the seasonings and method are quite different from Shrimp Saag, even though they are both spinach based curries.

400g (14 oz)	Chicken, boneless/skinless (see below)
420g (15 oz)	Onions, peeled and cut into rings
60g (2.1 oz)	Green Chilies, fresh (see notes below)
30g (1 oz)	Garlic, peeled
25g (0.85 oz)	Ginger, peeled
150-175g (6 oz)	Spinach, frozen (see page 235)
120g (4 oz)	Passata
150ml (2/3 cup)	Chicken Stock or water
65g (2.3 oz)	Coconut Oil (in all)
1 T	South Indian Coating (Vol. 3, page 243)
2 whole	Bay Leaves
5cm (2 inches)	Cinnamon Stick
8-10 drops	Liquid Smoke (optional)
1 T	Cumin Seeds, whole
1 teaspoon	Mustard Seeds, preferably black
1 teaspoon	Coarse Salt
1 1/2 teaspoons	Turmeric
1/2 teaspoon	Kashmiri Mirch (optional)
3/4 teaspoon	Dark Brown Sugar, idieally Muscovado

ADDITIONAL NOTES

You can use chicken breasts, as I showed in the video, but more flavorful results will be obtained using boneless/skinless thighs. Use green chilies that are medium-hot. This dish is not supposed to be extremely hot. Don't use Jalapeño chilies because the flavor is not right for this.

PROCEDURE

1. Put the frozen spinach in a bowl to warm up at room temperature. If you are using chicken breast meat, tenderize it with a Jaccard device, as in

Volume 2 (page 182 and on). Then cube up the chicken and put it in a bowl. Add the South Indian Coating and 20g (0.7 oz) of the coconut oil and massage it well into the meat. If you don't have the South Indian Coating, use a teaspoon of Garum Masala. Transfer to a baking dish.

3. Set a shelf in the oven 15cm (6 inches) from the broiler element. Put the dish under the broiler for about 10 minutes. Broilers vary, so check it. When it is done, set it off to the side. Save the juices that run off the meat.

4. Melt the remaining 45g (1.5 oz) of butter or ghee in a large nonstick pan on medium to medium-high heat. When it has foamed up, add the onions. Stir occasionally, but not constantly.

5. After about 8 minutes, add the bay leaves and cinnamon stick. Lower the heat. Continue cooking for 5 more minutes. During this time, cut up the ginger and the garlic coarsely. Set aside.

6. Add the cumin seeds, mustard seeds and coarse salt. Cook 3 minutes. Dice the green chilies while this is cooking.

7. Remove the bay leaves and add the garlic and ginger. Cook 5 minutes.

8. Add the diced green chilies. If you feel it won't be spicy enough, then add an extra half teaspoon or so of Kashmiri Mirch. Cook 5 more minutes.

9. Add the tomato purée (passata). Increase the heat to medium-high (#7). Cook for about 5 minutes until you smell the tomatoes caramelizing.

10. Add the juices from the chicken in Step 3. Cook 2-3 minutes more.

11. Add the chicken stock (or water). As soon as the gelatin of the stock melts, transfer it to a blender and purée. Clean out the pan that it was cooking in, and pour the puréed sauce (curry) back into the pan. Add the turmeric and dark brown sugar. Consider adding a few drops of green food coloring. This is common in Indian restaurants. Bring to a slow simmer.

12. Add the spinach and the yoghurt to the pan. Add the liquid smoke at this time, if desired. Stir to incorporate. Taste and adjust seasoning with salt or MSG. Add the previously cooked chicken. Mix the chicken in.

13. Turn the heat down to low and cover. Cook for 15 minutes. Add a little lemon juice, if desired.

⟡

Steak Diane

This is a classic dish dating back many decades. This is better than the original, especially with the Lovecraft Coating.

200g (7 oz)	Steak, Tenderloin
90ml (3 oz)	Beef Broth, room temperature
50g (1.75 oz)	Butter (in all)
35ml (1.25 oz)	Cognac or Brandy
30ml (1 oz)	Tawny Port (see note below)
2 T	Shallots, peeled and minced
2 teaspoons	Lovecraft Coating (see note below)
1 clove	Garlic
2-3 large	Mushrooms, ideally Cremini
2 teaspoons	Lemon Juice
1/2 teaspoon	Dijon Mustard
1/2 teaspoon	Corn Starch
to taste	Black Pepper, freshly ground
2 teaspoons	Chives, fresh (or 1/2 teaspoon dry if necessary)

LOVECRAFT COATING

The recipe for making this is in Volume 3 on page 242. Although this is optional, it really helps the dish. Aside from the tertiary flavor that this brings to the dish to elevate it, this coating enables the meat to have a nice dark caramelized color on it in only about a minute of cooking time, which means it will still be tender when you are done. You can substitute semolina for the texture, but it won't have the same depth of flavor.

PORT WINE

This is an important part of the flavor. Do not use an inexpensive generic brand of port. The foul taste will come through and ruin it. Port keeps for a very long time unrefrigerated, so it makes a good quality wine to keep on hand.

PROCEDURE

1. Cut the mushrooms in pieces (not too small). Put them in a bowl and squeeze the lemon juice over them using a sieve to keep out seeds.

2. Mix the corn starch in with a tablespoon of the beef stock at room temperature. Now mix this slurry back into the rest of the beef stock.

3. Cut the meat into two thin horizontal slices and then pound it out gently with a mallet under cling film, as you would for making schnitzel.

4. Sprinkle the top-facing side with the Lovecraft coating. Press in.

5. Heat 30 grams (1 oz) of the butter in a nonstick pan on a medium-high setting (#7). Smash the clove of garlic against the side of a knife. When the butter foams up, put the garlic in. Stir to infuse the garlic for a minute.

6. Add the mushrooms. Cook until they are golden.

7. Transfer the mushrooms and butter to a small bowl and reserve. Put another 20 grams (0.75 oz) of butter into the same pan. When the butter foams up, put the meat in, seasoned-side down. Season the side facing up with salt and black pepper while it cooks for a total of about 1 minute.

8. Flip the meat over and cook for about 45 seconds.

9. Remove the meat to a platter. Lower the heat to medium (#5) and add the shallots to the pan. Cook for about 1 1/2 minutes with stirring.

10. Add the beef broth and the mustard. Stir well. Simmer until the sauce thickens visibly (about 2 minutes).

11. Add the tawny port wine. Stir. Return the steaks to the pan as well as whatever juices ran off of them while they were resting. Also add the mushrooms and the butter they were cooked in to the pan. Pile the mushrooms on top of the steaks. If you are forced to use dried chives, add those now. Simmer for about 2 minutes.

12. Add the cognac to the sauce and wait a few seconds. Flambée for about 15 seconds, then put a lid on briefly to extinguish the fire.

13. Cook to thicken a bit more, then plate. Add fresh chives over the top.

"Toothpick Lamb"
in Green Mango Chili Sauce

Perfect as an appetizer for a Tiki themed party, or even better as a course in a Rijsttafel (see page 3).

250g (8.8 oz)	Lamb Tenderloin (see note below)
150g (5.3 oz)	Mango, somewhat unripe
45g (1.5 oz)	Shallot
30ml (1 oz)	Pistachio or Peanut Oil
30g (1 oz)	Green Serrano Chilies (plus more for garnish)
15g (0.5 oz)	Garlic cloves, peeled
15g (0.5 oz)	Ginger, grated
1 teaspoon	Turmeric
2 teaspoons	Muscovado or Dark Brown Sugar
1 teaspoon	Salt
1/4 teaspoon	White Pepper, ground
30ml (1 oz)	Apple Cider Vinegar
2-3 T	Mint, fresh - cut in chiffonade
1 teaspoon	Nam Pla (Thai fish sauce)
1/4 teaspoon	Black Pepper, ground
1 - 2 T	Cilantro, freshly minced
350ml (12 oz)	Vegetable Oil (for frying)

THE LAMB

The only cut of lamb that this dish will work well with is the tenderloin. Plus it is easy to trim and cut into slices the right size.

PROCEDURE

1. Be sure to remove any strips of sinew before slicing into 2.5cm (1 inch) pieces.

2. Peel and coarsely chop the mango. The weight is counted after removing the skin and pit.

3. Coarsely chop the shallot, green chilies, and garlic. Put all of these into

the cup of a stick blender along with the pistachio (or peanut) oil, the grated ginger, turmeric, dark brown sugar, dry mustard, salt and ground white pepper. Purée.

4. Put the cubed lamb in a bowl and add 60 grams (2 oz) of the puréed mixture from Step 3. Stir to combine and preferably vacuum seal, if possible. Refrigerate at least 2 hours.

5. Heat a good nonstick skillet on a medium heat. Gently fry the rest of the mango-chili paste. Don't add any more oil to the pan.

6. When it starts to sizzle, lower the heat slightly. Cook 5 minutes, stirring with a silicone spatula occasionally.

7. Add the vinegar and stir. Cook for another 2 minutes, or until it starts to thicken.

8. Add the chiffonade of fresh mint, the nam pla (fish sauce) and the black pepper. Reduce heat to very low. Cook for 4 minutes with stirring.

9 Transfer this off to a bowl. Refrigerate if it will be kept for over 2 hours.

10. Take the sauce out of the refrigerator. Lay the pieces of marinated lamb down on sheets of paper towel. Do not press down. Let it stand for about 15 minutes for the *excess* marinade to gently drain into the towel and for the lamb to warm up.

11. Heat about 350ml (14 oz) of vegetable oil in a 1 liter sauce pan to 170°C (340°F). The temperature will drop after adding the lamb.

12. Fry half the lamb a time. Cook for about 1 minute and 10 seconds, then remove the pieces with a spider directly to the metal bowl with the thick sauce. Do not drain the meat first. Stir the meat around to coat the sauce evenly.

13. Use a blowtorch liberally, caramelizing the top of each piece. Do not skip this important step.

14. Stir in the fresh cilantro and additional minced green chilies and a dash of MSG, if you are so inclined. Then either serve with toothpicks in each piece or in a Rijsttafel.

Louisiana Gumbo

One day I made this with the legendary Paul Prudhomme
back in the 1980's. I've reduced the heat substantially here.

135g (4.75 oz)	Vegetable Oil, or (better) Olive Oil
90g (3 oz)	Flour
1 liter (35 oz)	Chicken Broth
350g (12.3 oz)	Andouille Sausage (see notes below)
200g (7 oz)	Onions, peeled
100g (3.5 oz)	Celery
90g (3 oz)	Okra (see notes below)
50g (1.8 oz)	Green Bell Pepper
50g (1.8 oz)	Red Bell Pepper
2 (or more) whole	Red Serrano Chilies
30g (1 oz)	Garlic, peeled
60g (2 oz)	Crawfish, tail meat or substitute shrimp
180g (6.3 oz)	Tomatoes, fresh
120g (4.2 oz)	Tomato Purée (passata)
1 or 2 whole	Bay Leaves

Fresh Parsley, Sage and Thyme
Tabasco Sauce and Scallions

ANDOUILLE SAUSAGE

If you can't get Andouille, then use the smokiest coarse-grained pork sausage you can get, but <u>not</u> Chorizo. Andouille is made from smoked pork, garlic and other seasonings. Then after it is in the casing, it is smoked a second time (double smoked). You can amp up a conventional smoked pork sausage by smoking it a second time yourself.

OKRA

There are three choices here. Fresh okra roasted on metal skewers over charcoal is *the best*, but often impossible due to weather and difficulty in obtaining fresh okra. You can substitute frozen okra, or even the dry powdered okra in some ethnic food stores. Use 10g (0.3 oz) of the latter.

PROCEDURE

1. If you are using fresh okra, then put it on skewers like you were roasting marshmallows and cook it over coals before starting the rest of this recipe. After it is cooked, store it in a closed container until needed Refrigerate it if it is going to be more than a few hour. If you are using frozen okra, then thaw it and bring it to room temperature before starting.

2. Heat a 4 liter stainless steel pot on a medium heat. When the pan is warm, add the oil. Wait until it is just over 100°C (210°F).

3. Add the flour and stir. Traditionally only a wooden spoon should be used, but silicone is okay. You need a very dark roux for this, which typically takes at least 20 minutes to form with frequent stirring.

4. While this is cooking, if you are using frozen okra then put it in a ceramic baking tray and broil it. Position the shelf 15cm (6 inches) from the broiler element. It may take 10-20 minutes to broil well. Don't burn it.

5. Also while this is going on, make a conical incision and remove the stems from the tomatoes. Then cut them into quarters. Cut each quarter into 2 or 3 pieces, as shown in the video (3:40 to 4:05).

6. Coarsely chop the onions, bell peppers and chilies. Take a vegetable peeler and trim the coarse threads from the celery, then chop that up, too.

7. Keep stirring and watching the roux during these steps. Turn the heat down a bit as it begins to darken to keep it from burning. Sometime around now, put the chicken broth in a separate pot on a back burner and begin heating it on a medium-low setting.

8. When the roux is dark brown, add the tomatoes. Turn the heat down to very low, letting the residual heat do most of the work in caramelizing the tomatoes. Try to turn the tomato pieces around so that the skin-side is facing the bottom of the pan. Cook for about 6 minutes.

9. Now add the onion, bell pepper, celery and red chilies from Step 6 and turn the heat back up to medium. Stir and cook 2-3 minutes.

10. Cut the okra up coarsely (regardless of whether you used frozen or fresh), and add that to the pot, too. Stir and cook for another 7 minutes.

11. Chop up the garlic and leave it to sit in the air while this cooks.

GUMBO SPICE BLEND

2 teaspoons	Cumin Seeds
1 teaspoon	Black Peppercorns
1 teaspoon	Cayenne
1 teaspoon	Oregano, dried
1 teaspoon	Gumbo Filé (see text in Step 12)

---

12. Also while this is cooking, make the spice blend by combining the cumin seeds, cayenne, black peppercorns, oregano and gumbo filé in an electric spice mill and grinding to a powder. If you can't get gumbo filé, then add 4-5 whole allspice. It isn't the same, but it is better than nothing.

13. When the 7 minutes is up, add the chopped garlic to the pot. Stir and cook for another 2-3 minutes.

14. Add the ground spices from Step 12. Stir and cook for 3 minutes.

15. Add the tomato purée (passata). Reduce heat slightly and stir frequently for about 8 more minutes. Cut up the sausage into pieces during this time.

16. Add the warm chicken broth from Step 7. Also add the sausages. Bring it up to a simmer with occasional stirring. Adjust heat to maintain at a simmer for about 1 1/2 hours.

17. Make a bouquet garni by tieing together the bay leaf, fresh parsley, sage and thyme branches. If you have the green part of a leek, wrap them up in that before tieing for a more secure package. Alternatively, use a wire bouquet garni cage as shown on page 233. Drop the bouquet garni in and continue simmering for another 45 minutes to an hour.

18. Fish out the bouquet garni and discard it (or empty the contents in the trash if you are using the metal enclosure type). Add the crawfish tail meat (or shrimp) and cook for 5 more minutes. Taste and adjust salt level.

19 Plate up with minced scallions over the top and Tabasco sauce on the side. Serving over rice is traditional.

TWO CAJUN PREACHERS

Reverand Fontaine was the minister of the local Baptist church and Pastor Lapierre was the leader of the Cajun Covenant church across the way.

The two of them were standing at the edge of the road, pounding a sign into the ground that read:

"Da End is Near! Turn Yo Sef 'Round Now Afore it be Too Late!"

A car whizzed past them and the driver yelled out of his window, "You crazy religious nuts!"

A few seconds later they heard screeching tires, a crash and then a big splash!

Fontaine shook his head sadly and then asked Lapierre, "Do ya tink maybe da sign should jussay...

"Bridge Out"?

Paul Prudhomme, 1982

Jambalaya

A Louisiana classic that is very closely related to another Cajun/Creole classic, Étouffée. The main differences are that rice is served separately for Étouffée and it is made with a roux. Jambalaya has the rice cooked in with it together. Jambalaya can be further divided into the type with mushy very cooked rice and the type where the rice grains are more like a pilaf. This recipe lets you choose which way you want it, but you will need to pay careful attention to several key steps along the way.

140g (5 oz)	Basmati Rice (rinsed well with cold water)
140g (5 oz)	Andouille Sausage (see notes on page 132)
140g (5 oz)	Large Shrimp, raw (peeled and deveined)
70g (2.5 oz)	Chicken Thigh, boneles/skinless, cubed
70g (2.5 oz)	Ham, diced
70g (2.5 oz)	Bay Shrimp, previously cooked is okay
70g (2.5 oz)	Red Bell Pepper
70g (2.5 oz)	Onion
30g (1 oz)	Celery, peeled of tough outer fibers
20g (0.7 oz)	Garlic, sliced
2 or more	Green Serrano Chilies, minced finely
3 whole	Tomatoes, canned Italian
350ml (12.5 oz)	Chicken Stock
45ml (1.5 oz)	White Wine, dry
3/4 teaspoon	Smoked Paprika, Picanté (hot type)
3/4 teaspoon	Oregano, dried
1/2 teaspoon	Black Pepper, ground

PROCEDURE

1. If you are making this so the rice is not mushy, cook the rice in a separate pot using the chicken stock. Reserve the rice for adding later.

2. Cube the red bell pepper, onion and celery. Take care with knifework here because the final product will look sloppy if you have irregular size pieces. You want them all to be about 6.5mm (1/4 inch) each.

3. Heat a pan on medium and add about 2 tablespoons of oil to it. When the oil is warm, but not very hot, add the smoked paprika. Cook for just a few seconds to flavor the oil. Take care not to burn it.

4. Add the diced ham. Increase heat slightly. Sauté 2 minutes. Stir.

5. Add the red bell pepper, onion and celery. Stir and cook for 4 minutes.

6. Add the green chilies, garlic and canned tomatoes. Squeeze the tomatoes to help break them up. Stir and cook for another 4 minutes.

7. If you are making this in the mushy rice style, this is when to add the washed rice. Stir frequently. You want the rice to absorb the flavors and the mixture to dry out some. Turn the heat down as it cooks to prevent the mixture from burning. There is a fine line between caramelized and burnt, so be careful. In all you want to cook this for about 6 minutes.

8. Add the white wine and deglaze the pan, scraping the bottom.

9. When it is nearly dry again, add the chicken stock and simmer for 5 minutes if you are making the mushy rice style. If you are making this in the pilaf rice style, you already used the chicken stock in Step #1, so skip the simmering here and move to the next step.

10. Add the bay shrimp, oregano and black pepper. Simmer for another 3 minutes, stirring occasionally.

11. Add 240ml (1 cup) water and the sausage cut in 1cm (0.4 inch) lengths. Stir to combine. For the mushy rice style, put a lid on and simmer slow 20-30 minutes. Otherwise cook with no lid until it is thick again.

12. Add the raw chicken pieces and the pre-cooked rice from Step #1 if you are using that method. Stir. Turn the heat down low. Put a lid on and wait 8 minutes.

13. Add the large shrimp and stir them in. Turn off the stove and let the residual heat finish cooking the shrimp for 5 more minutes.

14. Plate up, adding the sliced scallions over the top. Offer Tabasco sauce at the table.

＋

Chicken Parmesan
Novel Method

The carrots in the coating add color, texture and nutritional value. More important, it keeps the coating crisp. This can be made with chicken thighs, but it will not look as good.

250g (8.8 oz)	Tomatoes, fresh (see note below)
200g (7 oz)	Chicken Broth
120g (4 oz)	Tomato Purée (passata)
30g (1 oz)	Garlic cloves, peeled (in all)
1 1/4 teaspoons	Hungarian Spice Mix (see note below)
1/2 teaspoon	Thyme, dried
1/2 - 1 teaspoon	Brown Sugar
3 whole	Chicken Breasts
80g (2.8 oz)	Carrots (see Step #1)
2 whole	Eggs
60g (2 oz)	Parmesan Cheese, freshly grated
60g (2 oz)	Bread Crumbs
about 70ml (2.5 oz)	Olive Oil
about 100g (3.5 oz)	Flour
(to taste)	Mozzarella Cheese, wet-pack

HUNGARIAN SPICE MIX

The recipe for this is on page 229 of Volume 3 in this series. A quick shortcut version can be prepared by combining 3/4 teaspoon Paprika with about 1/4 teaspoon each of Onion Powder and Cayenne. Naturally this is not going to be as good, but it will work.

THE TOMATOES

If you can't get fresh vine-ripened tomatoes, then you can substitute canned whole Italian tomatoes. In that case, cut the stems off of the canned tomatoes (discard them) and proceed with Step #1, but skip <u>only</u> Step #2.

PROCEDURE

1. Boil the carrots until they are tender. The weight is measured *after* they have been boiled and cooled.

2. If you are using fresh tomatoes, make a conical incision and remove the stem end. Then quarter them. Cut each quartered slice into about four pieces so there is a somewhat flat skin-side. See the video for details.

3. Heat a stainless steel 4 liter pot on a medium heat. When it is fairly hot (not smoking hot), add the olive oil. Swirl to coat the bottom. Now arrange the tomato slices skin-side down. Do not stir them. Cook for 6 minutes, paying attention that there is no burning (by smelling).

4. Still without stirring, add the tomato purée. You can put a splatter guard over it, but don't cover it with a lid. Chop the garlic, but don't add it yet.

5. After about 6 minutes, finally stir it, scraping up any fond.

6. Add the Hungarian Spice (or the substitute). Cook 30 seconds.

7. Add half of the chopped garlic, chicken broth and thyme. Adjust the heat to maintain at a good simmer (but not a rolling boil) for 15 minutes.

8. Transfer to the cup of a stick blender and purée. Taste and adjust with salt and add a little brown sugar. Blend again, then rub through a sieve.

9. Rinse out the stick blender cup, then put the other half of the garlic in it along with the boiled carrots and eggs. Purée. Put it into a bowl.

10. Trim the chicken breasts into even shaped pieces, then slice each one in half along the thin-side. Review the video if you are not clear about this.

11. Combine the Parmesan cheese with the bread crumbs. Transfer half of it to a bowl. Set up another bowl containing the flour.

12. Heat up a large nonstick pan on the stove. When it's hot, add enough oil to bring the level up to about 1 cm (just under half an inch).

13. Put three of the pieces of chicken into the flour one by one. Coat well, then shake off excess. Next, put each piece into the carrot and egg batter. Finally, into the Parmesan and bread crumbs. Press the coating into the chicken to make it stick.

14. When the oil reaches about 150°C (300°F), fry only 3 of the chicken

pieces at a time. Don't crowd the pan! Increase the heat to maintain the temperature. After about 4 minutes, they should be golden brown on the side facing the pan. Turn them over and cook the same time on the other side. When you have done three pieces of chicken, use the other half of the Parmesan and bread crumbs for the second group of three. This way you won't be trying to coat the pieces with bread crumbs that are already saturated with the egg and carrot mixture.

15. At this point you can put the chicken pieces in a sealed storage container in your refrigerator for up to 3 days before finishing. Ideally you want to proceed immediately, but that's rarely possible in a restaurant.

16. Preheat oven to 210°C (410°F) if the chicken is at still warm from having just been fried. If it is cold from the refrigerator, then set your oven to 165°C (330°F) because a lower temperature will allow extra time for the chicken to warm through before the cheese melts. Position a shelf in the oven 15cm (6 inches) from the broiler element (you will switch it to broil later).

17. Spoon a little of the sauce from Step 8 down onto individual au gratin or casserole dishes (no lid). Place a chicken piece on the sauce, then add more sauce on top and mozzarella cheese (to taste).

18. When the oven is at temperature, put the casserole dishes in. Watch them until the mozzarella has melted, but the sauce is not burned. The time will vary depending on the temperature. Judge it by when the cheese is well melted.

19. Switch the oven to broil and carefully watch until the cheese is golden brown, but not burnt.

20. Put folded napkins down on plates, and then the individual dishes straight from the oven onto the napkin, which will keep them from sliding around on the plates. A chiffonade of fresh basil is a nice touch. Buttered spaghetti or angel hair pasta makes a great side dish, although that's contrary to Italian tradition.

Poached Shrimp

These are the perfect shrimp for either a classic shrimp cocktail or a salad such as a Shrimp Louie.

up to 300g (10.5 oz)	Shrimp, raw
450ml (16 oz)	Water
50ml (1.75 oz)	Dry Vermouth, or substitute White Wine
2 teaspoons	Citric Acid
2 teaspoons	Apple Cider Vinegar
2 teaspoons	Salt
1 teaspoon	Sugar
1 teaspoon	MSG (optional)
1/2 teaspoon	White Pepper, ground
1/2 teaspoon	Garlic Powder
1/4 teaspoon	Smoked Paprika
2 whole	Bay Leaves (depending on size)

PROCEDURE

1. Defrost the shrimp (if necessary) in cold water. If you have shrimp shells (saved or from the shrimp you are about to poach) fry them in a little oil in the same pot you will be poaching the shrimp in (see next step).

2. Put all of the ingredients except the shrimp into a 1 to 2 liter pot. Bring to a simmer on a medium heat.

3. When the poaching liquid comes to a simmer, lower the heat way down and cover. Simmer for another 10 minutes.

4. If you added shrimp shells, then pass the liquid through a sieve. Discard solids and return the broth to the pan. Heat back up to a simmer.

5. Add the shrimp. Poach until they are just firm. The exact time will depend on the size of the shrimp, but typically 1 to 2 minutes. Then transfer them to an ice bath.

Chipotle Chicken

Because this needs to marinate for 4-6 hours, but should not be left in the marinade overnight, it is best to plan ahead and start this early on the day that you want to have it for dinner.

3 whole	Chicken Quarters (see notes below)
60g (2.1 oz)	Chipotle Chilies in Adobo, canned
140g (4.9 oz)	Onion, peeled and sliced
25g (0.9 oz)	Garlic cloves, coarsely chopped
80g (2.8 oz)	Mushrooms, stem ends trimmed, chopped
80g (2.8 oz)	Heavy Cream
2 teaspoons	Dark Brown Sugar, ideally Muscovado
1 Tablespoon	Cilantro, minced (plus more for garnishing)
Flour and Vegetable Oil for frying	

NOTES ON INGREDIENTS

Chipotles in Adobo Sauce is a canned product available in most grocery stores (even in Finland, surprisingly).

I suggest buying chicken quarters and doing the minor butchery work yourself. Not only is this usually less expensive than buying drumsticks and thighs already sectioned up, but you will probably get the rib sections to use in this recipe, which will improve the flavor.

PROCEDURE

1. After sectioning the chicken quarters (assuming you are doing that), set the rib pieces aside and store in the refrigerator for use later.

2. Use a blowtorch to burn off any stray pinfeathers. Depending on where you get your chicken from there may be a lot or none at all.

3. Put the chipotle chilies into a blender. Try not to get all chilies or all Adobo. You want mostly chipotles with some of the Adobo sauce.

4. Add the garlic, mushrooms and 90ml (3.2 oz) of water. Blend to purée.

5. Coat the chicken pieces (not the rib sections) with the paste. Wear gloves or your hands will have a chipotle aroma for the rest of the day! Make sure the pieces are all coated evenly.

6. Put into a box with a tight fitting lid and refrigerate for 4 to 6 hours. Do not leave it overnight or the texture of the chicken will not be good.

7. Now remove the box of marinated chicken from the refrigerator so it begins to warm up to room temperature while you get the next steps done.

8. Heat a tablespoon or so of vegetable oil in a pressure cooker. Brown the rib sections well on a medium-high heat (if you have them, otherwise move to the next step).

9. Reduce heat to medium-low. Add the onions to the pan, breaking up the slices into rings. Continue cooking until the onions are browned but not burnt. Stir frequently to prevent burning. This will take a while.

10. Add the dark brown sugar and another 90ml (3.2 oz) of water. Once the sugar is dissolved, turn the heat off and wait for boiling to stop.

11. Add the chicken pieces. Scrape out whatever marinade is clinging into the storage container and add that to the pot, too.

12. Turn the heat back on and bring to a boil before putting the pressure cooker lid on. Then set a timer for 7 minutes. Keep it at pressure.

13. Turn the heat off and wait 5 minutes before opening it up.

14. After 3-4 minutes with the lid off, transfer the chicken pieces to a platter. Pass the liquid from the pot through a sieve. Discard all solids.

15. Leave the chicken pieces on a rack to drain and cool for 1-2 hours.

16. Blowtorch the chicken skins as shown in the video (optional).

17. Put the strained liquid into a pot and reduce the volume by half.

18. Add the cream and reduce to thicken. Adjust seasoning with MSG and salt. When it is thick, stir in the cilantro. Take it off the heat.

19. Preheat oven to 190°C (375°F). Toss each piece of chicken in a bowl with flour, then fry them 2-3 at a time skin-side down in vegetable oil to crisp them up. Brown them and then place on a metal tray.

20. Spoon sauce over the pieces and place in the oven 5 minutes.

21. Garnish with cilantro.

Italian Roasted Cabbage

This recipe can be made vegetarian (see below). This uses the trick explained in Volume 3 in which the cabbage is enzymatically transformed to have an artichoke-like flavor.

400g (14 oz)	Cabbage (no stem or any thick ribs)
60g (2 oz)	Onion
60g (2 oz)	White Beans, canned
60g (2 oz)	Pancetta - optional (see notes below)
30g (1 oz)	Parmigiano-Reggiano, freshly grated
2 cloves	Garlic, peeled
2 whole	Bay Leaves
1 teaspoon	Coarse Salt
1 teaspoon	Austrian Spice Mix (see Volume 3, page 220)
3-4 T	Parsley, fresh
1-3 teaspoons	Vodka Chili Elixir (page 210) or Sriracha

THE PANCETTA

You can substitute bacon if you need to, and you can leave this out altogether to make it a vegetarian dish. In that case you will need olive oil, as explained in Step #3 of the procedures below.

PROCEDURE

1. Put the cabbage and onion in a food processor and cut into small pieces, but not a purée.

2. Coarsely cut the pancetta and put it into a large nonstick pan on a medium heat. Place a splatter guard over the pan and let the fat render for about 15 minutes. If you use cut up slices of bacon, it will take less time.

3. If there is too much fat, soak some up with a paper towel and discard it, or pour it off for use in cooking something else another time. If you are not using any meat, then use 30ml (1 oz) olive oil in the hot pan.

4. Add the cabbage and onion mixture to the pan. Then add the Austrian

spice mixture, salt and bay leaves. Stir and cook for 5-6 minutes.

5. Lower the heat slightly and put a lid on the pan. Do not remove the lid again for *approximately* 15 minutes. The exact amount of time will have to be determined by you the first time you make this, since there are several variables (the heat put out by your stove's burners, the thickness of the pan you are using, and how well the lid you have on the pan seals in the steam). If it is burning by then, you either have your burner too hot, or the pan is too thin, or the lid is not sealing.

6. Mince the parsley and garlic during the time this is cooking. Also drain the beans on a sieve, then rinse with cold tap water.

7. When the time is up, remove the lid and stir the contents well before adding the beans, the garlic, 2 tablespoons of the parsley and the Vodka Chili Elixir (or Sriracha). Stir well and continue cooking with no lid for another 4-5 minutes.

8. Remove and discard the bay leaves. Add the Parmigiano-Reggiano and turn the heat off. Stir in the cheese using the residual heat.

9. At this point you can refrigerate it in a closed container for a couple of days if you need to. When you are ready to serve the dish, transfer portions to individual au gratin dishes, or one large ovenproof casserole dish, if you prefer family-style service. Top with bread crumbs (fresh bread crumbs is better than dried here). Arrange a shelf about 10cm (4 inches) from the broiler element. Watch the time closely because it will go from raw to black quickly. The total broiling time should be about 5 minutes, but broilers vary. Under a restaurant salamander, this is browned nicely in less than one minute.

10. Top with a little more minced fresh parsley. Add some crushed red pepper flakes, if you are so inclined. Serve with wedges of fresh lemon.

Greek Lamb and Orzo Stew

This is a bit more complicated than the traditional method, but the flavor is well worth it, being deeper and richer.

450g (16 oz)	Lamb, trimmed
100g (3.5 oz)	Tomato Purée (passata)
90g (3 oz)	Red Onion, peeled and diced
75ml (2.6 oz)	Red Wine, dry
1 1/2 teaspoons	Oregano, dried
1 1/2 teaspoons	Beautiful World Seasoning (Vol. 3, page 233)
3/4 teaspoon	Cumin Seeds, whole
1/2 teaspoon	Black Peppercorns
1 stick	Cinnamon, whole
1 teaspoon	Coarse Salt
200g (7 oz)	Tomatoes, vine ripened
110g (3.9 oz)	Orzo (or other pasta)
25g (0.9 oz)	Parmesan, freshly grated
3-4 T	Feta, mild cow-milk type

PROCEDURE

1. Trim the lamb of silver skin and any tough ligaments. Also remove any very large pieces of fat (small bits are good). Save the large pieces of fat. Then cube the lamb up into pieces roughly 3-4cm (1.2 - 1.6 inches).

2. Put the lamb in a bowl and mix with a teaspoon of coarse salt.

3. Heat a 3 or 4 liter pot on the stove on a medium setting (#4) Put the lamb fat from Step 1 into the pan and cover with a lid or a splatter guard. Cook for about 10 minutes to get some fat rendered.

4. Increase the heat to high (#8 out of 10) and cook for about 3 more minutes, stirring occasionally and then replacing the lid or splatter guard.

5. Remove the lamb fat and put all of the lamb meat into the pan at once. Stir almost constantly for 1 to 1 1/2 minutes to coat the lamb with the fat and get the pink off of it.

6. Transfer the lamb to a bowl. Immediately while the pan is still smoking hot, add the tomato purée (passata) and scrape to pick up the fond.

7. Turn the heat off. Add the red wine and stir well. Let it stand 5 minutes. Pour this over the lamb that was partially cooked in Step 5.

8. Put the oregano, cumin seeds and black peppercorns in an electric spice mill and grind well. Put this into the bowl with the meat as well as the Beautiful World Seasoning (if you are using it - it is optional) and stir.

9. Now stir in the diced red onion and transfer to the braising dish.

10. Put the stick of cinnamon on top and then the cover. Put it into a preheated 160°C (320°F) oven for 3 1/2 hours.

11. Open the dish up halfway through cooking (after about 2 hours) and stir the contents before returning it to the oven. If it looks dry, it means your braising vessel is not well sealed, or your oven is out of calibration and running too hot. Add a little water in that case, and either get a better braising pot for next time, or have your oven repaired, as the case may be.

12. While the meat is braising, boil the orzo pasta in lightly salted water until just a little less than *al dente* (since it will be cooked the rest of the way with the lamb later. When the pasta is done, put it in a bowl and toss it with a teaspoon of olive oil to keep it from sticking to itself.

13. Also while the meat is braising, prepare the tomatoes if you have a second oven with a broiler (otherwise you will have to wait until the lamb is done cooking.) Cut the tomatoes into slices and put them on a metal baking sheet. Set a shelf about 10cm (4 inches) from the broiler element and turn fan assist ON if you have it. Put the broiler on maximum temperature and cook until there is good deep caramelization (see the video for how they should look).

14. When the braising time is up, remove the cinnamon stick and discard it. Stir in the par-cooked pasta and the charred tomatoes. Transfer the contents to a casserole dish (no lid) and put the feta on top, dotting it around evenly. Put the Parmesan on top next.

15. Set a shelf about 12cm (5 inches) from the broiler element. Put the casserole dish in for about 10 minutes, but broilers vary so watch it close.

✦

Sweet and Spicy
Stir Fried Walnut Shrimp

This is a version of a classic home-style Chinese dish but using the Vodka Chili Elixir and honey in place of the bottled sweet chili sauce that is more usual.

16 large	Shrimp, thawed if they were frozen
2 T	Vodka Chili Elixir (page 210)
2 T	Peanut Oil
10g (0.3 oz)	Ginger, peeled and chopped
15g (0.5 oz)	Garlic, peeled and chopped
15g (0.5 oz)	Shallots, peeled and thinly sliced
2 whole	Scallions, cut into 2.5cm (1 inch) batons
1 Tablespoon	Black Beans in Chili Oil (page 233)
25g (0.9 oz)	Walnuts, halves
1 Tablespoon	Honey
3 Tablespoons	Corn Starch
1/2 teaspoon	Baking Powder (not baking soda)
3/4 teaspoon	MSG (optional)
Vegetable oil for frying, Sesame Seeds for garnish	

PROPORTION OF INGREDIENTS

Normally the exact proportion of ingredients is left up to the chef. The amounts shown here are only a guideline. In keeping with tradition, feel free to change the proportions to suit your own tastes.

THE SHRIMP

Traditionally this is made with shell-on (and head-on) shrimp. The problem is that the shell fragments are chewy and get stuck between your teeth. If you grew up in China, you are probably used to this and it is part of the dish. Otherwise you will be more likely to enjoy them without the shells. Devein them, anyway (or purchase them already deveined).

PROCEDURE

1. Dry the shrimp off on paper towels. Then put them into a bowl with an excess of corn starch. Toss to coat them evenly.

2. Heat oil for deep frying to 170°C (340°F) for shrimp without shells. For shrimp with the shells, heat the oil to 180°C (355°F). Deep fry for about one minute depending on the exact size of the shrimp. If they are extremely large, then fry a bit longer. Don't forget they will receive additional heat later, and overcooking makes shrimp tough.

3. Heat a wok or a 3-4 liter stainless steel pan on a very high heat. Do <u>not</u> use a nonstick pan. When the pan is hot, add the peanut oil. Wait a few seconds for it to come up to temperature.

4. Add the ginger and the garlic. If you want a quality dish, don't use a ginger-garlic paste from a jar. Cook for 30 to 45 seconds, being careful not to burn the garlic.

5. Add the scallions. Cook for about 1 1/2 minutes, stirring.

6. Add the shrimp and the shallots. Sprinkle the Vodka Chili Sauce on.

7. Stir. After another minute add the black beans in chili oil.

8. Turn the heat off and drizzle with the honey. Add the MSG at the last moment.

9. Transfer to a plate and sprinkle some sesame seeds over the top.

HOLLYWOOD RESTAURANT VARIATION

Several popular Los Angeles area Chinese-American restaurants make this by doubling the amount of honey and stirring in some mayonnaise just before plating on a bed of iceberg lettuce leaves. Usually candied walnuts are added, too. The patrons of these restaurants are primarily Jewish, so the recipes have been adjusted to suit their tastes. Although I never understood why they refuse pork but eat shrimp, since both are equally forbidden by their religion.

South Indian Curry
Lamb or Vegetarian

This is a recipe that I developed many, many years ago. I put a video up on YouTube showing it, but I have made a few corrections and minor improvements. Be sure to use Sambar Masala for this. It is critical for the authentic taste.

apx. 700g (1.5 lbs)	Lamb, bone-in foreshank (see notes below)
* 300g (10.6 oz)	Potatoes, peeled (only for vegetarian version)
150g (5.3 oz)	Cherry or Pear Tomatoes, ripe (fresh)
25g (0.9 oz)	Butter
120g (4 oz)	Shallots, peeled
30g (1 oz)	Garlic cloves, peeled
2 teaspoons	Sambar Masala (see notes on page 100)
1 to 2 teaspoons	Kashmiri Mirch (ground red Indian chilies)
2 teaspoons	Coriander Seeds, whole (in all)
1 teaspoon	Paprika, ideally Bittersweet
3/4 teaspoon	Mustard Seeds, whole
1/2 teaspoon	Fenugreek seeds, whole
1/4 teaspoon	Asafoetida, also known as Hing
40g (1.4 oz)	Red Chilies, fresh
80g (2.8 oz)	Onion, peeled
1 T	Tamarind Paste
2 teaspoons	Dark Brown Sugar (ideally Jaggery)
2 teaspoons	Gram Flour or Pea Flour (peasemeal)
3 whole	Bay Leaves (in all)
1 T	Methi (dried fenugreek leaves)
2 teaspoons	Coconut Oil, or Ghee
2 T	Flour
1-2 T	Cilantro, freshly minced (garnish)
1 T	Lemon Juice, fresh (at the end)

THE LAMB

Instructions for making this vegetarian appear in the procedures below. If you are using lamb, get your butcher to cut one foreshank into halves.

PROCEDURE

1. Put 1 liter (1.1 quarts) of water in a pressure cooker. Coarsely chop the red chilies and onion. Add them to the water along with 2 teaspoons of salt, 1 teaspoon of the coriander seeds and 2 of the bay leaves. Add the lamb and bring it up to a simmer on a high heat.

VEGETARIAN SUBSTITUTIONS

Instead of lamb, put 300 grams (10.6 oz) of peeled potatoes in. You can also use some carrots if you like. Be sure to use large pieces. If they are small, they will turn to mush. If you have my book, *Vegetables for Carnivores,* then add 1 tablespoon of the Deep Undertones Spice Blend. This will greatly improve the flavor without adding any meat.

---

2. When bubbles break the surface, put the lid on and watch for steam starting to vent. Now lower the heat to keep it at the point where steam is just barely leaking out. Maintain for 1 ½ hours for lamb, or 20-30 minutes for potatoes. The exact time for potatoes varies with the type they are.

3. While this is cooking, heat a small pot on a medium heat. Add the butter. After it melts, add the paprika, a bay leaf and a teaspoon of salt. Cook for 2 minutes, lowering the heat if needed so it doesn't burn.

4. Put the cherry tomatoes in a mixing bowl and pour the seasoned butter over them. Discard the bay leaf. Let them sit in the butter 4-5 minutes.

5. Add the flour to the bowl and mix well using your fingers. Make sure the tomatoes are all coated as well as possible.

6. Put the tomatoes on a wire rack over a baking sheet. Position a shelf in the lower third of the oven. Roast at 150°C (300°F) for 1 ½ hours.

7. When the time is up, let them cool at room temperature. Set aside.

8. Heat a small heavy-bottomed sauce pan on a medium setting. When it is warm, add the coconut oil (or ghee) and wait a minute before adding the other teaspoon of coriander seeds along with the mustard seeds, the pea flour, the fenugreek seeds and the asafoetida. Also add two of the roasted tomatoes from Step #7 (the rest will be used later). Stir frequently. After

about 4 minutes the mustard seeds will have started to pop. Then take it off the heat promptly.

9. After it cools for a few minutes, scrape the contents out to a food processor with a small work bowl, or a mortar. Grind to a paste. Don't attempt to use an electric spice mill for this because it will ruin the mill.

10. Put the dried methi leaves in an electric spice mill along with 1/2 teaspoon of coarse salt and the Sambar masala. Also add the Kashmiri mirch to taste. If you want it extremely hot, use up to 2 tablespoons. Just 1 teaspoon is mild. Grind to a powder. Set aside for later use.

11. When the time on the pressure cooker is up, release the pressure promptly in this case. Drain the lamb (or potatoes in the case of the vegetarian version) on a sieve over a bowl to collect the broth. Place the lamb on a plate to cool. Discard the solids from the sieve.

12. In the case of lamb, transfer the broth to a fat separating pitcher (there is no fat from potatoes, of course). Put the tamarind paste in a bowl and pour about 250ml (1 cup) of the hot broth over it. Stir to dissolve. Reserve the fat from the fat separating pitcher in the case of the lamb (if it was fatty enough to have any). The extra broth you have is quite salty and spicy, and it has no further use in this recipe. You can throw that out.

13. When the lamb has cooled, cut the meat away from the bones. Discard the bones and trim off any gristle. Cut the meat into large cubes that would fit on a tablespoon. Don't cut it too small. If there are a few small pieces, that's okay. Same in the vegetarian version using potatoes: Cut into cubes, but not too small.

14. Heat a 4 liter stainless steel pot on a medium setting. When it is warm, add 30 grams (1 oz) of the reserved lamb fat, or ghee if you are making the vegetarian version. If you do not have enough lamb fat, make up the difference with ghee or coconut oil. Chop the shallots while this comes up to temperature, then add them to the pot. Cook for about 5 minutes. Chop the garlic up coarsely during this time.

15. Add the garlic to the pan. Cook for about 2 minutes.

16. Turn the heat down to low and add the ground spice mixture from the electric spice mill in Step #10. Stir for about 45 seconds.

17. Add the tamarind broth from Step #12. Scrape the bottom to dissolve the fond. Increase heat to medium and bring to a simmer.

18. Add the rest of the roasted tomatoes from Step #7. Also add the dark brown sugar. Cook for 2 minutes.

19. Add the mixture from Step #9. Also add the lamb (or potatoes) back in at this point, UNLESS...

PRESENTATION DECISION

In Indian home style cuisine, the lamb or potatoes would be added back in now. This results in better flavor in the meat (or vegetables) but the pieces will break up some and look less attractive. In a restaurant, the curry (sauce) is finished completely and then combined with the meat only when being reheated in a skillet for serving. It is up to you.

20. Stir. Put a lid on the pot and reduce the heat to low. Simmer for at least 10 minutes. When it has thickened, it is ready.

21. This can be stored for several days in the refrigerator without fear of it spoiling because of all the spices. When it comes time to serve, reheat it with a little water on a pan, adding the lamb (or potato) as it warms.

22. Garnish with a little freshly minced cilantro and lemon wedges on the side.

Lamb Biriyani

This is a recipe that I have been asked for probably more than any other. The secret is in the advance preparation of the lamb, which is even better if you have the ability to cook it over hot coals on a barbecue. It is not a requirement, though.

200g (7 oz)	Lamb Tenderloins
5g (0.17 oz)	Red Curry Powder (page 201)
1 Tablespoon	Vegetable Oil
2 teaspoons	Cumin Seeds, whole
1 teaspoon	Coriander Seeds, whole
2-4 whole	Dried Red Chilies, small (stems removed)
1/2 teaspoon	Black Peppercorns, whole
1/4 teaspoon	Fennel Seeds, whole
1/4 teaspoon	Black Mustard Seeds, whole
1/2 pod	Star Anise
1 teaspoon	Coarse Salt
1 teaspoon	Methi (dried fenugreek leaves)
1 Tablespoon	Ghee or Coconut Oil
140g (5 oz)	Onion, sliced into thin rings
2	Bay Leaves
1	Cinnamon Stick, ideally real cinnamon
20g (0.7 oz)	Garlic cloves, minced
15g (0.5 oz)	Ginger, peeled and minced
90g (3.2 oz)	Passata
400ml (14.1 oz)	Chicken Stock (or water +1/2 Knorr gel)
2 teaspoons	Tamarind Paste
175g (6.2 oz)	Basmati Rice
30g (1 oz)	Pistachios, shelled (or substitute Cashews)

Also: Fresh Cilantro and sliced limes for garnish.

PROCEDURE

1. Combine the red curry powder and the vegetable oil. Rub this mixture into the lamb tenderloins. Refrigerate overnight in a sealed container.

2. If you have a charcoal barbecue, sear the seasoned lamb tenderloins.

Do not cook them all the way through. Use a high heat and concentrate on cooking the outsides. If you do not have a barbecue, do this on a cast iron grill pan on a high heat. Then cool the meat at room temperature. You can do this stage in advance and refrigerate the meat for up to 3 days ahead.

3. Combine the cumin seeds, coriander seeds, dried chilies, black peppercorns, fennel seeds, black mustard seeds, star anise and coarse salt into a cup. Then toast the spices on a hot pan until they barely start to smoke. Transfer to a bowl to cool down at room temperature.

4. Add the methi to the spices. Grind in an electric spice mill. Reserve.

5. Heat a pressure cooker with the ghee or coconut oil. When it is warm add the sliced onion, cinnamon stick and bay leaf. Fry on a medium heat until the onion is just barely starting to brown.

6. Now add the minced garlic and ginger. Cook 2 minutes with stirring.

7. Add the ground spices. Stir. About 30 seconds later pour in the passata and continue cooking 4-5 minutes with stirring.

8. Add the chicken stock and the tamarind paste. Bring to a good simmer.

9. Wash the basmati rice well with cold water, then add to the pressure cooker. Do not stir! Add the pistachios (or cashews) on top and do not stir.

10. Close the lid on the pressure cooker and set a time for 15 minutes.

11. Turn the heat off and set a timer for 10 more minutes.

12. Release the pressure. Discard the bay leaves and cinnamon stick. Stir in a dash of MSG if desired. Turn the contents out onto a sheet pan and allow to rest at room temperature for about 15 minutes before transferring to a storage container in the refrigerator.

This is a restaurant recipe, so it is not intended to be eaten the moment it comes out of the pressure cooker. It is still on the moist side. The idea is that you heat a nonstick sauté pan with ghee and fry the biriyani on a high heat to finish it up when you are ready to serve a portion, adding fresh cilantro at the end, finely sliced red onion or shallots and a spritz of lime juice.

Sookhi Urad Dal

The term sookhi (pronounced soo-key) means dry. Most Indian dal recipes are so wet they should be called soups. In much of India, urad dal is topped with Tadka, which is spiced ghee. In the North, especially Punjab, they also make a dryer style of dal that incorporates the Tadka and is usually more pleasing to westerners who don't enjoy a big pool of liquid fat covering their "soup". The flavors are milder and richer due to the influence of being closer to Europe and generally being wealthier than in the South. This is also a perfect dish for Rijsttafel (see page 3). This recipe is essentially the same as the esteemed Punjabi restaurant I worked at in Los Angeles, as chronicled in my "40 Years in One Night" book.

100g (3.5 oz)	Urad Dal, white
45g (1.5 oz)	Shallots
15g (0.5 oz)	Green Chilies, fresh
5g (0.2 oz)	Ginger, peeled and chopped
1/2 teaspoon	Garlic Powder
1 Tablespoon	Ghee or Coconut Oil
1/2 teaspoon	Cumin Seeds, whole
3/4 teaspoon	Red Curry Powder (page 201)
1/4 teaspoon	Asafoetida (also known as hing)
2 teaspoons	Tomato Paste, the Italian kind in a tube
25g (0.9 oz)	Cilantro, chopped
1 Tablespoon	Butter (not ghee)
1/4 teaspoon	MSG (optional)

Sliced lime and additional cilantro for garnish.

URAD DAL

This comes in two kinds, black and white. This recipe uses the white, which is also sometimes called Urad Gota. The black and white are not interchangeable because both the flavor and the cooking times differ.

PROCEDURE

1. Rinse the urad dal very well. You do not need to soak it, but you do need to submerge it in water half a dozen times, draining it each time.

2. Put the urad dal into a pressure cooker along with 175ml (6.2 oz) of water and a teaspoon of salt. Bring to a strong simmer before putting the lid on. Cook for 8 minutes.

3. Turn off the heat. Let rest 5 more minutes before releasing the pressure. You can prepare this up to three days in advance if you store it in the refrigerator (as is done in restaurants). You will need 200 grams of this, which should be about what you have.

4. Put the shallots, green chilies, ginger and garlic powder into a food processor and grind to cut everything into small uniform pieces.

5. Heat a nonstick skillet with the ghee (or coconut oil).

6. When it is hot, add the cumin seeds. Fry them for a minute, taking care not to burn them. If you do burn them, throw it out and start over.

7. Add the shallot mixture from the food processor (Step #3 above) and fry on a medium heat until the shallots are just turning golden.

8. Now add the red curry powder and asafoetida. Cook 30 seconds.

9. Add 200 grams of the cooked urad dal (Steps #1 and 2 above). Stir and continue cooking for about 2 minutes.

10. Add 150ml (5 oz) water. Stir together then cover the pan. Cook 5 minutes with the lid on.

11. Remove the lid and add the tomato paste and the butter. Stir and continue cooking slowly until the urad dal is soft but not mushy. It should not have any bite to it. This is not *al dente* pasta.

12. Add the chopped cilantro and MSG (if using). Stir and cook 1-2 more minutes. Add salt to taste.

Serve with the ubiquitous Indian garnishes of sliced lime and sprigs of fresh cilantro.

Chicken Tikka Masala
Murgh Makhani or Butter Chicken

This was adopted as a national dish of Britain, but there is considerable debate about it's origin. For more on this see the brief history of the naming that follows after this recipe. At any rate, very few western restaurants do it right, taking shortcuts and adding sugar to correct bitterness. Making this properly involves quite a few steps, as shown here in its entirety. Note that the procedure differs slightly from the video years earlier.

500g (1.1 lbs)	Chicken, boneless/skinless thighs
FOR THE MARINADE	
1 1/2 teaspoons	Dried Ginger, ground
1 teaspoon	Paprika
1 teaspoon	Kashmiri Mirch, or 1:1 paprika/cayenne
1 teaspoon	Cumin Seeds, whole
1 teaspoon	Coriander Seeds, whole
1 teaspoon	Garlic, granulated
1 teaspoon	Sugar
1 teaspoon	Salt
1/2 teaspoon	Black Peppercorns
1/2 teaspoon	Fenugreek Seeds (Methi)
2.5cm (1 inch)	Cinnamon Stick, ideally true cinnamon
4 whole	Cloves (the spice - not garlic)
2 whole	Brown Cardamon Pods
120 g (4 oz)	Yoghurt or Kefir
1 T	Lemon Juice
1/2 teaspoon	Red Food Coloring, powdered (optional)

PROCEDURE

1. Begin by making the marinade. Combine all of the ingredients listed above (except the yoghurt, lemon juice and food coloring) in an electric spice mill and grind to a powder. Pass the powder through a fine mesh sieve. Discard any solids that would not pass through.

158

2. Put the yoghurt, lemon juice and red food color in a bowl with the ground spices. Whisk to combine.

60g (2 oz)	Ghee or Coconut Oil
30g (1 oz)	Butter
2 T	Coconut, dry and unsweetened
6-8	Green Cardamon Pods, whole
1 teaspoon	Nutmeg, ground
1 whole	Bay Leaf
6 whole	Allspice
22g (0.75 oz))	Garlic, cut in large pieces
700g (1.5 lbs)	Tomatoes, ripe
15g (0.5 oz)	Green Serrano Chili Pepper
22g (0.75 oz)	Ginger, fresh
60g (2oz)	Onion, peeled
1 teaspoon	Cumin Seeds, whole
1 teaspoon	Paprika
1/2 teaspoon	Cayenne (optional - see text)
350ml (1.5 cups)	Chicken Stock
45ml (1.5 oz)	Heavy Cream
2-3 T	Yoghurt or Kefir (not lowfat)
1/2 teaspoon	Curry Powder
3/4 teaspoon	Liquid Smoke (optional - see Step #16)
2-3 T	Cilantro, freshly chopped
1 whole	Lemon

3. Use a sharp knife to make light slashes in the chicken thighs, but don't cut them up. Massage the marinade well into the chicken. Put in a closed container and refrigerate overnight. That is, between 4 and 16 hours.

4. Take the chicken out of the marinade one piece at a time. Remove the excess marinade with a pastry brush that has been dipped in vegetable oil. If you leave the chicken heavily coated with the marinade, the spices will burn and make the dish bitter. You don't have to get all of the marinade off (you can't, anyway). Then thread the chicken onto either metal skewers or wooden skewers that you soaked in water ahead of time. Cut the chicken into halves length-wise to help not hang too far off of the skewers.

5. When you have all of the chicken ready, cook it over charcoal outdoors if possible. If not, then arrange it on an inverted colander as shown in the

video so that it can be roasted in the oven. If your oven is too small, then broil them on a rack, turning the pieces over halfway through cooking.

6. Put the cooked chicken skewers on a plate to cool. Squeeze fresh lemon juice over them. These can be made up to 3 days ahead of time.

7. Begin making the sauce. Note that the amount of green cardamom pods and nutmeg will vary with the quality and freshness of the product you have. If you have very strong cardamom, then you might need to use less. Heat a 3 or 4 liter pot on a low setting (#3 out of 10). Put in the 60 grams (2 oz) of the ghee (or coconut oil). Add the dry coconut, green cardamom pods, whole allspice, bay leaf and the ground nutmeg. Cook gently for 2 minutes.

8. Add the garlic. Stir occasionally for 5 minutes.

9. While this is cooking, make a conical incision around the stem-end of each tomato and remove the bitter part. Chop the tomatoes coarsely.

10. Add the tomatoes and stir. Increase heat to medium (#5). Cook for just over an hour, stirring occasionally to keep it from sticking to the bottom. When it starts to get thick, lower the heat a bit more (#4 out of 10).

11. While this is cooking, split and scrape the green chilies of the seeds and membranes. Then coarsely chop them. Also peel and coarsely chop up the ginger during this time. Then cut up the onion coarsely.

12. On another burner, heat a pan on medium-high. Add the 30g (1 oz) of butter. When it has melted, then add the chilies, ginger and onions prepared in Step #11, as well as the teaspoon of cumin seeds. Cook for a few minutes with stirring until the cumin seeds have puffed slightly.

13. When the oil has started to separate from the tomatoes in the first pan, add the teaspoon of paprika to it. If you want this to be a bit spicier, add the 1/2 teaspoon of cayenne at this point. Stir, then add the cooked chilies, ginger, onions and cumin seeds from the second pan to this one. Cook for 5-6 minutes more with occasional stirring.

14. Add the chicken stock and stir. Turn off the heat and let it cool for

about 10 minutes at room temperature.

15. Transfer to a blender and purée for a full minute. Pass the contents of the blender through a sieve, rubbing to get as much as you can through.

16. Rinse out the pan you were using and put the liquid that passed through the sieve into the same pan again. Add the heavy cream, curry powder and if you didn't cook the chicken over charcoal outside, then add the liquid smoke to the sauce, too. Stir, then taste and adjust salt.

17. Cut up the chicken and add it to the sauce. Simmer for about 10 minutes gently. Finish with freshly chopped cilantro. Serve with wedges of lemon.

Chicken Tikka Masala, Butter Chicken and Murgh Makhini are all interchangeable names in my opinion since no two recipes are identical and all are extremely similar. While some argue that it was created in the U.K. by immigrants from Bangladesh, the dish is virtually identical to a classic Punjabi Indian dish. There is yet another version of the story where it was supposedly invented in Scotland by a Scottish cook (no, not Gordon Ramsay!) Because no two recipes agree about anything other than chicken and tomatoes, I consider all three names to be equally valid for the dish. Take your pick! The one thing that everyone agrees on is that it is truly delicious.

Massaman Chicken Curry

Now famous for having been voted #1 among the 50 most delicious recipes in the world. Note there are some small changes here from the original 2013 video on YouTube.

500g (1.1 lbs)	Chicken, boneless, skinless thighs
1 full recipe	Massaman Curry Paste (page 196)
1 bunch	Cilantro, fresh
300g (10.6 oz)	Potatoes, peeled and cut in large cubes
2 teaspoons	Curry Powder (see note below)
70g (2.5a oz)	Shallots, peeled
30g (1 oz)	Ginger, peeled
30g (1 oz)	Garlic, peeled
30g (1 oz)	Lemongrass, peeled and tender core minced
3 T	Thai Basil, fresh
2 T	Dark Brown Sugar
1 T	Nam Pla (Thai fish sauce)
60g (2 oz)	Cashews
400g (1 can)	Coconut Cream, unsweetened
120ml (4 oz)	Chicken Stock, ideally homemade
1 whole	Lime
2 T	Peanut Oil or coconut oil
1 teaspoon	Thai Spice Mix, optional (Volume 3, page 225)

THE CURRY POWDER

You can use a commercial curry powder, since it is only being used to give the potatoes some color and background flavor.

PROCEDURE

1. Put 500ml (17.6 oz) water in a saucepan on the stove. Add 1 teaspoon of salt and 1 tablespoon of curry powder to the water, along with the potatoes. Bring to a boil. Maintain for about 2 minutes.

2. Move the pan from the heat to an unoccupied burner or trivet. Cover. Let stand until cooled down to room temperature.

3. Heat the peanut oil in a nonstick skillet. When it is hot, fry the cashew nuts in it, turning frequently. Take care not to burn them. Fry until golden, then set aside in a bowl until later when they will be used.

4. Divide the cilantro into the root end (coriander stems) and the upper leaves. Set the leaves aside for now. Soak the stems in a bowl with cold water to clean them of any clinging dirt.

5. Coarsely chop the shallots, ginger and lemongrass. Cut the garlic cloves into halves. Heat a small stainless steel pan on a high heat. When it is very hot, add the shallots, ginger, lemongrass and garlic. Dry toast these in the pan until there is color and some little black flecks, but be very careful not to actually burn them.

6. Now add 30ml (1 oz) water to the pan and quickly cover with a lid. Turn the heat down to very low and let them cook for about 2 minutes.

7. Transfer the contents to a regular blender (not a stick blender cup). Add half of the cashews from Step #3, the coriander from Step #4, the Massaman Curry Paste and the coconut cream. Grate about half of the zest from the lime in, too. Purée.

8. Rub the mixture through a sieve. Discard the solids that won't pass.

9. Transfer to a 3 or 4 liter stock pot on a medium heat. Add the brown sugar and nam pla (Thai fish sauce). When it comes to a simmer, lower the heat down to keep it around 70°C (160°F).

10. After about 5 minutes, chop up the Thai basil and add it. Cube up the raw chicken and add that to the pot, too. Cook for about 5 minutes.

11. Add the chicken stock and the Thai Spice Mix (optional). Maintain the heat just below 70°C (160°C) for about an hour.

12. Squeeze the lime now to get about 30ml (1 oz) of juice and add it. Stir and then add the previously cooked potatoes and the rest of the fried cashews. Increase the heat slightly to 80°C (180°F) and stir until thicker. Don't reduce it too much and over cook it.

13. Chop up the rest of the cilantro (the leaves) and add that at the end of the cooking time.

✛

Hunan Cauliflower

Hunan (not "human"!) is a region of China well known for the fiery cuisine. If you like super, super spicy Chinese food, I implore you to try this! The recipe can be either vegetarian or made with shrimp. The original recipe called for over twice this amount of small red chilies. Most people find that inedible, so I have reduced the amount to something manageable. Either way it is extremely hot, so consider yourself warned!

300g (10.6 oz)	Cauliflower (weight is after trimming)
apx. 150g (5.3 oz)	Medium Shrimp (optional - see note below)
45ml (1.5 oz)	Peanut Oil
40ml (1.4 oz)	Lime Juice, fresh (in all)
15g (1/2 oz) or more	Thai Red Chilies, stem removed, chopped
25g (0.9 oz)	Shallots, peeled
12g (0.4 oz)	Ginger, peeled and sliced or grated
12g (0.4 oz)	Garlic, peeled and coarsely chopped
2 teaspoons	Brown Sugar, ideally Muscovado
1/2 teaspoon	Turmeric
1/2 teaspoon	Shrimp Paste
1/2 teaspoon	MSG
1/4 teaspoon	Black Pepper, ground
small bunch	Cilantro, fresh
1 whole	Star Anise
5cm (2 inch)	Cinnamon Stick
1 whole	Scallion, sliced into thin strips

ADDING SHRIMP

I suggest adding shrimp. Grind equal parts of salt, white peppercorns and Sichuan peppercorns coarsely. Mix these with medium-sized shelled and deveined shrimp. Toss with peanut oil. Either sear them well on a cast iron pan, or stir fry them quickly. Reserve until the end of the recipe.

PROCEDURE

1. Cut the cauliflower into 6-7mm (1/4 inch) slices. There will be small pieces that fall away as you do this, but don't worry about that. You will use all of the cauliflower, but you want the larger slices in there as well. When you get near the center and your slice includes the stem, cut the stem away and use it for something else. Your goal is to have a lot of pieces that are vaguely shrimp-like in shape. The origin of this dish is Buddhist monks who often imitate meat and fish with cut vegetables.

2. Into the cup of a stick blender put the peanut oil, half of the lime juice, half of the red chilies (coarsely chop them first), the shallots, ginger, garlic, brown sugar, turmeric, shrimp paste and black pepper. Also, divide the cilantro into stem/root ends and leaves. Rinse the root ends well and add those to the stick blender, too. Reserve the leaves for later. Purée.

3. Heat a very large nonstick pan on medium. When it gets warm add the purée from the stick blender. Add the rest of the Thai chilies, the star anise and the cinnamon stick. Stir.

4. When it starts to bubble, reduce the heat slightly. Cook 3-4 minutes.

5. The oil should have started to separate by now. Add the cauliflower. Stir well to make sure the cauliflower is evenly coated in the mixture. Then count the time and cook for 3 minutes.

6. Add 30ml (1 oz) of water and put a lid on it. Reduce the heat to medium-low. Allow it to steam for 6 minutes without stirring.

7. Remove the lid. If you are using shrimp, stir them in now so that the residual heat will warm them up. Continue cooking to drive off excess moisture and make sure the cauliflower is tender but not mushy. Remove the star anise and cinnamon stick at this time, too.

8. Add the rest of the lime juice, the MSG and half of the cilantro leaves (cut finely). Reserve some larger cilantro leaves for the final garnish. Stir well. Taste and add salt if you think you need it.

9. Transfer to a plate and add the rest of the fresh cilantro and the sliced scallions.

✦

Secret to Chow Mein

This magical sauce will give your homemade chow mein a restaurant flavor, and you can keep it in a bottle for fast meals.

40ml (1.4 oz)	Oloroso Sherry
40g (1.4 oz)	Oyster Sauce, Lee Kum Kee
30g (1 oz)	Hoisin Sauce, Lee Kum Kee
30ml (1 oz)	Rice Wine Vinegar, ideally 9%
20ml (0.7 oz)	Mirin
20ml (0.7 oz)	Soy Sauce
2 teaspoons	Dark Brown Sugar, ideally Muscovado
12g (0.4 oz)	Sesame Oil
1/2 teaspoon	Turmeric
1/2 teaspoon	Lemon Zest, freshly grated
1/2 teaspoon	Black Pepper, ground
1 teaspoon	MSG

MAKE THE SAUCE IN ADVANCE

The secret is this sauce. Combine all of the above ingredients into a small saucepan. Heat gently and whisk to dissolve the sugar. Do not boil. Then cool for a few minutes before straining through a sieve. This can be stored in a squeeze bottle at room temperature for up to two weeks.

PROCEDURE

1. Boil Chinese egg noodles until soft (but not squishy). Drain and dry them very well. Now fry them in a little hot peanut oil until they start to get crisp. You can do these steps in advance. Set aside until ready to use.

2. In a wok or nonstick pan, heat more peanut oil. Fry garlic and ginger until fragrant. Add chopped onion and other items in the order that goes from that which takes the longest to cook to things that cook the fastest. Don't forget to put the noodles back in at the right point and then squirt in a generous amount of this sauce. Add water if you made it too thick.

3. Garnish with scallions.

Balinese Curry

This is a good example of how a spice paste makes it easy to have a delicious meal with complex flavors ready to eat fast. To step it up beyond a fast meal, see notes on the next page.

250g (8.8 oz)	Pork Neck, Chicken Thighs or Confit Duck
50g (1.75 oz)	Shallots, peeled and sliced into rings
60g (2 oz)	Coconut Cream, unsweetened
40g (1.4 oz)	Base Ganep Paste (see page 198)
20g (0.7 oz)	Green Serrano Chilies (see note below)
2 Tablespoons	Cilantro, freshly chopped
1 Tablespoon	Lime Juice, fresh
1 Tablespoon	Peanut Oil, or substitute Vegetable Oil

CHILI PEPPERS

This amount is for medium heat. If you like very spicy food you can add more chilies. For extra mild, remove seeds and membranes.

PROCEDURE

1. Dice the chilies. Cube the boneless/skinless meat. Combine both in a bowl and add the Base Ganep paste. Mix well to coat the pieces. You can cook this right away or leave to marinate for up to 2 hours.

2. Heat a nonstick skillet with high sides on a medium setting. Add the peanut oil. When it is hot, add the sliced shallots. Fry until translucent.

3. Add the marinated meat. Scrape in any Base Ganep that's clinging to the bowl. Increase the heat. Cook without much stirring so that the meat can brown some. Take care not to actually burn it, but <u>do</u> brown it nicely.

4. Lower the heat. Add the coconut cream. Bring to a simmer and add the ingredients from next page (if using) and the cilantro. Cover 2-3 minutes. Mix in the lime juice and 1/4 teaspoon MSG (optional). Serve over rice.

Balinese Curry
Extended Version

If you liked the recipe on the previous page, just wait until you try this expanded version!

IN ADDITION TO THE RECIPE ON THE PREVIOUS PAGE

150g (5.3 oz)	Potatoes, peeled
2 teaspoons	Curry Powder
150g (5.3 oz)	Large Prawns, shelled and deveined
1/2 teaspoon	White Peppercorns, whole
1/2 teaspoon	Crushed Red Chili Flakes
1/2 teaspoon	Coarse Salt

POTATOES

The exact cooking time is impossible to state because every type of potato is different. The point is to cook the cubed pieces until they are just barely tender, however long that might take. It was 15 minutes here.

PROCEDURE

1. Cube the potatoes into fairly large pieces. Heat about 500ml (17.5 oz) of water in a pot. Add the curry powder and 2 teaspoons of salt. Boil potatoes until they are just tender but not mushy. They will be cooked a second time, so be sure not to overcook them now. Drain and reserve.

2. Put the white peppercorns, red chili flakes and coarse salt into an electric spice grinder. Pulse to a coarse grit. Don't turn it into a powder!

3. Dry the prawns then trim off the tails. Put them into a container and mix in the spices. Add 1-2 teaspoons vegetable oil. Marinate for an hour.

4. Heat a cast iron pan <u>very</u> hot. Char the shrimp for about a minute on each side. Reserve.

5. Add the prawns and potato as explained in Step #4 of the recipe on the previous page.

Thai Shrimp Salad
Farang Style

Western foreigners in Thailand are called Farang. This salad is delicious, and everything you hope for in a Thai salad.

60g (2 oz)	Mayonnaise
30ml (1 oz) in all	Lime Juice, fresh
10g (0.3 oz)	Thai Red Curry Paste (page 200)
10g (0.3 oz)	Muscovado or Dark Brown Sugar
1 teaspoon	Nam Pla (Thai Fish Sauce)
3/4 teaspoon	MSG

Prawns (see Step #1 below) Cherry Tomatoes, Gem Lettuce, Roasted Peanuts, Cilantro, Honey, Thai Chili, Carrot, White Pepper

THE DRESSING

Combine <u>half</u> of the lime juice with the mayonnaise, the Thai red curry paste, the brown sugar, the nam pla and the MSG in a blender. Purée. This improves greatly after refrigeration for 2-3 days. **Make it in advance!**

PROCEDURE

1. Prepare the prawns in the same way as on the previous page for the Balinese Curry (steps 2 through 4). Then put them in a bowl and sprinkle with the other half of the lime juice. This will finish them like ceviche.

2. Slice the gem lettuce in half. Trim the stems. Smear with vegetable oil and then season with salt and white pepper. Grill on the same pan that the shrimp were cooked on (the residue from the shrimp is part of the flavor).

3. Halve the cherry tomatoes, mince <u>one</u> Thai chili, crush the roasted peanuts, roughly chop the cilantro and finely grate the peeled carrot.

4. Slice the grilled lettuce and combine everything except cilantro and honey with dressing. Top with cilantro and a few drops of the honey.

Korean Cucumber Banchan

Banchan refers to that massive collection of little side dishes served to you in any good Korean restaurant along with whatever it is that you actually ordered. Some are simple things and some are fabulous creations of the chef that defy anyone else copying them. This is such a dish and it is a bit of work, but is wonderful as an accompaniment to Korean BBQ.

45g (1.5 oz)	Bok Choy—leaves only (see Step #1)
60g (2 oz)	Cucumber, European Type
2 teaspoons	Corn Starch
1 Tablespoon	Peanut Oil
1/2 to 1 whole	Red Chili, minced (see notes below)
1/2 teaspoon	Sesame Oil
1 teaspoon	Lime Juice
1/4 teaspoon	MSG
1/2 teaspoon	Sesame Seeds

THE CHILI

The amount and variety of chili is up to you, of course. This should not be blazing hot, though. A single red serrano chili or a single Thai red chili is sufficient. You can always add more if you insist.

PROCEDURE

1. Pick through the bok choy and cut away stems. Discard any damaged parts. The weight is counted only of the picked leaves.

2. Put the leaves in a bowl and toss with the corn starch.

3. Drizzle the peanut oil over the leaves and mix together.

170

4. Preheat oven to 130°C (265°F) oven with fan assist ON. Spread the leaves out on a metal baking sheet and roast for 30 minutes.

5. Cool to room temperature and then scrape off to transfer to a bowl. Season with salt and MSG, crushing the leaves to pieces.

6. Peel the cucumber or leave the skin on, as you prefer. Slice the cucumber lengthwise. Scrape out the seed pods. Now slice into small cubes. Marinate in the lime juice for a minutes.

7. Leaving the lime juice behind mostly, mix the cucumber around in the bowl with the roasted bok choy.

8. Season with MSG. Stir in the finely diced chilies and the sesame oil.

9. Portion out to small decorative bowls and garnish with sesame seeds. Once it is mixed together, it needs to be served within a few minutes.

TYPICAL ARRAY OF BANCHAN IN A GOOD KOREAN RESTAURANT
Imagine having to produce a dozen such little dishes as the one in this recipe for a quality Korean dinner. That's what restaurants do.

Mastering Gravies
Mushrooms or any Meat

This is a one-size-fits all gravy recipe. All you have to do is choose what stock and mushrooms you are using.

400g (14.1 oz)	Stock (see notes below)
115g (4 oz)	Mushrooms (see notes below)
60ml (2 oz)	Cream, light
1 medium	Shallot, peeled
1 clove	Garlic, peeled
45g (1 oz)	Stock Fat (see notes below)
2 T	Flour
2 whole	Bay Leaves
1/3 teaspoon	Red Pepper Flakes
1/4 teaspoon	Coffee, instant (strong)
1/4 teaspoon	Black Peppercorns, whole

Butter (amount varies on whether you have stock fat or not)
Sprigs of fresh Rosemary, Sage, Tarragon and Parsley
(or substitute 1/2 teaspoon each of the dried)

STOCK AND STOCK FAT

Use beef stock for either beef or mushroom gravy. Use chicken, turkey or lamb stock for each of those respective gravies. With the exception of chicken, use the fat that was rendered from making the stock in the recipe. However, chicken fat is oily and unpleasant in a gravy, so substitute olive oil in the case of chicken. Also use olive oil if you don't have stock fat.

MUSHROOMS

You should use wild mushrooms (ideally porcini) with a stronger flavor for a mushroom gravy, but if you are making chicken gravy (for example) then stick with plain champignons (button mushrooms) so that the mushroom flavor stays in the background.

PROCEDURE

1. Heat a heavy 3 or 4 liter stainless steel pot on a medium-high (#7 to 8) setting. When it gets hot, add 30 grams (1 oz) of the stock fat (or olive oil in the case of chicken or mushroom gravy). If you are using stock fat, then use a splatter guard and heat it until the splattering from the traces of water have boiled off.

2. When the fat comes up to temperature, add the whole mushrooms (trim the stem end a bit, but otherwise don't cut them up). Stir them to coat with the fat, then don't stir too much so they can brown. Cook for 4-5 minutes.

3. Turn the heat off and move the pan away. Use a slotted spoon to remove the mushrooms to a bowl. Add 30 grams (1 ounce) of butter. The butter will quickly melt and brown. Stop it from burning from the residual pan heat by adding 90 grams (3 oz) of the stock after about 30 seconds. Now stir to combine. Scrape to pick up any fond.

4. **This is the trickiest part of the recipe**, and the point where your chances for failure are the greatest. Put the pan on a low to medium-low flame and stir occasionally. After 5-10 minutes you will see the fat has separated into a pale clear liquid and there are brown spots in it. Turn the heat off. The trick is that those brown spots will kind of blossom and soon burn if you don't cool the pan down a bit. Aside from moving it off the heat, add another 22 grams (0.75 oz) of cold butter and whisk. Then use a metal spatula to scrape the bottom of any bits clinging there. Whisk to dissolve the fond as best as possible. By now it should have cooled enough not to burn. Now whisk in the flour.

5. Put the pan back on a low heat and cook the flour in, forming a roux. Meanwhile tie the fresh herbs together with a short length of twine, or put in a metal "herb cage" (see page 233). If you are using dried herbs, just assemble half a teaspoon of each. Mince the shallot and the garlic during this time, too.

6. When the roux is blonde in your estimation, add the shallots and stir.

7. After the shallots are translucent add the rest of the stock. Also add the garlic, the bouquet garni (or the dried herbs), chili flakes, coffee and black peppercorns. Also add the liquid that ran off of the mushrooms you cooked earlier. Cook 5 minutes.

8. Coarsely chop the browned mushrooms and add them. Continue simmering for about 15 minutes.

9. Remove the bundle of herbs. Do not purée the mixture! (see page 10 as for why not). Pass this mixture through a sieve. The solids are of no further use in this.

11. Rinse out the pan you were using. There should not be any visible fond left. Now add the strained liquid back into the same pan.

12. Add the cream and half a teaspoon of salt. Set the heat to medium and slowly bring to a simmer with frequent stirring. Bubbles should just barely be breaking the surface. Cook like this for 5-6 minutes.

13. Pass through a sieve again. If you want an especially refined gravy, rub the contents through a chinois (fine mesh strainer, also known as a China cap). In Michelin star restaurants it is not uncommon to pass it through three times, but you lose some each time.

15. I suggest adding 1/2 teaspoon of MSG at this point. Taste and adjust the seasoning with salt. It should not need any pepper, but if you insist then use finely ground white pepper so that it doesn't have black flecks in it. When serving in a gravy boat, add a sprig of one of the herbs on top. Choose the garnish herb that compliments the type of gravy you made:

Chicken = Thyme
Turkey = Sage
Beef = Rosemary
Mushroom = Tarragon
Lamb = Parsley

Swedish Meatballs

The quintessential Swedish Smörgåsbord staple that's been relentlessly humiliated at Ikea stores for decades now. This very non-traditional recipe makes use of mushrooms to produce a meatball that is more tender and has better flavor.

360g (12.7 oz)	Reindeer Meat, or substitute Beef
160g (5.6 oz)	Pork Belly or other fatty cut
60g (2 oz)	Mushrooms
1 slice	Rye Bread, crust trimmed
1 slice	Sourdough Bread, crust trimmed
60g (2 oz)	White Onion
45ml (1.5 oz)	Light Cream or substitute milk
120g (4 oz)	Heavy Cream
120g (4 oz)	Crème Fraîche or Smetana
1	Egg Yolk
1/4 teaspoon	Nutmeg, freshly grated
SEASONING MIX	
1 teaspoon	Earl Gray Tea
3/4 teaspoon	Coarse Salt
1/2 teaspoon	Brown Sugar
3/4 teaspoon	White Peppercorns
1/2 teaspoon	Dill, dried
4-5 whole	Allspice, whole
1 teaspoon	Finnish Spice (Volume 3, page 232)

The Finnish Spice is optional but delivers the best results

PROCEDURE

1. Cut the meat into cubes. Trim any large pieces of connective tissue.

2. Coarsely chop the mushrooms. Put them into the cup of a stick blender along with about 120ml (4 oz) of water. Purée. Add the rest of the water and purée again.

3. Pour the purée from Step 2 over the cubed meat and mix well. Leave it to stand at room temperature for between 1 and 3 hours.

4. Butter both the rye and white bread. Heat a nonstick skillet on a medium heat and put both pieces in, buttered-side down. After 6-7 minutes, flip the pieces over so that the dry side is now in the melted butter. Continue cooking slowly, flipping occasionally.

5. Put all of the Seasoning Mix ingredients in an electric spice mill and grind to a powder.

6. As the slices of bread become toasted well, lower the heat to keep them from burning, and continue to flip over every few minutes to dry. When you are satisfied that they are as dry as possible, set them aside.

7. Pick the meat out of the puréed mushroom solution. Refrigerate the liquid for later use in this recipe.

8. Cube up the fatty pork and chop the white onion coarsely. Mix together with the meat that was marinated with the mushrooms and pass through a meat grinder two times using the medium-fine plate. Clean the meat grinder between the first and second pass.

9. Break up the fried bread into the bowl of a food processor. Grind to coarse pieces. Add the spice mixture from Step 5 and run the processor again. Add the egg yolk and light cream. Process again.

10. In a mixing bowl, combine the ground meat with the contents of the food processor. Don't over mix it, or the meatballs will be tough.

11. Sprinkle a plate with flour. Form meatballs and put them on the plate. When you have made about 24 meatballs, sprinkle more flour over the top and jostle the plate around carefully to coat the meatballs in the flour on all sides.

12. Heat a very large nonstick skillet on a medium-high setting. Put about a tablespoon of butter into the pan. Let it melt well, swirling the pan to coat evenly. Now add all of the meatballs at once. Normally this would be too many because the meat will partially steam instead of just browning, but Swedish Meatballs are an unusual exception where you actually want them to partially steam in their own juices.

13. After a few minutes, begin turning the meatballs around <u>gently</u> to help them cook evenly on all sides. See the video if this is not clear. You aren't trying to get them deep, dark brown. You just want to firm up the outside and get rid of the pink color. They will be cooked more later in the sauce.

14. Transfer the meatballs off to a bowl to reserve. Add the mushroom purée that the meat soaked in to the pan the meatballs were just fried in.

15. While this is coming to a simmer, whisk together the crème fraîche (or smetana) and the cream in a bowl.

16. After the mushroom mixture has simmered for a few minutes (it will coagulate some, but don't worry about that), add the cream mixture. Stir.

17. Return the meatballs to the pan so that they can poach in the cream. Simmer gently with no lid so that the sauce can thicken. During this time, add a little freshly grated nutmeg. Turn the meatballs over occasionally.

18. As it finally gets close to being thick enough, now taste it and add salt as needed. It may need a little more freshly ground white pepper, too. Do not add black pepper to this under any circumstances. When it is almost ready to serve, add a little freshly minced dill.

FINAL TOUCHES

For best results, either leave them under a lid for another hour, adding a little water from time to time to keep them from drying out (this simulates the steam table used in Smörgåsbords) or refrigerate them and reheat 2-3 days later. They are best reheated gently in a covered pan with a little water and *not* in a microwave.

Serve over mashed potatoes or buttered noodles. Traditionally this is served with lingonberry jam and sliced pickles. However, unless you grew up with those condiments on the side, you may find that the dish is better off without them.

Romesco de Peix

The name is Catalan for fish with Romesco sauce. This is a Catalan fish and tomato soup that's thickened to the point where it could be called a stew. There are many recipes for this ranging from the plain and simple to more elaborate and sophisticated recipes such as this. This recipe is for 2-4 portions, depending on if this will be a first course or a main.

280g (10 oz)	Canned Italian Cherry Tomatoes (in all)
100g (3.5 oz)	Onions, coarsely chopped
60g (2 oz)	Red Bell Pepper
45g (1.5 oz)	Olive Oil, extra virgin - preferably Catalonian
15g (0.5 oz)	Garlic cloves
1 1/2 teaspoons	Sherry Vinegar
2 whole	Bay Leaves
1 Tablespoon	Ground Almonds
1 teaspoon	Picanté Pimentón (hot smoked paprika)
1 Tablespoon	Parsley, freshly chopped
1/2 teaspoon	Salt
1/4 teaspoon	Black Pepper, ground
60ml (2 oz)	Cava or substitute champange or dry white wine
240g (8.5 oz)	Shrimp Stock or substitute chicken stock
1/8 teaspoon	Saffron
8-12	Mussels, fresh
8-12 medium	Shrimp, raw peeled and deveined
90g (3 oz)	Whitefish, boneless (see Step #1 below)
1 Tablespoon	Lemon Juice

To serve: Additional fresh Parsley, Catalonian Sauce (page 204)

PROCEDURE

1. There are a great many fish sold as "whitefish" including cod and even haddock sometimes. Choose a smaller species. Dry fillets off and season with salt. Heat a nonstick pan on a medium-low flame and add a little vegetable oil. When the oil is warm (but not hot) place the fillet down on it. Cook slowly until it is about half done.

178

2. Turn the fillet over. Wait a minute and then shake the pan to make sure the fillet is not stuck to the pan. Loosen it if necessary. Now add the lemon juice. Turn off the heat and cover the pan. Wait 3-4 minutes.

3. Remove the fish to a plate and set it aside for now. You don't need to refrigerate it unless you are going to delay cooking the rest of the recipe for more than a couple of hours.

4. Use tongs to hold the red bell pepper slices over an open flame to char them, or alternatively use a blowtorch.

5. Add the charred bell pepper to a blender along with 200 grams (7 oz) of the canned cherry tomatoes, the onion, garlic cloves, sherry vinegar, olive oil, salt and black pepper. Purée.

6. Heat a large nonstick skillet on a medium flame. Add the puréed vegetables and the bay leaves. Cook slowly with occasional stirring. A splatter guard will keep your stove and floor clean.

7. After the mixture has thickened some, add the pimentón and the ground almonds. If you can only get regular smoked paprika, add 1/2 teaspoon cayenne. Continue cooking until the mixture thickens from the almonds.

8. Add the cava and the fresh parsley. Stir and cook until thick again.

9. Remove from the heat and transfer to a blender. Purée. Rinse the pan it was cooking in and then transfer the puréed mixture back to the pan.

20. Add the shrimp stock, the saffron and the rest of the canned cherry tomatoes. Bring back to a slow simmer.

8. Scrub the mussels under running cold water. Flake the whitefish.

9. Add the mussels, the shrimp and the whitefish all at the same time. Put a lid on and simmer until the mussels have opened.

10. Sprinkle more freshly chopped parsley on top before serving.

11. The Catalonian sauce may be added directly to bowls or offered in a small pitcher on the side. Be sure to serve some crusty sourdough bread and butter as an accompaniment.

Hasselback Potatoes

This is a simple recipe that relies on only a few simple things to be executed perfectly to achieve outstanding professional results. Most of the recipes you see online are terrible because they violate the three essential rules of this recipe.

2 medium	Potatoes, waxy type - Red Rose are good
30g (1 oz)	Butter, melted
15ml (0.5 oz)	Olive Oil
1-4 cloves	Garlic, peeled
1 teaspoon	Beau Monde Seasoning (Vol. 3, page 233)
3-4 branches	Thyme, fresh
3/4 teaspoon	Sea Salt (see note below)

THE THREE SECRETS

First, select potatoes that are waxy. Otherwise they will crumble. Second, cut the slices thin. Thick slices are the mark of an amateur and it will not cook right. Potatoes are inexpensive. Here is an opportunity to improve your knife skills. Watch the video for how it is done. Finally, baste them with the pan juices repeatedly during cooking, as detailed in the procedure here. The juices aren't doing you any good in the bottom of the baking tray.

SEA SALT

Salt is an especially important ingredient with potatoes. You will help this be its best with a quality sea salt, and ideally a smoked salt. The best choice is Halen Môn Gold Smoked Sea Salt (see Volume 2, page 49 for more about this). The alder smoked salt on the same page is too smokey for this. That one is better suited to steaks and lamb.

PROCEDURE

1. Choose potatoes that are symmetrical. Scrub the potatoes, but don't peel them. Hold a sharp chef's knife at a slight angle so that the cutting board prevents you from cutting all the way through. See the video if this is not clear. Make thin cuts along the entire length of the potatoes, making sure not to cut all the way down.

2. Coarsely chop the garlic. Put the olive oil, melted butter and garlic into a stick blender cup. Purée.

3. Strain it through a sieve to remove solid bits of garlic that would burn and become bitter.

4. Coat the potatoes as evenly as possible by putting them into the garlic butter and smearing it between the cuts. Keep the extra butter for Step 6.

5. Put them in an ovenproof casserole dish and roast at 180°C (355°F) for about 45 minutes. During this time, whisk in the Beau Monde seasoning to the garlic butter that didn't stick to the potatoes in Step 5.

6. Use a silicone brush to put the garlic butter down between the layers of potato (which will have opened up some now). Lay branches of thyme over the potatoes. Increase oven to 200°C (390°F). Roast for 20 minutes.

7. Drain the juices from the pan into a bowl. Pour the juices back over the top of the potatoes. Sprinkle with sea salt. Roast another 20 minutes.

8. Drain juices and pour back over potatoes once again. Roast until tender inside and crisp at the edges.

9. When plating, drizzle some of the final pan juices over the top, using a sieve to prevent any bits of charred thyme from getting mixed in. Put fresh thyme branches over the top when serving.

Banana Fritters

The traditional method of making these is to mash up the bananas and fry them. Those are usually quite greasy, and probably why they fell out of favor sometime in the 1970's. These are not greasy at all, but they are a bit more work.

2 small or 1 very large	Banana, ripe.
1 whole	Egg
15g (0.5 oz)	Rice Flour
15g (0.5 oz)	Corn starch
½ teaspoon	Baking Powder
30ml (1 oz)	Cream
2 teaspoons	Dark Brown Sugar
5-6 whole	Allspice
1/8th teaspoon	Salt
25ml (0.8 oz)	Dark Rum (see note below)
25g (0.8 oz)	Butter
about 50g (1.8 oz)	Flour, all-purpose
Powdered Sugar, Whipped Cream	

THE DARK RUM

Use a good deep dark rum, preferably Jamaican or a nice aged one from Barbados. Whatever you do, avoid Bacardi's *Carta-Negra* because when you reduce it by cooking you concentrate the bug repellant and paint thinner notes. Even if you can stomach it in a drink, it is horrible here.

PROCEDURE

1. In a bowl, combine the egg, rice flour, corn starch, the cream, baking powder and a pinch of salt. Whisk to combine.

2. Grind the allspice with the brown sugar in an electric spice mill.

3. Cut the banana on the bias (diagonal slices) about 7.5 mm (0.3 inches) thick.

182

4. Put the banana slices in a bowl and add the ground up sugar and allspice. Toss the bananas in the mixture to bruise them. They will develop a dark brown sticky coating.

5. Add the flour to the bowl and toss to coat the banana pieces. Wait about one minute.

6. Pick the banana slices out of the flour and transfer to a clean bowl.

7. Pour the batter (the egg mixture) over the floured bananas. Stir to combine gently, taking care not to break up the banana pieces.

8. Melt the butter in a nonstick skillet on a medium (#6 out 10) heat.

9. When the butter has foamed up, transfer the banana pieces to the pan carefully, one at a time. Then add a little more of the batter on top of each banana piece with a spoon, letting it drip down the sides a bit.

10. After 3-4 minutes, turn the heat down slightly (#5 out of 10) and turn the banana pieces over.

11. After 1-2 minutes, move the pan off of the heat (leave the burner on) and wait about 45 seconds before adding the rum. Pour it around evenly and not directly on the bananas. Flambée. The flame should not be an explosive fireball, but a rather long-lasting blue flame that dances between the pieces in the pan. If pieces of batter start to burn, blow out the flames.

12. When the flame is nearly out, but not completely, move the pan back to the hot burner. This will reinvigorate the fire.

13. When the flame is out completely, turn the banana pieces over again.

14. Sprinkle with a little powdered sugar. Lower the heat to #2 to #3.

15. After about 2 minutes, turn the banana pieces over again.

16. After another 2 minutes, turn the pieces over for the last time.

17. After about a minute, transfer to a plate. Pour the pan sauce over the banana fritters and top with whipped cream. A garnish of a mint leaf or berries is common.

Chocolate Chip Cookies
Secret Recipe

This recipe is based on the notes of the French baker who started a mini-empire in Los Angeles back in the 1980's. If you read my "40 Years in One Night" book, you know how I got the recipe! The brand lives on in name only now as a factory made product sold in some American chain stores. The recipe was changed long ago to increase profits. If you lived in Beverly Hills in the mid-1980's, you might remember these as the most incredible cookies anyone had ever tasted—and how there was always a line of people waiting for them fresh from the oven. The price was over $8 per cookie in today's money! But that was okay in Beverly Hills. It's also why the recipe was changed.

150g (5.3 oz)	Butter, softened at room temperature
60g (2.1 oz)	Muscovado Sugar, or Dark Brown Sugar
40g (1.4 oz)	Sugar, white granulated
170g (6 oz)	Pastry Flour
90g (3.2 oz)	Eggs (see notes below)
1 Tablespoon	Cream
1/2 teaspoon	Vanilla Extract
1 teaspoon	Baking Powder
1/2 teaspoon	Baking Soda
55g (2 oz)	85% Chocolate Bar, Lindt or better
25g (0.9 oz)	Pecans or Macadamia Nuts (optional)

THE EGGS

One of the frequent problems with baking recipes that have been adapted to home kitchens is that the amount of eggs gets rounded up to the nearest whole egg. That won't provide optimum results. Beat 1 whole egg with 1 egg yolk and then weigh out the 90 grams (3.2 ounces).

PROCEDURE

1. Note that only the finest Danish butter was used. Every ingredient was the best quality. Equip a stand mixer with the paddle attachment. Put the softened butter, dark brown sugar and white sugar into the bowl.

2. Run the mixer slowly at first and then faster to cream the mixture. Stop to scrape down the sides as needed. You will need to do this at least twice.

3. Stop the mixer and add the eggs, cream and vanilla. Mix some, but don't obsess about this because it will come together in the next step.

4. Replace the paddle with the whisk attachment on the mixer. Add the flour, baking powder and baking soda. Run the mixer to make a homogeneous batter, once again stopping to scrape down the sides as needed (and it will be needed several times).

5. Chop the chocolate and the nuts into fairly large pieces. You want them to be quite visible as chunks in the cookies.

6. Remove the bowl from the mixer and stir in the chocolate and nuts by hand using a spatula. Now put the mixture into a sealed storage container and refrigerate for a minimum of 2 hours. Overnight is better.

7. Preheat oven to 187°C (370°F) with fan assist on. Unless you have a very good modern stove with a digital readout of the internal oven temperature, use an oven thermometer because the exact temperature is important if you want perfect results. Line a baking sheet with parchment paper. Take pieces of the stiff batter and roll into meatball-like shapes of about 35 grams (1 to 1 1/4 oz) each. Place down on the parchment leaving plenty of room between them. The better spheres you roll, the more circular you cookies will come out. You will need to cook them in several batches unless you have a commercial oven that uses full size sheet pans.

8. Bake for 11 minutes with the rack positioned in the lower third of the oven (see page 23). Do <u>not</u> place on a solid metal sheet in the oven!

9. Remove from the oven and lift off the cookies to a wire rack to cool. They need to rest for a minimum of 15 minutes. Control yourself.

Pinwheel Beignets

This is a dessert that is related to beignets, but without any yeast. This uses choux pastry, as some beignets do. Multiply all of the ingredients to scale up as much as desired.

200ml (7 oz)	Water
100g (3.5 oz)	Flour
20g (0.7 oz)	Butter
1 whole	Egg
2 teaspoons	Brown Sugar (see note below)
1/2 teaspoon	Salt
1/4 teaspoon	Baking Powder (not soda)
1/4 teaspoon	Orange Zest, freshly grated
1/4 teaspoon	Vanilla Extract

Sugar - ideally half Cane Sugar and half Coconut Sugar
Vegetable Oil (for frying)

OTHER APPLICATIONS

This recipe can be adapted to savory applications. In that case, omit the brown sugar and vanilla.

PROCEDURE

1. In a sauce pan, heat the water, butter and salt until it is boiling and the butter has all melted.

2. Put the flour in a bowl. Pour the hot water and butter solution onto the flour. Stir with a spatula to form a stiff dough. Let it cool for 4-5 minutes

3. Transfer the contents of the bowl to a stand mixer. Add the egg, brown sugar (if you are using it), baking powder, orange zest and vanilla.

4. Using the whisk attachment, beat until it is smooth. Don't over blend it, but make sure it is homogeneous.

5. Put the contents into a piping bag with a 1.25cm (0.5 inch) straight tip, or just snip the end of the plastic piping bag to that size if it is disposable.

6. Put parchment paper squares down. Pipe spirals onto the paper of whatever size you like. I prefer small ones - about 10cm (4 inches) in diameter is generally a good size.

7. Heat a nonstick skillet with enough vegetable oil to come up to approximately 8mm (0.3 inches). If this is a savory application, then I suggest using about 20- 25% duck fat.

8. When the oil is about 165°C (330°F) then put the pinwheels in, paper-side facing up. After about 30 seconds, you should be able to peel the paper off cleanly.

9. Fry until golden on both sides, turning as needed. This will typically take about 7-8 minutes.

10. Drain on paper towels briefly, then transfer to a large pan containing the sugar. Turn over and slide back and forth some to coat.

12. Let cool for at least 5 minutes before serving. If you did everything correctly, you should have something that looks like the image below. Serve with vanilla ice cream.

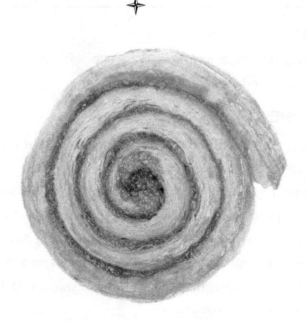

Chocolate Ice Cream
with No Ice Cream Machine

This (scaled down) recipe was used in a place relying on an old second-hand ice cream machine for our signature dessert. We could go through 5 kilograms (over 10 pounds) of it in one night. Knowing it was only a matter of time before the machine broke down and it would take time to repair or replace, I created this recipe as an emergency backup plan. As predicted, the day came when the machine billowed smoke and stopped cold (no pun intended). So this recipe was implemented that same afternoon. We told the waiters to apologize for this new different ice cream. That night reports from our regular guests hailed this new ice cream as far superior. I agree, but the key is keeping it at a precise temperature. Too cold and it is an icy rock. Too warm and it is a puddle, but get it just on the verge of melting and it is really a thing of beauty. The old machine was tossed.

250ml (8.5 oz)	Cream
150g (5 oz)	Milk
100g (3.5 oz)	Sugar
3	Egg Yolks
15g (1/2 oz)	Cocoa Powder (see notes below)
1 teaspoon	Vanilla Extract
2 sheets	Gelatine

COCOA POWDER

It is important to use pure 100% cocoa powder and not a hot chocolate mix if you want a quality end product. Dutch processed is the best.

While other flavors are possible, chocolate works especially well because the dry cocoa powder contributes to the texture..

PROCEDURE

1. Combine all ingredients except the gelatine in a saucepan. Heat on low and whisk.

2. Continue whisking frequently while monitoring the temperature. As soon as steam begins to come off the surface, put the gelatine sheets in cold water to soak for 3-4 minutes. Be careful not to let it boil and don't over-soften the gelatine.

3. When the gelatine is soft, whisk it in. Continue whisking and monitor with a thermometer. Your target is 85°C (175°F).

4. Turn the heat off but leave it in the pot for another 3-4 minutes, whisking occasionally. This ensures the entire mixture is at temperature and not just the area you put the thermometer in at.

5. Pour into a bowl and let stand at room temperature for an hour before transferring it to a container with a lid. Put it in the freezer for 2 hours.

6. By now it should have started to thicken. Take it out of the freezer and stir it one more time, incorporating some air into it by whisking.

7. Return to the freezer. It will be ready to eat in another few hours (depending on your freezer). After a full day it will become too firm in most home freezers, so you should transfer it to your refrigerator 2-3 hours ahead of when you plan to eat it. It should be firm but not a rock. You may want to divide the portions into separate containers in your freezer.

Christmas Fruitcake

Fruitcake gets more bad publicity than any other dessert because they are so often old and nearly inedible. This one is moist, flavorful and insanely good—and I don't say that lightly!

150g (5 oz)	Butter, slightly softened
80g (2.8 oz)	Sugar
80g (2.8 oz)	Dark Brown Sugar, ideally Muscovado
120ml (4 oz)	Milk
3 whole	Eggs
150g (5 oz)	Pastry Flour
25g (0.9 oz)	Molasses (see note below)
1/2 teaspoon	Nutmeg, ground
1/4 teaspoon	Allspice, ground
1/2 teaspoon	Salt
1 1/2 teaspoons	Baking Powder (not baking soda)
1 teaspoon	Orange Zest, freshly grated
1/2 teaspoon	Vanilla Extract
90g (3 oz)	Candied Cherries, red (see note below)
90g (3 oz)	Crushed Pineapple, canned (drained)
45g (1.5 oz)	Raisins, preferably golden
30g (1 oz)	Walnuts, coarsely chopped
30ml (1 oz)	Cognac or Brandy
Copius amounts of Grand Marnier for curing (see recipe)	

CANDIED CHERRIES

These are usually sold in small plastic tubs in the baking section. While they are famously synthetic tasting on their own, ignore that here.

MOLASSES

Ideally you should substitute *Almost Rum* brand syrup for the molasses if you live in the U.S. Unfortunately international shipping on this product from the company is insanely expensive ($100 per bottle!) However, I did acquire mine in Italy, so perhaps you can find it somewhere in Europe.

PROCEDURE

1. Heat the cognac in a small sauce pan until vapors rise. Turn the heat of and add the raisins and candied cherries. Let this stand while you continue.

2. Equip a stand mixer with the paddle attachment. Put the butter, sugar and dark brown sugar into the bowl and beat to cream the mixture.

3. Add the eggs, molasses, milk, nutmeg, allspice, vanilla extract, orange zest and salt. Change to the whisk attachment. Run the machine slowly at first, then faster to make a smooth mixture.

4. Stop the mixer. Add the pastry flour and the baking powder. Run slowly at first, stopping to scrape down the sides until a batter is formed.

5. In a separate bowl combine the crushed pineapple (pressed to remove liquid) and walnuts with the soaked raisins and candied cherries in the cognac. Mix in a teaspoon of flour to make it slightly more goopy.

6. Butter and flour a 10x25cm (4x10 inch) loaf pan. Scrape in the batter from the mixer bowl. Then divide out the fruit mixture over the top evenly with your fingers. Press the fruit down just a little. When it gets warm in the oven, the fruit will sink into the mixture. If you just blended it in, then the fruit would all end up on the bottom as it cooks.

7. Bake at 175°C (350°F) for 60 minutes.

8. Cool on a rack for about 15 minutes before turning it out. Then let it cool to room temperature. This is important. Don't move it. Be patient!

9. Sprinkle with Grand Marnier then wrap it up in cheesecloth. Add more Grand Marnier on the cheesecloth. Wrap up in a zip-lock bag. Refrigerate.

10. Every 3-5 days open it up and sprinkle a little more Grand Marnier to soak into the cheesecloth, then rewrap and return to the refrigerator. You can keep doing this as long as you care to, but I suggest repeating this at least five times. It will only improve with age. I once had a fruitcake like this that I kept adding Grand Marnier to for over two years!

Spice Pastes

Flavors are transported more efficiently when they are in a liquid medium, especially oil or fat. Spice pastes are a common trick in many restaurant kitchens as a way to speed the service of dishes with complex flavors because almost all of the work is done ahead of time and most spice pastes can be kept for days in a refrigerator without the risk of spoilage.

GEORGIAN ADJIKA SPICE PASTE

This is a product that most Russians buy in jars these days, but it's rarely seen in stores elsewhere. This is better than the factory made stuff.

60g (2 oz)	Red Serrano Chilies, fresh (stems removed)
50g (1.75 oz)	Walnuts, shelled
40g (1.4 oz)	Green Apple, peeled and sliced
25g (0.9 oz)	Garlic cloves, chopped coarsely
25g (0.9 oz)	Red Bell Pepper, chopped
30ml (1 oz)	Vegetable Oil, or ideally, unfiltered sunflower Oil
1 teaspoon	Coriander Seeds, whole
1 teaspoon	Fennel Seeds, whole (or better, Khmeli-Sunelii)
3-4 whole	Dried Red Chilies, crumbled (see notes below)
1/2 pod	Star Anise
1 teaspoon	Fenugreek seeds, whole
1 teaspoon	Oregano, dried
1/2 teaspoon	Thyme, dried
1/2 teaspoon	Black Peppercorns, whole
1/2 teaspoon	Coarse Salt
2 teaspoons	Cilantro Leaf, dried (available in bottles)
1 teaspoon	Paprika
1 teaspoon	Lemon Zest, grated
1/2 teaspoon	Muscovado Sugar, or Dark Brown Sugar
50ml (1.75 oz)	White Wine Vinegar (or champagne vinegar)

DRIED CHILIES

Ideally you want to use the dried red serrano chilies from Volume 1 of my cookbook series. You can substitute dried Arbol chilies if you need to.

PROCEDURE

1. Toast the walnuts in a hot pan, being careful not to burn them. Then cool at room temperature before grinding in a food processor. Set aside.

2. Combine the apple, garlic cloves, red bell pepper and fresh chilies in a food processor and grind to small pieces. Heat the vegetable oil in a nonstick skillet and fry this mixture on a medium-low heat until the garlic aroma is gone (roughly 6 minutes). Then set aside.

3. Toast the coriander seeds, fennel seeds, dried red chilies and star anise in a hot pan. The moment that it smolders, remove the contents to a dish to cool.

4. Combine the toasted spices from Step #3 with the fenugreek (or Khmeli-Sunelii), oregano, thyme, black peppercorns and coarse salt. Grind in an electric spice mill to a powder. Take care that the dried serrano chili is completely ground up as well. It will probably need to be broken up by hand first.

5. Put the ground toasted walnuts from Step #1 and the ground spices from Step #3 into the cup of a stick blender. Add the cooked vegetable contents from Step #2 along with the dried cilantro leaves, paprika, grated lemon zest, muscovado sugar and white wine vinegar. Blend to a paste. Stop to scrape down the sides when necessary and continue until it is as homogenous as possible. This may take a few minutes. Be patient.

6. Bottle and refrigerate. The vinegar aroma will subside after a fewdays because the acetic acid will react with other ingredients. Let it remain in the refrigerator for at least 24 hours before using, and 3 days ideally.

Although this will keep in the refrigerator for a long time without actually spoiling, the flavor will gradually fade as it ages, so it is best used within a week or two.

BLACK TRUFFLE MEAT PASTE

Based on one of the kitchen preparations used by 3 Michelin Star chef, David Bouley. This is especially well suited to roast lamb and sous vide cooking of beef, veal and other meats. See the recipes on pages 107 and 108 for sample applications.

60g (2 oz)	Black Olives, pitted (drained well)
60g (2 oz)	White Miso Paste
60ml (2 oz)	White Wine, dry
30ml (1 oz)	Black Truffle Oil (see notes below)
2 1/2 teaspoons	Thyme leaves, fresh (or 1 t. dried)
1 teaspoon	Black Peppercorns, whole
1/2 teaspoon	Coriander Seeds, whole
1/2 teaspoon	Sumac

NOTES ON INGREDIENTS

Note that all of the saltiness comes from the miso paste, but not all miso is equally salty. The best quality miso is much less salty, so if you have the good fortune of using a very high quality product, you may need to add salt to this. Yellow Miso may be substituted with good results, too.

The truffle oil used by top chefs is actual black truffle trimmings blended with olive oil in a Vitamix. Be aware that cheap "black truffle" oils are just vegetable oil with chemical flavorings (see page 231).

PROCEDURE

1. Put the black peppercorns, thyme, coriander seeds and sumac into an electric spice mill. Grind to a powder.

2. Put the black olives, miso paste, white wine and black truffle oil into the cup of a stick blender. Add the ground spices from Step 1. Purée.

3. Store in a jar in the refrigerator for up to a week.

WHITE TRUFFLE FRICASSEE PASTE

This works especially well as a marinade on chicken and guinea fowl or rabbit. See the recipe on page 110 for an example. I don't recommend using this with sous vide cooking because it will overpower the meat's flavor and also produce a bad texture on the surface. It should be regarded only as a cold marinade. Also, don't combine this with garlic in any way. Garlic and white truffles are a forbidden combination in classic French cuisine.

90g (3.2 oz)	Mushrooms, coarsely chopped
50g (1.75 oz)	Olive Oil, extra-virgin
30ml (1 oz)	White Wine, dry or Dry Vermouth
10g (0.35 oz)	Thyme, fresh (see notes below)
1 teaspoon	White Truffle Butter (see page 230)
1/2 teaspoon	White Pepper, ground
1/2 teaspoon	Lovage, dried (or dried Tarragon)
1/2 teaspoon	Cardamom, ground
1/2 teaspoon	Salt
1/2 teaspoon	MSG (optional)

THE THYME

There are different types of fresh thyme. Some have tough woody branches, while the best kind has very soft stems (easier to find in Europe). If you can't get the soft type, then pick only 6 grams (0.2 oz) of the leaves and discard the tough woody stems. If you absolutely must use dried thyme, then substitute 2 teaspoons of it (not recommended).

PROCEDURE

1. Put all of the ingredients into a blender. Purée.
2. Ideally use immediately. You can store for up to 1 day only.

MASSAMAN CURRY PASTE

This is considerably different from the simplified recipe in the old YouTube video years ago, but it is also much superior in both taste and authenticity. With its staggering list of ingredients, you know why the flavor is so complex. Be sure to add the ingredients one at a time in sequential order so that you don't accidentally leave something out. Don't forget the water in Step #7, too!

65g (2.3 oz)	Carrot, peeled and chopped coarsely
1 1/2 teaspoons	Coarse Salt
2-3 whole	Kaffir Lime Leaves, dry
1 teaspoon	Coriander Seeds, whole
1/2 teaspoon	Cumin Seeds, whole
1/2 teaspoon	White Peppercorns, whole
1/4 teaspoon	Fenugreek Seeds, whole
1/4 teaspoon	Cardamom, ground
60g (2.1 oz)	Peanut Butter, smooth and unsweetened
60g (2.1 oz)	Shallots, peeled and chopped
50g (1.75 oz)	Coconut Milk, canned
25g (0.9 oz)	Garlic Cloves, chopped
15g (0.5 oz)	Thai Chilies, stems removed and chopped
15g (0.5 oz)	Ginger, peeled and chopped finely
15g (0.5 oz)	Muscovado or Dark Brown Sugar
1 Tablespoon	Maggi Seasoning (liquid)
10g (0.35 oz)	Coriander Roots & Stems, washed and chopped
10g (0.35 oz)	Lemongrass (see notes below)
1/2 teaspoon	Shrimp Paste
1/2 teaspoon	Turmeric, ground
1/2 teaspoon	Cinnamon, ground
1/2 teaspoon	Mace, ground (or substitute nutmeg)
1/4 teaspoon	Cloves, ground (the spice, not garlic)

LEMONGRASS

Peel the lemongrass and discard the tough outer layers. There will only be a small amount of soft, tender and useable plant in each stalk. Then mince the tender part because it is too fibrous to rely on the food processor to make smooth.

PROCEDURE

1. Simmer the carrot chunks in lightly salted water until they are tender but not mushy. This will take 20 minutes or more depending on the exact size of the carrots and the heat setting.

2. Remove and cool the carrots at room temperature. Then place them in a food processor with the coarse salt. Also crumble the kaffir lime leaves in, discarding any tough stems. Grind well.

3. Spread the mixture out on a silicone mat on a baking sheet. Roast at 180°C (355°F) for 25 minutes.

4. Stir the mixture around to prevent burning at the edges and then return it to the oven for 10 more minutes.

5. Allow this to cool to room temperature.

6. Put this into an electric spice mill (don't worry if it is a little damp still because the spices it will be ground with will absorb the moisture). Add in the coriander seeds, cumin seeds, white peppercorns and ground cardamom. Grind until it is a homogeneous powder.

7. Transfer this into a food processor and add all of the rest of the ingredients plus 30ml (1 oz) of water. Grind to a paste.

This also makes an outstanding addition to many soups and stews in small amounts.

The exact history of Massaman Curry is not known. It is one of the earliest true fusion dishes with roots in Thailand, Malaysia, India and Iran (which was known as Persia back then). There is no *one* true recipe and locals are opinionated about how spicy it should be and things like whether to include tomatoes, whether to use ginger or galangal, etc. This recipe has been received very favorably from natives of all four regions as well as westerners, although some do think it should be hotter. Most don't, but you can add more chilies.

BASE GANEP

This is the most common spice used in Balinese cooking. Almost every savory dish begins with this as the base, although there are many slightly different versions. This recipe is a bit more complex than some, but it came from cooking in Bali years ago.

25g (0.9 oz)	Macadamia Nut Oil or Vegetable Oil
25g (0.9 oz)	Candlenuts or Macadamia Nuts (see next page)
3-5 whole	Red Serrano Chili Peppers, chopped (no stems)
1 stalk	Lemongrass
1 Tablespoon	Palm Sugar, or substittute Muscovado
50g (1.75 oz)	Shallots, peeled and coarsely chopped
20g (0.7 oz)	Ginger, peeled and chopped
10g (035 oz)	Coriander stems and roots, washed and chopped
50g (1.75 oz)	Coconut Cream
15g (0.5 oz)	Garlic cloves, chopped
1/2 teaspoon	Shrimp Paste
1 teaspoon	Coarse Salt
1 teaspoon	Turmeric
1/2 teaspoon	Coriander Seeds
1/2 teaspoon	Cumin Seeds
2 whole	Java Long Peppercorns (see notes below)
1/4 teaspoon	Nutmeg, ground
2 whole	Daun Salem leaves (see notes below)
1/4 teaspoon	Cinnamon (if Daun Salem is not used)

DAUN SALEM

Otherwise known as Indonesian Bay Leaf. The aroma and flavor are quite different from Laurel (California Bay) or the Mediterranean Bay grown mostly in Turkey. To complicate matters further, there is also Indian Bay, which is even more like cinnamon in its aroma. Purists object to substituting western bay leaves for either Daun Salem or Indian Bay because the aroma is different. However, the chemistry is similar and neither one acts directly, as explained in great detail in Volume 3 of this series. So, if you can't obtain Daun Salem, then the best substitution you can make is bay leaves plus add a little cinnamon.

NOTES ON OTHER INGREDIENTS

Candlenuts are the preferred authentic ingredient, but they are hard to find in much of the world and are fairly similar to Macadamia nuts.

Java Long Pepper (peppercorns) has an unusual aroma and taste, and these can also be hard to find. Substitute 1/2 teaspoon black peppercorns.

PROCEDURE

1. Put the first two ingredients (the oil and the nuts) into a small food processor and grind up for about 30 seconds. There may be some small chips of the nuts left, but they will break up later.

2. Grind up the coriander seeds, cumin seeds, Java long pepper and coarse salt in an electric spice mill. Grind to a powder, then rub through a sieve. Discard any solids that won't pass through the sieve.

2. Trim the outer tough membrane of the lemongrass away, then slice it up finely. Put this into a blender along with all of the other ingredients except the Daun Salem (or bay leaves if you are using those). Also add the nuts and the oil from that in Step #1 and spices from Step #2. Purée.

2. Heat a nonstick skillet on medium. When it gets warm, fry the puréed spice paste and the Daun Salem leaves (or bay). Fry the mixture gently. You do not want to caramelize it with high heat. Stir almost constantly for 6-7 minutes. Lower the heat if needed.

4. Turn the heat off and continue stirring, cooking with the residual heat in the pan for another 2-3 minutes.

5. Remove the Daun Salem leaves (or bay leaves) and transfer to a dish to cool at room temperature. Then store in the refrigerator. It will not spoil for a long time, but it will gradually lose flavor. You can freeze it to extend it's life. Otherwise it is best used within a week.

THAI RED CURRY PASTE

Most recipes tell you to use the stuff you buy in a jar, but that's not cooking—and it isn't nearly as flavorful as this is.

40g (about 4)	Red Serrano Chilies, fresh
1 Tablespoon	Vegetable Oil
40g (1.4 oz)	Garlic cloves, coarsely chopped
20g (0.7 oz)	Galangal, peeled and minced
1 Tablespoon	Nam Pla (Thai fish sauce)
1 1/2 teaspoons	Kashmiri Mirch (ground red chilies)
10g (0.35 oz)	Lemongrass, peeled and minced
10g (0.35 oz)	Red Thai Chilies, stems removed
10g (0.35 oz)	Coriander Roots (from fresh cilantro)
1 teaspoon	Shrimp Paste
1 teaspoon	Lime Zest, ideally from Kaffir Lime
2 teaspoons	White Pepper, ground
1 teaspoon	Cumin, ground
1/2 teaspoon	Coriander Seed, ground
45g (1.5 oz)	Peanut Oil
15ml (0.5 oz)	Lime Juice, fresh

PROCEDURE

1. Slice the fresh red serrano chilies lengthwise. Scrape out the seeds and membranes a bit if you want to limit the heat some.

2. Heat the vegetable oil in a small skillet and place the chilies in it, cut-side down. Leave them there on a medium-low heat until they are quite brown on the cut side. Do not turn them over. Cook only that side.

3. When cooled to room temperature, chop coarsely and put in a food processor. Add all of the rest of the ingredients except the peanut oil and lime juice. Grind as much as possible, frequently scraping down the sides.

4. Transfer the contents to a blender, or to a stick blender cup. Add the lime juice and peanut oil. Purée vigorously. You want this smooth.

5. Store in a glass jar in the refrigerator. This will keep for several weeks, but it will gradually lose its potency.

RED CURRY POWDER

There are hundreds of different curry powders on the market and in recipes. Most of them are yellow due to the turmeric and/or curry powder (which also gets its color from turmeric). Red curry powders are frequently associated with Thai cooking if you try to search online. This is because true Indian cookery is seldom seen on the Internet. Authentic Indian curries often contain no turmeric.

1 1/2 teaspoons	Cumin Seeds
1 teaspoon	Coriander Seeds
1/2 pod	Star Anise
4 whole	Allspice
2.5cm (1 inch)	Cinnamon Stick
3/4 teaspoon	Coarse Salt
1/4 teaspoon	Mustard Seeds
1 teaspoon	Muscovado Sugar
1 teaspoon	Paprika
1 teaspoon	Kashmiri Mirch (an Indian chili powder)
1/2 teaspoon	Ginger, dried powder

PROCEDURE

1. Combine the cumin seeds, coriander seeds, star anise, allspice, cinnamon stick, coarse salt and mustard seeds into a small dish.

2 Heat a metal pan (do <u>not</u> use a nonstick pan) on a high heat. When it is hot, add the mixture from #1 (above).

3. As soon as the mustard seeds begin to vigorously pop, pour the contents of the pan back into the dish and leave to cool for a few minutes.

4. Add these toasted spices into an electric spice mill along with the rest of the ingredients. Grind to a powder.

5. Bottle and store as a powder for up to a month. **Mix with oil to make a paste only as needed.** See page 154 for an example.

A COLLECTION OF COLD SAUCES THAT CAN DOUBLE AS SALAD DRESSINGS

All of these use Ultra Tex 8 (see page 229) to thicken them into commercial style packaged sauces. Leave this ingredient out to use them as salad dressings or as thin sauces. Note: greater thickening power is obtained from whisking Ultra Tex 8 in instead of blending.

TARTARE SAUCE

This is great as a dressing on seafood salads, or with the Ultra Tex 8, this is an elegant topping to steamed asparagus in the style of Sauce Gribiche, only better. Top with fresh dill or parsley.

200g (7 oz)	Mayonnaise
45g (1.5 oz)	Sweet Pickles
15g (0.5 oz)	Shallots
15ml (0.5 oz)	Lemon Juice, strained
15ml (0.5 oz)	Champagne Vinegar, or white wine vinegar
1 Tablespoon	Parsley, freshly minced
10g (0.3 oz)	Sugar
1 teaspoon	Dijon Mustard
3/4 teaspoon	White Pepper, ground
3/4 teaspoon	Salt
1 1/2 teaspoons	Ultra Tex 8 (optional)

PROCEDURE

1. Combine all ingredients in a blender. Refrigerate before use. It will thicken as it cools.

CATALONIAN SAUCE

This is primarily suited to fish and vegetables. In Catalonia there is a fish and tomato soup that has a sauce like this added as a topping. Barcelona is close to Marseille, and the French influence is clear. Be sure to use a quality olive oil for this and not the type you would be more likely to cook with. The reason for passing this through a regular sieve before the chionis is that it will save you a lot of time because the fine mesh will get clogged quickly otherwise.

120g (4 oz)	Fennel
120g (4 oz)	Catalonian Olive Oil, extra-virgin
50g (1.75 oz)	Red Onion
45ml (1.5 oz)	Lime Juice
30g (1 oz)	Mayonnaise
2 Tablespoons	Capers, ideally salt-packed
1 teaspoon	Turmeric
1 teaspoon	Salt
1 teaspoon	Tarragon, dried
1 teaspoon	Sugar
1 teaspoon	Absinthe or Pernod (don't leave this out)
1/2 teaspoon	Mint, dried (or 1 1/2 teaspoons fresh)
1/2 teaspoon	MSG
1 teaspoon	Ultra Tex 8 (optional)

PROCEDURE

1. Trim the root end of the fennel off. You can include some of the stem and fronds, but use mostly the bulb.

2. Soak the capers in water for 2-3 minutes and then rinse well.

3. Add all of the ingredients to a blender. Purée.

4. Pass through an ordinary sieve. Discard solids that wouldn't pass.

5. Pass through a chinois (China cap) or the finest mesh of a tamis. Once again discard solids that would not pass. Store in the refrigerator.

TANGY INDONESIAN

Great with barbecued shrimp. This can also be used as a BBQ glaze for pork (leave out the Ultra Tex 8 in that case). Ketjap-Manis (also called Kecap manis) is Indonesian sweet soy sauce, and is a fundamental ingredient in their cuisine. It can be hard to find in some countries, so you can substitute a mixture of soy sauce, dark brown sugar and molasses in the ratio of 6:8:1, respectively. This is then heated with a slurry of corn starch to dissolve the sugar and thicken the mixture into a viscous syrup. The result is good, but not quite the same thing. Incidentally, the word Ketjap is adapted from the Chinese word for sauce, which is where the western word ketchup originated, and not the other way around as many assume.

120g (4 oz)	Ketjap-Manis (see note below)
45ml (1.5 oz)	Rice Vinegar
30g (1 oz)	Shallots
30g (1 oz)	Red Serrano Chilies, stems removed
30ml (1 oz)	Lime Juice
15g (0.5 oz)	Sugar
1 Tablespoon	Tomato Paste, Italian tube type
1 stalk	Lemongrass, tender inner part only
2 cloves	Garlic
1 teaspoon	White Pepper, ground
3/4 teaspoon	Salt
1/4 teaspoon	Liquid Smoke
1/2 teaspoon	Ultra Tex 8 (optional)

PROCEDURE

1. Combine all ingredients except Ultra Tex 8 in a blender. Purée.

2. Rub through a tamis with the second finest mesh. Discard solids, which will mostly be chili skins, seeds and the tougher fibers of the lemongrass.

3. Whisk in the Ultra Tex 8 if you are using it. Refrigerate at least overnight before use so the flavors can blend.

TACO HELL

An ideal choice for a Tex-Mex taco salad with lettuce, tortilla chips, cheddar cheese and avocado. That is, if you are not too sensitive to spicy food—then you can regard this as a hot sauce for tacos, and think back to the days when that one particular fast food chain still had a sauce that was actually spicy, because that is very much the flavor of this. Note that dried cilantro means the leaf, and not ground coriander seed.

120g (4 oz)	Tomatoes, whole canned Italian
45g (1.5 oz)	Jalapeño Chilies, stems removed
25g (0.9 oz)	Shallots
25ml (0.9 oz)	Red Wine Vinegar
1-2	Garlic Cloves (depending on size)
1/2 teaspoon	Cilantro, dried (or 2 teaspoons fresh)
1 teaspoon	Cumin, ground
1 teaspoon	Salt
1 teaspoon	Sugar
3/4 teaspoon	MSG
1/2 teaspoon	Citric Acid (or 2 teaspoons lime juice)
1/2 teaspoon	Ultra Tex 8 (optional)
1/8 teaspoon	Black Pepper, finely ground
1/8 to 1/4 teaspoon	Red Food Color, powdered

PROCEDURE

1. Pour the canned tomatoes into a bowl. Lift the tomatoes themselves into a container on a scale, leaving most of the juice behind. You can use the juice and other tomatoes for another recipe. You don't need it here.

2. Add the tomatoes and all of the other ingredients (including the chili's seeds and membranes) into a blender. Purée.

3. Rub through a sieve. Discard solids that would not pass. Store in the refrigerator. The heat will diminish some over several days.

YUZU MAYO

A successful sushi restaurant in Los Angeles created a signature lobster roll flavored with a sauce identical to this one. To reproduce their roll, prepare a nori-wrapped cut roll with cold previously cooked lobster and a little of this sauce inside. After cutting the lobster roll, stand up the pieces and put a dollop of the sauce mixture on top of each. Use a blowtorch to cook the mixture, which changes the flavor. Then add a little tobiko and a little lemon juice. The same procedure can be used with some whitefish with good results too, too. Yuzu juice can usually be found in Asian grocery stores. Be sure to get 100% Yuzu. Horseradish is preferred to wasabi in this case because of the color. This should be nearly white. It can be used as a dipping sauce for fish or as a topping on a broth with soba (Japanese buckwheat noodles).

150g (5.3 oz)	Mayonnaise, ideally Kewpie
30g (1 oz)	White Miso Paste
25ml (0.9 oz)	Sake (Japanese rice wine)
2 teaspoons	Yuzu Juice
1	Egg Yolk
1 Tablespoon	Soy Sauce
1 Tablespoon	Rice Wine Vinegar
2 teaspoons	Horseradish, prepared (or Wasabi)
1 1/2 teaspoons	Sugar
1 1/2 teaspoon	Ginger, dry ground
1 1/2 teaspoons	Ultra Tex 8

PROCEDURE

1. Combine all ingredients except the Ultra Tex 8 in a blender. Purée.
2. Whisk in the Ultra Tex 8. Refrigerate overnight before using. It will thicken as it cools.

MOROCCAN SAUCE

Mushrooms are a popular ingredient in Moroccan cuisine. A vegetarian dish of mushrooms and couscous is elevated by this sauce. It is also an exotic dipping sauce or salad dressing.

70g (2.5 oz)	Mushrooms, ideally Cremini
30g (1 oz)	Onion, sliced
1 Tablespoon	Vegetable Oil
50ml (1.75 oz)	Champagne, or dry white wine
2 cloves	Garlic, coarsely chopped
1/4 teaspoon	Black Pepper, ground
1/4 teaspoon	Salt
1 teaspoon	Ras el Hanout
15ml (0.5 oz)	Lemon Juice
60g (2 oz)	Mayonnaise
1 teaspoon	Sugar
1 teaspoon	MSG
1/2 teaspoon	Maggi Seasoning (liquid)
1/4 teaspoon	Ultra Tex 8 (optional)

PROCEDURE

1. Cut the mushrooms into large slices. Heat the oil in a nonstick pan and fry the mushrooms for 2 minutes.

2. Add the onion slices and continue frying until the onions are browning.

3. Add the champagne, the garlic and the salt and pepper. Reduce the heat. Cook for 3 minutes.

4. Add the Ras el Hanout. Stir and cook until the mixture is thick.

5. Turn off the heat and let cool 10 minutes.

6. Add the lemon juice and scrape the contents into a blender, or the cup for a stick blender. Add the mayonnaise, sugar, MSG and Maggi seasoning. Purée.

7. Pass through a sieve. Discard solids that wouldn't pass through.

2. Whisk in the Ultra Tex 8. Refrigerate. It will thicken some as it cools.

CREAMY ITALIAN

This is a classic salad dressing flavor from decades ago that has gradually eroded into factory-made and artificially flavored bottles loaded with enough preservatives that the shelf life is practically infinite. This is how it was made in the best restaurants long ago. This works well as a sauce on grilled chicken over pasta, too! The Ultra Tex 8 is only needed if you want to make this into a thick dipping sauce.

60g (2 oz)	Cherry Tomatoes, fresh
60g (2 oz)	Olive Oil, good quality Italian extra-virgin
30ml (1 oz)	Lemon Juice
25ml (0.9 oz)	Cream
15g (0.5 oz)	Parmigiano-Reggiano, grated
15g (0.5 oz)	Sugar
10g (0.3 oz)	Basil Leaves, fresh
3g (0.1 oz)	Parsley Leaves, fresh
1 Tablespoon	Marjoram, fresh (or 1/2 teaspoon dried)
7.5g (0.25 oz)	Garlic cloves, coarsely chopped
1	Egg Yolk
1 teaspoon	Red Wine Vinegar
1/2 teaspoon	Salt
1/4 teaspoon	Black Pepper, ground
1/2 teaspoon	Ultra Tex 8 (optional)

PROCEDURE

1. Combine all of the ingredients except the olive oil, cream and the Ultra Tex 8 into a blender and purée. A Vitamix blender is ideal here. An ordinary blender or stick blender will not be able to make it perfectly smooth.

2. Add the olive oil and cream. Blend to emulsify.

3. Whisk in the Ultra Tex 8 if you are using it.

4. Store refrigerated. Best used within 2 days.

Vodka Chili Elixir
and Seafood Cocktail Sauce

The use of alcohol, such as wine, to extract flavors that are not very soluble in pure water is an ancient technique going back thousands of years, but the specific combination of vodka and red chilies is not like anything else you have ever tried.

100g (3.5 oz)	Red Chilies, coarsely chopped (see note below)
60ml (2.1 oz)	Rice Wine Vinegar, red type if possible
25g (0.9 oz)	Garlic cloves, peeled and coarsely chopped
45ml (1.5 oz)	Vodka (in all - see recipe)
30g (1 oz)	Sugar
1 teaspoon	Shichi-mi Tōgarashi (七味唐辛子)
3/4 teaspoon	Salt
100ml (3.5 oz)	Water, ideally Perrier mineral water

RED CHILIES

Ideally you want to use ripe (red) New Mexico or Hatch chilies for this. You can substitute other varieties, but the flavor and amount of heat will vary accordingly, of course. Do not use Jalapeño or Thai chilies because their flavor profiles are incompatible.

PROCEDURE

1. Heat a stainless steel pan until very hot. Do not use nonstick (the coating will be damaged and toxic fumes will be released) and do not use cast iron (the surface will leach iron salts into the sauce from a chemical reaction) or aluminum (again, a reactive pan can not be used on acidic ingredients at a high temperature). Only stainless steel will do.

2. Add the chopped red chilies to the pan with no oil or fat. Roast them until there is some blackening (and acrid fumes galore!) About 4 minutes.

4. Leave them in the pan, but turn the heat off. Stir for 2 more minutes.

5. Add the water. Continue stirring until the steam has subsided.

6. Transfer to the cup of a stick blender. Add 30ml (1 oz) of the vodka as well as the sugar, salt, chopped garlic, Shichi-mi Tōgarashi (Japanese mixed pepper blend) and vinegar. Purée.

7. Rinse out the same pan previously used and add the puréed contents of the stick blender cup to the pan. Bring to a simmer on a medium heat.

8. Maintain at a simmer with occasional stirring for about 8 minutes until it has thickened noticeably.

9. Pass this through a food mill using the fine plate. You can not use a sieve for this and get good results.

10. Add the rest of the vodka to the sauce that passed through the mill. If you did everything right, you should have around 150 grams (5.3 oz). This can be kept in a closed bottle in the refrigerator for at least a month. Ideally you should leave it rest in the refrigerator for at least a day before you use it. The flavor will be better. It won't spoil, but it does gradually get weaker after weeks of storage.

11. To use this as a unique hot sauce directly (rather than an ingredient in cooking), put some in a squeeze bottle and add a little more vinegar.

SPICY SEAFOOD COCKTAIL SAUCE

This is especially well suited to shrimp cocktails. Oysters or breaded and deep fried scallops are also beautiful with this.

85g (3 oz)	Ketchup
25g (0.9 oz)	Vodka Chili Elixir
15g (0.5 oz)	Horseradish, prepared cream style
1 teaspoon	Lemon Juice, fresh
1/4 teaspoon	Ultra Tex 8 (optional)

Simply whisk all of the ingredients together and refrigerate.

NASTOYKAS

Nastoyka is vodka that has been infused with berries, fruits, spices, seeds, herbs, chili peppers, or some combination of those things. The principle difference between Nastoyka and the infused vodkas made in other nations is that the flavoring agents are generally allowed to steep for no more than 48 hours, and often less than that. This means that only the most volatile components of the flavoring are released into the vodka, giving a brighter and generally more natural and floral flavor.

In the past, making Nastoyka was a common hobby for grandfathers in Russian villages. Annual competitions were held in the same spirit as a county fair is in the United States. These days there are many different commercial nastoykas sold in Russian stores and making your own is likely to receive chuckles because it is now regarded about the same as making moonshine, even though there is no distillation involved.

Previously there was a recipe for a Lingonberry Nastoyka (Volume 1, page 142), Horseradish Nastoyka (Volume 2, page 209) and Coriander Nastoyka (Volume 3, page 254), but nastoykas can be even more complex in the same way that Coca-Cola has many ingredients. This craft that has mostly died out. Commercial nastoykas are usually simple single flavors. The reason is that consumers won't buy something with an unfamiliar flavor. Such nastoykas worked fine in rural villages where neighbors sample each other's concoctions, but that's not what mass marketing is all about. Recently a Russian company has gotten around this obstacle with two complex mixtures. One is a simulation of rum and the other of whiskey.

They are both infused vodkas and labeled as nastoykas in the fine print. You can see this in the photo here as the first word just under the drawing of the captain, "НАСТОЙКА" (in Cyrillic).

So why would someone buy a simulation of rum or whiskey instead of the real thing? Vodka is cheap in Russia, but other liquors are usually expensive. So a product that tastes like rum but is priced only slightly more than vodka has a place in the market.

In case you are wondering why the rest of the label is in English, that's to give the impression that it is imported and of better quality. These simulations are actually pretty good—but only if you don't taste them side by side with the real thing. The way to enjoy such nastoykas is to drink them on their own and not think of them as a substitution. They are typically chilled in the freezer along with cold shotglasses to serve them in straight up. In that same spirit (no pun intended), the following nastoyka recipe was met with admiration in Russia, jokingly being complimented as making me an honorary village grandfather.

GIN NASTOYKA

Aside from being very drinkable directly, you can also use it to "doctor" commercial gins, as explained in my book, Cocktails of the South Pacific, by adding a little of this to commercial gin.

400ml (14 oz)	Vodka
10 whole	Marjoram leaves, fresh
2 whole	Sage leaves, fresh
1 1/2 teaspoons	Sugar
1 stalk	Lemongrass, minced (inner part only)
1/4 teaspoon	Coriander Seeds, whole
1/4 teaspoon	Absinthe, or substitute Pernod
10 whole	White Peppercorns, lightly crushed
8 whole	Juniper Berries, crushed
1/4 teaspoon	Sichuan Peppercorns
2 drops	Orange Oil (see page 217)
2 drops	Lemon Oil (see page 217)

PROCEDURE

1. Combine all of the ingredients in a wide-mouth jar with a lid. Allow the mixture to steep for 10 minutes only, shaking the jar several times.

2. Strain off half of the solution to a stoppered bottle. Make sure all of the solids go back into the original jar . Allow to steep for another 2 hours.

3. Strain again into a clean bottle. Now pour the previously strained liquid (the portion you strained after 10 minutes) over the solids left behind in the sieve. Combine the two clear solutions and discard the solids from the sieve. You can pass this through a "jelly bag" to make it more clear, if desired. Store in the freezer along with shotglasses. Serve with a small wedge of lemon or lime.

ORANGE SYRUP & NASTOYKA

This is an orange syrup primarily for cocktails, but also useful in plating desserts.

1 large	Orange
300g (10 oz)	Sugar, white granulated
6 drops	Orange Oil (see page 217)

PROCEDURE

1. Peel the outermost layer of the orange using a vegetable peeler. Put this into a saucepan.

2. Juice the orange. Put the saucepan on a scale and then add the juice. Add enough water to bring up the total weight to 300 grams (10.5 oz).

3. Add 300 grams (10.5 oz) of sugar to the pan. Heat on a medium flame to bring to a slow simmer for 15 minutes.

4. Turn off the heat and allow it to steep for another 15 minutes before pouring it through a fine mesh sieve. Add the orange oil. This is now your orange syrup.

To make it into the nastoyka, follow the next steps:

1. You don't need to use all of the syrup for this. You can use some as nastoyka and some as regular syrup, such as you will need for the *Medicinal Purposes* cocktail (page 222). For each 100ml (3.5 oz) of orange syrup add 220ml (7.75 oz) vodka plus 1/2 teaspoon of whole cloves (the spice), 1/2 teaspoon coriander seeds and 1/2 teaspoon of fenugreek seeds. Allow it to steep for 1 to 2 days. Shake occasionally.

2. Strain and discard the solids. This is an Orange Nastoyka. Store in the freezer. Serve very cold in chilled shotglasses or snifters. This is like a lovely complex liqueur.

Cocktails

As of the time of this writing, I am working on a sequel to my *Cocktails of the South Pacific and Beyond*. These drinks were all developed after the publication of my last cocktail book. There are no duplicate recipes.

Some of the recipes in this volume make use of citrus oils. A convenient set of three (lemon, lime and orange) produced by Boyajian rather inexpensively and available on Amazon. Other brands are fine. These are extremely potent. Use only a few drops!

THE TASTE OF CAPTAIN'S RUM NASTOYKA

For those wondering what the Russian *Captain's Rum Nastoyka* (page 213) tastes like, this is very similar. Multiply the ingredients to scale it up, naturally. I realize some might consider adding the Austrian Stroh "rum" to this is cheating, but Stroh is a thing all by itself with very little in common with any other actual rum. By the way, avoid Stroh 54, which tastes like gasoline and hairspray.

90ml (3 oz)	Vodka
25ml (0.9 oz)	Lemon Juice
20ml (0.7 oz)	Creme de Cassis, Merlet
10ml (0.3 oz)	Stroh 60
1/2 teaspoon	Amaro Montenegro

Combine all ingredients. Put in the freezer until cold along with shotglasses to chill for serving. This is surprisingly good, but it isn't *really* rum, of course (unless you don't know what rum tastes like).

THE STAGGERING DEAD

This was actually created before *The Walking Dead* series. Loosely based on the classic *Zombie,* this is a great modern version and higher octane than you would likely find in most licensed bars.

60ml (2 oz)	Dark Rum, ideally Havana Club *7 Year*
15ml (1/2 oz)	Grand Marnier
22.5ml (3/4 oz)	Pineapple Juice
15ml (1/2 oz)	Lemon Juice, fresh
7.5ml (1/4 oz)	Orange Juice, fresh
7.5ml (1/4 oz)	Passion Fruit Liqueur, Marie Brizard
1 teaspoon	Lime Juice, fresh
1/2 teaspoon	Absinthe, or substitute Pernod
1/4 teaspoon	Orange Zest (see directions)

Combine all ingredients except the orange zest. Grate the zest onto a sieve and pour the rest of the ingredients through the zest. Press down to express the liquid. Shake with ice. Pour into a chilled lowball glass (including ice from the shaker). In a shotglass mix:

1 teaspoon	151-proof Rum
3/4 teaspoon	Luxardo Maraschino Cherry Syrup (from jar)

Drizzle over the ice cubes. The syrup should look a bit like blood. Add a straw.

DIAMOND PALACE

I was challenged to invent a cocktail that pairs perfectly with Indian curries. No small challenge, but this one works very well.

60ml (2 oz)	Gin, ideally Finsbury in this unusual case
15ml (1/2 oz)	Drambuie
1 teaspoon	Bigallet *China-China* liqueur
1 teaspoon	Aquavit
1 teaspoon	Lemon Juice, fresh
a pinch	Red Curry Powder (see page 201)

Don't use regular curry powder. Shake with ice. Double strain into a chilled Nick and Nora glass. Add a curl of lime peel.

REINDEER TEARS

Based on a Finnish cocktail, but altered here for a wider audience. Extremely easy to make, which made this a favorite of bartenders.

45ml (1 1/2 oz)	Citron Vodka, Absolut
30ml (1 oz)	Mesimarja, Arctic Brambleberry Liqueur
22.5ml (3/4 oz)	Lemon Juice

Shake gently with cracked ice and dump all into a highball glass. Ideally mix in some lingonberries left over from the nastoyka as in Volume 1, page 142. Add a splash of seltzer water and a straw.

OVER, UNDER, SIDEWAYS, DOWN

Originally called a Yardbird. When one particular customer at the bar ordered these neat, each time peering into the glass from all angles before gulping it down, this new name seemed even better.

30ml (1 oz)	Cognac, Hennessy *VSOP*
15ml (1/2 oz)	Diplomatical *Planas,* white rum (47% ABV)
15ml (1/2 oz)	Heering Cherry Liqueur
15ml (1/2 oz)	Vodka
22.5ml (3/4 oz)	Lemon Juice, fresh
1 teaspoon	Roasted Hazelnut Syrup, 1883 brand
1 teaspoon	Campari
1 dash	Seville Orange Bitters, Scrappy's

Combine all ingredients. Shake with ice and strain into a chilled Nick and Nora glass with ice. Add a spiral curl of lemon for garnish.

Nick and Nora glass.

DARQUIRI

Daiquiris got a bad reputation in the disco era for being snow cones for adults, but the *real* Daiquri from Cuba is quite potent and sour by comparison (see below). This *Darquiri* is made with dark rum. While not as sour as the traditional Daiquiri (because tastes have changed over the decades) this is still very much a real cocktail and not a snowcone. This calls for two Cuban liquors. The Havana Club rum may be substituted with Matusalem *7 Year Solera* without any problem, but there is no substitute for Legendario's *Elixir De Cuba*. Come to the dark side!

60ml (2 oz)	Dark Rum, Havana Club *7 Year*
30ml (1 oz)	Lime Juice, fresh
30ml (1 oz)	Legendario *Elixir De Cuba*
1 teaspoon	Maraschino Liqueur, Luxardo

Shake with ice. Strain into a large goblet with a large cube of ice. Reminisce fondly about Fidel while serving your guests.

FLORIDITA DAIQUIRI

This is the REAL *original* Daiquiri from the Floridita bar in Cuba that Hemingway made famous (although he always requested his less sweet). They put a life size bronze statue of Hemingway sitting at the end of the bar after he died. This recipe is from one of Floridita's original 1939 recipe cards, which I have. The only change I made is the Bacardi rum, because that was back when it was made in Cuba and was still a good product. Don't use Bacardi these days.

60ml (2 oz)	Light Rum, Plantation *3-Star*
15ml (1/2 oz)	Lime Juice, fresh
1 teaspoon	Sugar
1 teaspoon	White Grapefruit Juice, fresh
1 teaspoon	Maraschino Liqueur

Combine all ingredients. Shake with cracked ice and pour all into chilled glass. Add a straw.

(COCKTAIL) BOOK OF THE DEAD

This cocktail was created in Cairo back in the 1970's. It remains a personal favorite for balance and the interesting cooling effect.

45ml (1 1/2 oz)	Vodka
45ml (1 1/2 oz)	Dubonnet
7.5ml (1/4 oz)	Lime Juice
7.5ml (1/4 oz)	Orgeat (or 1 teaspoon Almond Syrup)

Combine in a shaker. Add ice cubes and shake vigorously. Double strain into a chilled rocks glass with a single large ice cube. Add a curl of lime peel as a garnish.

SUMO TAIHO

Taiho was Japan's most famous sumo wrestler. This is quite an expensive cocktail to produce. It is for the rich and famous because of several of the ingredients, not the least of which is the top shelf sake. You can make the cocktail with lesser ingredients, but it won't be the same. Just as the Diamond Palace cocktail (page 218) was the result of me being challenged to pair a cocktail with Indian curries, this cocktail was born of a challenge to create a cocktail for sushi. Normally sushi is consumed with sake, beer or tea. The alien idea of an actual cocktail that would compliment a random selection of nigiri sushi (not sashimi) was indeed a worthy challenge, but this recipe won the prize. Although it is a bit of a cheat using sake and yuzu as primary ingredients, I realize, but still the overall nature of this drink somehow belies its principle ingredients.

60ml (2 oz)	Sake, *Wing of Japan*
15ml (1/2 oz)	Gonzáles Byass *Noé* 30 Year Sherry
7.5ml (1/4 oz)	Yuzu Juice
7.5ml (1/4 oz)	Campari
1/2 teaspoon	Absinthe, Pernod *Recette Traditionnelle*
pinch	Salt

Shake with ice. Strain into a chilled small decorative goblet. Present with a humble bow and then be sure to charge up the wahzoo.

A ROSE BY ANY OTHER NAME

Another sake based cocktail. These have grown in popularity lately with the trend toward lower alcohol cocktails by some people. This bewitching cocktail has the distinct aroma and subtle taste of roses, but in a much more pleasant way than if rose extract were to be added. In fact, there is no actual rose in this; it is the symphony of flavors that give this gentle illusion. This name has been used before for other cocktails (as is so often the case these days), but I don't care because it is the perfect moniker for this creation. This is the perfect cocktail to serve either before or with the Royal Persian Rose Duck (page 118).

60ml (2 oz)	Sake
15ml (1/2 oz)	Lemon Juice, fresh
7.5ml (1/4 oz)	Maraschino Liqueur, Luxardo
5ml (1 teaspoon)	Grand Marnier
2.5ml (1/2 teaspoon)	Apricot Liqueur, Merlet *Lune d'Abricot*

Shake gently with ice. Strain into a chilled martini glass.

MEDICINAL PURPOSES

Long ago it became a folk myth in Hungary that paprika and vodka was a cure for many diseases. Soon paprika chilies were planted across the land. Hungary is still synonymous with paprika to this day. Long ago people would excuse their drinking saying it was for medicinal purposes. I explained this history in my *Cocktails of the South Pacific* book. Zwack is a Hungarian liqueur somewhat like Fernet Branca but much less harsh.

60ml (2 oz)	Vodka or Moonshine
30ml (1 oz)	Orange Syrup (see page 215)
15ml (1/2 oz)	Lemon Juice, fresh
2 teaspoons	Unicum Zwack Liqueur
2.5ml (1/8 oz)	Creme de Banana, ideally Tempus Fugit
1/4 teaspoon	Paprika, ideally Hungarian

Shake gently with ice. Strain into a chilled martini glass.

IVORY COAST HIGHBALL

This cocktail was created at Laava. One night a customer came to the bar asking for something "strong, but not too strong, with something like flowers and mint." I put this together based on another cocktail that used Green Chartreuse in place of the green Creme de Menthe here, and added the splash of seltzer to make it "strong, but not too strong." The guest absolutely adored it. As it turned out he was from the Ivory Coast of Africa where the national colors are orange and green. He assumed that I had recognized his nationality and made this orange and green cocktail just for him. I didn't tell him that is was pure luck, but he returned every single day of his vacation in Finland for another one of "his own" cocktail.

60ml (2 oz)	Gin, Tanqueray
15ml (1/2 oz)	Lemon Juice
15ml (1/2 oz)	Elderflower Liqueur, Giffard *Fleur de Sureau*
15ml (1/2 oz)	Green Creme de Menthe, Bols
5 drops	Orange Oil (see page 217)

Rub the rim of a chilled highball glass with a strip of orange rind. Combine all ingredients in a shaker and stir with ice. Dump entire contents into the highball glass. Add:

30ml (1 oz)	Seltzer Water

Twist the orange peel into a spiral as a garnish. Put a straw in and swirl it around to blend the seltzer with the rest of the mixture.

ONE FOR THE ROAD

This is a cocktail that an old cook would always order at the bar after work, then he'd sip it for two hours before finally going home.

60ml (2 oz)	Cognac, Hennessy, preferably *VSOP*
30ml (1 oz)	D.O.M. Benedictine
15ml (1/2 oz)	Vecchio Amaro del Capo

Shake with ice and strain into a chilled martini glass. Garnish with a wedge of fresh lime so the guest can squeeze it in for themselves.

PRESSURE COOKER TIMES

This table assumes you are using a traditional stove top pressure cooker and not an instant pot (see page 34). While you can find many tables online, the information is often faulty, and these times are only to give you a ballpark idea. Your equipment and specific details of your recipe will factor in. I have only included foods that I consider worthy of using a pressure cooker for.

PROCEDURE

Times are all based on the items being **boiled** in an <u>excess</u> of water, especially for beans. Pressure cookers can also be used to steam foods, but those times vary by recipe. Follow these steps:

1. Bring water to boil. Add salt (unless stated not to). Other seasonings may also be added without affecting the timing.

2. Meats should never be added frozen. Add food to be pressure cooked to pot. Wait for the water to return to a boil.

3. Secure lid and begin counting time. Make sure enough heat is applied to maintain pressure, but not so much as to cause splattering out of the relief valve.

4. When the time is up, turn off the heat. Wait 5 minutes to release pressure. Times may vary some with equipment.

FRUITS AND NUTS		
Apples, peeled and sliced	8-11	Varies with type
Apricots, dried	7	"Stewed Apricots"
Chestnuts, fresh	22	Finish in oven
Citrus Fruits, sliced with peel	15	For cocktail syrups
Cranberries, fresh	8	
Prunes	9	"Stewed Prunes'
Quince	10	

GRAINS		
Barley, flakes	10	
Barley, pearl	20	
Buckwheat, rinsed well	11	Not "instant" type
Bulgur	*7 or 11	* See note below
Kamut, previously soaked	15	
Oats, steel cut	16	
Oats, rolled	11	Not "instant" type
Quinoa	1	** See note below
Rice, brown	14	
Rice, jasmine (for stir fry)	6	*** See note below
Rice, wild	24	
Wheat Berries	45	

NOTES

None of the grains cited are the "instant" type. Those are best prepared following the package directions in a pan on the stove.

* Bulgur is a common ingredient in Russian soups and pirogi. Partially cooking it ahead of time produces better results overall. If you plan to eat it directly, then pressure cook it for the longer time.

** Quinoa only needs a minute at full pressure. The additional 5 minutes without heat applied will finish the cooking smoothly.

*** This is for preparing rice to make stir fried rice the next day. Cool the rice on a tray until it reaches room temperature, then stir in a little soy sauce and put it in a closed container and refrigerate overnight. The next day it will have the right consistency to make Chinese stir fried rice.

MEATS		
Beef Brisket	70	Season very well
Beef Ribs	55	Brown first
Wild Boar Roast (by size)	45-70	Finish on a BBQ
Chicken, bone-in pieces	11	Boiled, fully cooked
Chicken, whole up to 2kg	21	Boiled for soups
Duck Legs, bone-in	55	Brown first
Duck, whole up to 2kg	70	Boiled for soups
Elk Roast	30	Finish in oven
Goat Roast	20	Finish in sauce
Goose trimmings and bones	30	For stock or broth
Lamb Leg scraps or Shank	45	For stock or broth
Mutton Rack, with bones	60	Brown fat first
Pork, ham hock	45	
Pork, leg or shank	42	
Pork Stock, with bones	47	Brown first
Quail Stock, bones / scraps	11	Brown first
Rabbit, sectioned bone-in	15	Finish in sauce
Tripe	16	Finish in sauce
Turkey Legs, bone-in	50-70	Depends on size
Turkey Wings, browned first	35	For stock or broth
Veal Tongue	45	More time if large
Venison for Stock, with bones	40	Brown first

VEGETABLES		
Artichokes, whole (by size)	12-21	Add citric acid
Celery Root	15	Peeled, 2cm slices
Corn, still in husk	12	Add butter to water
Kohlrabi	17	Peeled, 1cm slices
Potatoes, whole	8-15	Varies with type/size
Rutabega or Turnips	8	Peeled, 1.5cm slices
Yams (Sweet Potatoes)	12	Peeled, 2cm slices

PEAS AND BEANS		
Black Beans, dry	28	Do not add salt
Borlotti Beans, dry	22	Do not add salt
Cannellini Beans, dry	44	Do not add salt
Chickpeas, dry (with salt)	65	Wait 10 mins. to open
Fava Beans, soaked 8 hours	40	Do not add salt
Great Northern Beans, dry	38	Do not add salt
Kidney Beans, dry	24	Do not add salt
Pinto Beans, dry	*35	Do not add salt
Scarlet Runner Beans, dry	21	Do not add salt
Split Peas, dry	27	
Urad Dal, rinsed well	**8 or 14	Time=White vs. Black

* **NOTES: These times are for the first cooking only. The pinto beans are to make refried beans. **See the urad dal recipe on page 156.**

PRO TIPS

This is a collection of advice—odds and ends that didn't neatly fit into any other section.

STEAMING VEGETABLES

The belief that steaming foods is healthier than other methods of cooking is an oversimplification. Both steaming and boiling are arguably healthier than frying, but fat is not the only issue. Although more nutrients are preserved during steaming as opposed to boiling, so are chemicals including pesticides and naturally present compounds such as oxalates that lead to kidney stones. Boiling removes 87% of oxalates! Steaming does not. However, the problem with boiling in the hands of a novice is that vegetables are easily overcooked and mushy. This is undoubtedly why surveys have found that most people prefer steamed vegetables over boiled for better taste. I can tell you that restaurants generally *parboil* vegetables first to preserve them longer with their fresh bright color. That is, they are partially cooked in boiling water and them plunged into an ice water bath. Then they are dried off, refrigerated and pan fried, or on request, steamed (though still previously boiled!) when needed. Of course a restaurant meal should not be taken as representative of what you should eat every day, but restaurants make a profit based on what tastes best, and frying parboiled vegetables in butter is a reliable way of pleasing guests.

ULTRA-TEX 8

While most of the inventions of molecular gastronomy are either implausible for a home kitchen (*e.g.* liquid nitrogen) or are just plain gimmicky, one exception is Ultra-Tex 8. This is an invaluable tool for thickening without heat. It is made from tapioca and is totally natural. Just a little stirred in (without any heating) will beautifully thicken sauces and salad dressings without adding any odd flavors—it is completely neutral in taste.

IMPROVING ZINFANDEL

My favorite red wine is Zinfandel, also known as Nebbiolo in Italy. A great zin will have a high alcohol concentration and be very fruit-forward, as the expression goes in the wine industry. To improve a bargain zinfandel by cheating, combine the following:

500ml   *Zinfandel, about 13.5% alcohol (moderate quality)*
150ml   *Port Wine, about 20% alcohol*
75ml   *Vodka, 40% alcohol*

Now you have just a little less than a regular size bottle of a fruitier wine with an alcohol content of 15.9%, which will taste much better to almost everyone. Only one person ever complained, but he owned a winery where zinfandel was produced, so no fair!

"INSTANT AGING" BY BLENDER

There are quite a few online sources now claiming that wine can be instantly aged by putting it in a blender to oxidize it. They taste it and compare the before and after. They invariably proclaim the one blended is better. Otherwise why post a video? The placebo effect is in the house. When double blind studies were performed, most people declared all blended wines to be inferior. No surprise there.

THAI FISH SAUCE — NAM PLA

The quality of this varies immensely. Unfortunately the type that one finds in a supermarket is usually the absolute worst. This kind usually smell like rotting fish and lacks any of the floral notes that are part of the Thai dish you are trying to make. I encourage you to purchase a quality product from an Asian market.

PANEER

A frequent ingredient in Indian cuisine is paneer, a type of unaged cheese from curds. Try substituting feta instead, especially the cubed chili-marinated one from Apetina for much more flavor.

WHITE TRUFFLES

The incredible high price of white truffles has spawned many fake white truffle oils on the market that are merely olive oil with some chemical flavoring. If you want the taste of actual white truffles without spending literally hundreds of euros on a single meal, the best product I have ever found is Savini Tartufi White Truffle Butter. They make several products that are similar, but this is the one you want:

The price is roughly 10 euros for only 80 grams, which sounds like a lot, but even a quarter of a teaspoon is potent.

BLACK TRUFFLES

The problem with most black truffle products is that they lack flavor. Even bottled whole black truffles are almost flavorless compared to fresh Italian black truffles. The black truffle powder from Giuliano is an amazing exception. You can't put nice pretty slices of black truffle on the plate, but the flavor is unparalleled. As with the white truffle butter above, this company makes many variations. Get the one shown below. Plus it is not even expensive!

CITRIC ACID and SODIUM CITRATE

A frequently encountered problem is when you want to cook something with lemon juice. Lemons derive most of their flavor from citric acid. The problem is that many of the other flavor molecules in the lemon break down when heated leaving bitter and unpleasant odd notes. The solution (as virtually every industrial food manufacturer knows) is citric acid. For instance, if you want a deep lemon flavor in your roast chicken, don't just stuff the cavity with lemons. The resulting lemon flavor will be weak. Instead finish the roasted meat with fresh lemon to add the missing natural flavor and aroma. A few drops of lemon oil can be mixed in, too (page 217).

When it comes to using it to control pH, as I said on page 18, Citric Acid is "problematic" with vegetables because it breaks down cell membranes under the high heat of caramelization leading to premature burning. So you need to use Sodium Citrate for that, where the acidic component will only be released slowly as the food cooks. Sodium Citrate is also the ingredient used to keep cheese sauces liquid, as I explained in Volume 2 of this series.

Citric Acid is okay to use for enhanced browning of meats, but remember that also leave a very strong lemon taste. Therefore it is generally not advisable to use on beef or venison. It's also not good for pork because the outside will brown before the inside cooks. It does work well on chicken and lamb chops, though (see page 107). Do not use it with butter or your butter will burn before the food cooks. Citric Acid is available in some larger supermarkets and most Indian specialty food shops. For more about this and how to make your own Sodium Citrate, see Volume 2, page 44.

LOBSTER LEG MEAT

One part of lobster meat that is often overlooked, or mangled in the process of trying to extract it, is inside of each of the small legs. To get this out smoothly, break the legs off from the body, then place each one on a cutting board with the cut-end facing away from you. Now use a rolling pin in a single motion from the claw-end to the cut end, and the meat will come out in a single piece rather like toothpaste being squeezed from the tube. This meat is not as glamorous as claw or tail meat, but still full of flavor.

BOUQUET GARNI CONTAINMENT

The metal "herb cages" sold are very convenient compared to the traditional wrapping up with cheesecloth or in the greens of a leek and tieing with string. However, they are not always a substitute because they will allow small particles such as dried herbs to pass through after they've been in boiling liquid for a while.

If you need the final product to be crystal clear, cheesecloth remains the only viable solution.

PRESERVED BLACK BEANS IN CHILI OIL

Preserved Black Beans in Chili Oil— most especially the one produced by Laoganma—is one of the secret ingredients of many top chefs. It is available in most Asian grocery stores as well as from online sources such as Amazon. When a recipe calls for a small amount of soy sauce, this just might be the way to amp it up. Despite the name saying it is in chili oil, it really isn't that spicy (especially in small amounts such as using it to replace a tablespoon of soy sauce). There are two recipes in this book that use this (pages 116 and 148).

Depending on the application you may need to purée it first because the beans will not dissolve during cooking, so the texture may be objectionable.

AFFORDABLE LOBSTER

An economical solution for actual lobster meat in a casserole or a sauce is the use of a canned pâté or mousse. These are mostly from France and are generally extremely affordable.

Two examples are shown above, containing 40% and 27% lobster meat respectively, and are priced at just a few euros.

SHRIMP TRIMMINGS AND SHELLS

After peeling and deveining shrimp, save the shells for use in making shrimp stock, sauces and bisques—but there's more. The little nub of meat that connects to the tail is the tough nugget that is not easily chewed. To level up your seafood game, cut this off where the dotted line is shown here. Add that to your box of shrimp trimming. Keep a closed box for these bits in your freezer. When you need them, you will have them waiting.

Not only will this make your stock much richer in flavor, but whatever dish you are preparing with shrimp will have lovely smooth and chunk-free shrimp.

MAKING YOUR OWN WINE VINEGAR

This is easy, but it does take a long time and the final production is a bit smelly. The most economical way is to accumulate leftovers of good wine in a single wine or champagne bottle. Of course you can just start with a full bottle and drink a little. When you have about 3/4 of a bottle, add a piece of dry pasta to it (any shape that will fit through the neck). Cover the opening with a piece of cheesecloth or other fabric that breathes and secure it with a rubber band. Don't cork the bottle. Then put it in a cabinet or closet where it is dark and wait about two months. Now there should be a layer of mold on top. That's your mother. No, I'm not insulting your mother. The name for that mold is "mother". You will use that to make your next batch of wine vinegar without pasta. So you pour the contents of the bottle through a sieve. Put some of the mold back into the bottle or a new clean bottle (you only need a little). Now you can feed your mother with fresh wine and start the process over again.

The vinegar you obtained needs to be pasteurized before you use it. To do this, put it in a pan and heat it to 75°C (that's 165°F). Then pour it through another (clean) sieve into a clean bottle. Don't contaminate your sterilized vinegar with anything you used to remove the mold from the first batch! This works for red wine, white wine and champagne.

FRESH vs. FROZEN SPINACH

Aside from being far more economical, to the surprise of most people, frozen spinach is superior in every application except (naturally) spinach salads. It is flash frozen immediately after being picked at the peak of freshness. Plus there is no chance of sand.

BAKING PAPER TRIVIA

Few people know that baking paper, also known as parchment paper, is manufactured in the same way that the rubber for tires is vulcanized. That is, it is ran through a bath of sulfuric acid. This creates sulfur crosslinks that make it highly resistant to burning as well as dissolving some of the cellulose, giving it a glossy surface.

SHOULD YOU BRING MEAT UP TO ROOM TEMPERATURE BEFORE COOKING IT ?

Recently there has been a challenge to the conventional wisdom of cooks around the world that meat should be brought out of the refrigerator and allowed to warm at room temperature for at least 30 minutes, and ideally 2 hours. In an attempt to capture headlines, some have reported that it did not make any difference to the internal temperature and claimed to have tested this notion with an instant read thermometer inserted into the center of a steak (sideways), declaring—sometimes with photos—that even after 2 hours there was no change to the internal temperature.

I was intrigued enough to test it out for myself, even though it was obviously false and the photos fake. Big surprise: Of course it isn't true. This is the problem with the Internet. It is an ocean of misinformation in an attempt to get people to click and then pass the story along for advertising revenue.

Now there is the factor of the *temperature gradient*. That is, if your "room temperature" is so cold that it close to the refrigerator temperature, then of course there won't be a huge change. For my test, a 2.5cm (1 inch) thick steak was left on a table in Finland on a cool day (pretty much the worst case scenario). After 45 minutes, the internal temperature had increased from 2°C to 12°C (35°F to 54°F). The temperature near the table was 18°C (64°F). After 2 hours it reached room temperature. Had it been warmer, it would have been less time to come up to 18°C (64°F). So go right on warming up meat first.

INDEX

Oven Position / Placement, 23

P

R

S

9 781934 939901